SHAKESPEARE, SPENSER
AND THE
CONTOURS OF BRITAIN

Reshaping the Atlantic Archipelago

SHAKESPEARE, SPENSER AND THE CONTOURS OF BRITAIN

Reshaping the Atlantic Archipelago

JOAN FITZPATRICK

UNIVERSITY OF HERTFORDSHIRE PRESS

First published in Great Britain in 2004 by
University of Hertfordshire Press
Learning and Information Services
University of Hertfordshire
College Lane
Hatfield
Hertfordshire AL10 9AB

British Library Cataloguing in Publication Data
A catalogue record for this book is available from the British Library

ISBN 1-902806-36-0 hardback
ISBN 1-902806-37-9 paperback

Design by Geoff Green Book Design, CB4 5RA
Cover design by John Robertshaw
Printed in Great Britain by J W Arrowsmith Ltd, BS3 2NT

Acknowledgements

I WOULD LIKE TO thank University College Northampton for awarding me the study leave which facilitated the writing of this book and the British Academy for supporting the research which helped toward the book with the award of an Overseas Conference Grant. Thanks also to: Kate Welch and Jim Shaw at the Shakespeare Institute Library; Willy Maley, for help with terminology; Jane Housham, my editor at University of Hertfordshire Press, for exceptional attention to detail; and to Gabriel Egan without whom this book would not have been written but who is responsible for none of its shortcomings.

This book is dedicated to my father,
Patrick Joseph Fitzpatrick

Contents

A note on geographical nomenclature   IX

A note on references   X

Introduction   1

Chapter 1 Pastoralism versus ruralism: 26
    Spenser's vision for Ireland

Chapter 2 Marrying waterways and resolving conflict   58
    in *The Faerie Queene*

Chapter 3 Internal insurrection and foreign invasion: 82
    Richard 2, *Cymbeline*, and *The History of King Lear*

Chapter 4 Celtic alterity and the force of prophecy: 120
    1 Henry 4, 2 Henry 4 and *Macbeth*

Conclusion   149

Works cited   171

A note on geographical nomenclature

THE 'ATLANTIC ARCHIPELAGO' of this book's subtitle is approximately the same as the 'Britain' of its main title, but in the difference lies much of the political and artistic energy with which I am concerned. Making 'Britain' stand as a label for all the islands on the eastern rim of the North Atlantic ocean, just north-west of the main continental land mass, was a politic project begun around the time of Shakespeare and Spenser and just now coming to a close. The politics of this project are discussed in this book's introduction, but here it is worth clarifying certain geo-political terms.

The 'Atlantic archipelago' (or more specifically the 'north-east Atlantic archipelago') consists of two large islands (the more westerly being Ireland and the more easterly consisting of England, Scotland and Wales) and many smaller islands. This means the same as an older expression, the British Isles, in which is encoded a history of colonial oppression of Ireland by its neighbour. Uniting the kingdoms of the easterly island into an entity called Britain was already a longterm expansionist political objective of that island's rulers when James I was proclaimed 'King of Great Britain' in 1604. No clear distinction between 'Britain' and 'Great Britain' is found in usages over the past 400 years, and both are applied to the geographical and political unit of the easterly island. An act of union in 1801 formed a 'United Kingdom of Great Britain and Ireland' that brought the westerly and easterly islands into a political unity, but this had to be reduced to a 'United Kingdom of Great Britain and Northern Ireland' when the Irish Free State broke away in 1921.

~~

A note on references

REFERENCES ARE GIVEN by parenthetical author and date,
followed by page numbers where relevant, keyed to the single list of
works given at the end of the book. Unless otherwise stated, all
quotations of Shakespeare are from the electronic edition of the Oxford
Complete Works edited by Stanley Wells and Gary Taylor (Wells et al. 1989)
and all quotations of Spenser are from A. C. Hamilton's edition (Spenser
1977) except *A View of the Present State of Ireland* (Spenser 1949) and the
shorter poems (Spenser 1989). Quotations from Shakespeare's source *King
Leir* are from Geoffrey Bullough's still unsurpassed collection (Bullough
1973a, 337–402) and those of Thomas Heywood's *If You Know Not Me You
Know Nobody, Part 2* are from the Malone Society Reprint (Heywood 1935).

Introduction

ECENT DEVOLUTION IN Scotland and Wales, the Good
Friday agreement in Northern Ireland, and proposals for regional
assemblies in England complicate simplistic notions of what are
meant by Britain, Britishness and the United Kingdom. The formation and
interrelation of national and regional identities have, in fact, been longterm
historical processes. Wales, effectively subjugated by Edward 1 in the late-
thirteenth century, was formally joined with England by the 1536 act of
union. The union of the crowns of England and Scotland, under James 1 in
1603, began a process which resulted in the abolition of Scotland's parliament with the 1707 act of union. Although Ireland was first colonized in the
twelfth century, the process of 'Making Ireland British' (as Nicholas Canny
recently called it) did not get fully under way until the establishment of the
early modern plantations. The Welsh assembly, the Scottish parliament,
and the Northern Ireland assembly, all of which were established in 1988,
suggest the unravelling of the forcibly yoked-together fiction which is the
'United Kingdom'; as Terence Hawkes put it, "the 'Great Britain' project ...
has now reached its conclusion" (Hawkes 2002, 4). The term 'Atlantic archipelago', sometimes favoured by critics responding to J. G. A. Pocock's plea
for a new British history (Pocock 1975), is not entirely satisfactory (Scotland
and Wales are not islands) but it is more neutral than 'United Kingdom'
which has become a rather ironic misnomer.

Tracing the conceptual reshaping of land in literature of the early
modern period offers an insight into present-day conceptions of nationhood and identity. This book considers the ways in which major literary

works by William Shakespeare and Edmund Spenser metaphorically manipulate the geographical reality of the north-east Atlantic archipelago for political and religious purposes. Fantasies of metamorphosis (unification, dissection, and even elimination of the landscape) abound, as do aspirations for the landscape to endorse a particular political agenda. In this sense human endeavours – economic, political, and religious – are privileged over geographical reality. In their responses to the centripetal and centrifugal forces bringing the north-east Atlantic archipelago into a political unity, and holding its elements apart, Spenser and Shakespeare form a useful axis for consideration of the literature. Spenser seems at first defensively conservative when compared to Shakespeare's radical and nuanced explorations of the relationship between nationhood (a matter of cultural affiliations) and state-formation. Too easily this binarism can be aligned with others, such as Spenser's apparently fundamentalist Protestantism and the emerging picture of Shakespeare's secret Catholicism. At the very least genre restrictions must be brought into such a discussion: it has been traditionally thought that poetry and prose afford Spenser a freedom to fantasize about control and to indulge in the role of literary creator, whilst Shakespeare was to some degree restricted by the practicalities of writing for the stage. But traditional views about Spenser and Shakespeare require some modification. By considering biography, reputation, genre, and, in subsequent chapters, each writer's approach to the imaginative manipulation of the landscape in their creative writings, I hope to show that Shakespeare and Spenser, though distinct, are more alike than has hitherto been observed.

Spenser

Spenser's first publication, an anonymous translation of 'Visions by Petrarch' and 'Visions of Du Bellay', appeared in Jan Van der Noot's *A Theatre for Worldlings* in 1569 and provides clues about his political and religious affiliations. Van der Noot was a Dutch Calvinist and his collection was, as A. C. Hamilton put it, an "apocalyptic and militantly anti-Catholic work" (Spenser 1977, viii). Spenser's first major work, *The Shepheardes Calender*, was published in 1579 and, due to its popularity, Spenser was praised as a pastoral poet throughout the 1580s and beyond. As we shall see in the next chapter, *The Shepheardes Calender* contains overt anti-Catholic propaganda as well as a Petrarchan encomium of Queen Elizabeth but it is Spenser's epic poem *The Faerie Queene*, the first part of which was published in 1590, which has established his modern reputation as a sensitive and gentle poet of romance. Contradictorily, it has also established him as a dominant force in the propagation of Elizabethan Protestant nationalism. Also published in 1590 was Spenser's *Letter to Raleigh* outlining what he referred to as his "general intention and meaning" for *The Faerie Queene*. It is unusual to have a writer's explicit explanation of his work and so the *Letter to Raleigh* is a most important document. Since Freud's discovery of the unconscious, and more especially since post-structuralism's analysis of the inflated 'author function', the survival of a poet's explanation of his work has been held to be something of a mixed blessing (it might mislead a reader into holding a particular view of the writing which the poem does not offer) but we may at least note that Spenser assumed his readers would read his poetry as allegory and was apparently keen that his poem should not be misinterpreted:

> knowing how doubtfully all Allegories may be construed, and this booke of mine ... being a continued Allegory, or darke conceit, I have thought good aswell for auoyding of gealous opinions and misconstructions, as also for your better light in reading therof, (being so by you commanded,) to dis-couer vnto you the general intention and meaning, which in the whole course thereof I have fashioned, without expressing of any particular purposes or by-accidents therein occasioned. (Spenser 1977, 737)

Colin Clout's Come Home Againe, "a post-1590 revision of the poet's persona as lover and poet" (Quitslund 1990, 81), was published in 1595, and 1596 saw the publication of the second part of *The Faerie Queene* (Books 4-6 and what may be the incomplete Book 7, also known as 'The Mutabilitie Cantos'). *A View of the Present State of Ireland* (hereafter 'the *View*'), a prose dialogue between Irenius and Eudoxus about how best to solve Irish resistance to English colonial rule, was not published until 1633, 34 years after Spenser's death, but it was probably written in the early-to-mid 1590s and most likely circulating in manuscript. It is not clear why this work was not published during Spenser's life-time; some critics believe that the *View* was suppressed because it dealt with Ireland, a sensitive subject at the time, but there is insufficient evidence to settle the issue categorically (Hadfield 1994).

The contradictory views of Spenser as ethereal poet on the one hand

and dogmatic political commentator on the other has its roots in the history of Spenser criticism. The Romantic poets, effusive in their praise of Spenser, were particularly preoccupied by the role of allegory. Although Coleridge believed that "no one can appreciate Spenser without some reflection on the nature of allegorical writing" (Coleridge 1918, 137), his contemporary William Hazlitt thought *The Faerie Queene* entirely escapist:

> If Ariosto transports us into the regions of romance, Spenser's poetry is all fairy-land. In Ariosto, we walk upon the ground, in a company, gay, fantastic, and adventurous enough. In Spenser, we wander in another world, among ideal beings. The poet takes and lays us in the lap of a lovelier nature, by the sound of softer streams, among greener hills and fairer valleys. He paints nature, not as we find it, but as we expected to find it; and fulfils the delightful promise of our youth. He waves his wand of enchantment – and at once embodies airy beings, and throws a delicious veil over all actual objects... . The love of beauty ... and not of truth, is the moving principle of his mind; and he is guided in his fantastic delineations by no rule but the impulse of an inexhaustive imagination. (Hazlitt 1908, 53-54)

Hazlitt advised readers who found themselves deterred or confused by Spenser's allegory to ignore it: "If they do not meddle with the allegory, the allegory will not meddle with them... . For instance, when Britomart, seated amidst the young warriors, lets fall her hair and discovers her sex, is it necessary to know the part she plays in the allegory, to understand the beauty of the following stanza?" (Hazlitt 1908, 57-58). The Victorian critic James Russell Lowell echoed Hazlitt when he suggested that the allegory was irrelevant and, moreover, dull: "But how if it bore us, which after all is the fatal question?" (Lowell 1875, 373). For Lowell "whenever in the 'Faery Queen' you come suddenly on the moral, it gives you a shock of unpleasant surprise, a kind of grit, as when one's teeth close on a bit of gravel in a dish of strawberries and cream" (Lowell 1875, 382). Lowell's view that Spenser's allegory is distracting and "perhaps, after all, he adopted it only for the reason that it was in fashion" (Lowell 1875, 377) was challenged by his contemporary Edward Dowden who in his essay "Spenser, the poet and Teacher" referred back to Milton's praise of Spenser as "sage and serious" and noted that "with all its opulence of colour and melody, with all its imagery of delight, the *Faery Queene* has primarily a moral or spiritual intention" (Spenser 1982-1884, 305, 330).

Spenser's reputation as a poet more concerned with beauty than truth, as Andrew Hadfield put it, a poet of "hazy, romantic pastoralism" (Hadfield 2001, 1), has persisted, but it co-exists with his reputation as an advocate of Elizabethan Protestant nationalism and a fervent supporter of Elizabeth. After Spenser's death his contemporary Richard Niccols referred to him as "that Fairie Queenes sweet singer" (Niccols 1610, Eee6r) and Karl Marx, more pithily, as "Elizabeths Arschkissende [arse-kissing] Poet" (Marx 1974, 305). Certainly Spenser begins his epic poem by apparently praising Elizabeth:

> ... O Goddesse heauenly bright,
> Mirrour of grace and Maiestie diuine,
> Great Lady of the greatest Isle, whose light
> Like *Phoebus* lampe throughout the world doth shine,
> Shed thy faire beames into my feeble eyne,
> And raise my thoughts too humble and too vile,
> To thinke of that true glorious type of thine,
> The argument of mine afflicted stile:
> The which to heare, vouchsafe, O dearest dred a-while.
> (*The Faerie Queene* 1.Proem.4.1-9)

Elizabeth is here presented not only as the poet's muse but also a divine figure and here, as throughout the poem, brightness is an indication of English Protestant virtue. In the Proem to Book 2 the narrator claims that any reader who supposes that Faery land does not exist should consider

> dayly how through hardy enterprize,
> Many great Regions are discouered,
> Which to late age were neuer mentioned.
> Who euer heard of th'Indian *Peru*?
> Or who in venturous vessell measured
> The *Amazons* huge riuer now found trew?
> Or fruitfullest *Virginia* who did euer vew?
> (*The Faerie Queene* 2. Proem. 2. 3-9)

The notion that light shines from Britain ("the greatest Isle") throughout the world is the kind of assertion that helps to confirm Spenser's reputation as the nationalistic poet of empire, as does the reference to the exploration of foreign lands. All that is great stems from Britain, and Faery land is a mirror for Elizabeth's rule:

> And thou, O fairest Princesse vnder sky,
> In this faire mirrhour maist behold thy face,
> And thine owne realmes in lond of Faery,
> And in this antique Image thy great auncestry.
> (*The Faerie Queene* 2. Proem. 4. 6-9)

Spenser continues to celebrate Elizabeth in the Proems to subsequent Books: in the Proem to Book 3 he praises her chastity and beauty (3. Proem.1 and 5); in the proem to Book 4 she is described as "that sacred Saint" (4.Proem.4.2), "The Queene of loue, and Prince of peace from heauen blest" (4.Proem.4.9) and in the proem to Book 6 the virtue of courtesy stems from her (6.Proem.6.1-9). Strangely there is no mention of her in the Proem to Book 5, an omission which is informed by Spenser's vision of a reshaped Ireland and which I will consider more closely in the conclusion to this study. In the *Letter to Raleigh* Spenser wrote:

> In that Faery Queene I meane glory in my generall intention, but in my particular I conceiue the most excellent and glorious person of our soueraine the Queene, and her kingdome in Faery land. And yet in some places els, I doe otherwise shadow her. For considering she beareth two persons, the one of a most royall Queene or Empresse, the other of a most vertuous and beautifull Lady, this latter part in some places I do expresse in Belphoebe, fashioning her name according to your own excellent conceipt of Cynthia, (Phoebe and Cynthia being both names of Diana). (Spenser 1977, 737)

The Faery Queene, also called Gloriana, never appears in the poem but it is likely that, aside from Belphoebe, Elizabeth is figured in the characters of Astraea, Una, Mercilla, Britomart, and perhaps some others (Wells 1983; Yates 1947).

Spenser develops his flattery of Elizabeth throughout *The Faerie Queene* but his advocacy of English Protestant nationalism is arguably most fully expressed in Books 1 and 5. The subject of Book 1 is Holiness with its champion, Redcrosse, representing not only this virtue but England itself via reference to its patron saint, George. Book 1 thus functions as a reminder that true holiness can be found only in those who champion the English queen as the divine representative of Protestant reform. Spenser tells us that Redcrosse's companion Una represents Truth (1.2.argument.2) but she may also represent Elizabeth. Through Una Spenser alludes to the queen in many ways: her beauty, specifically her pallor, chastity and moral goodness, function as a general compliment to Elizabeth, she wear's Elizabeth's colours (black and white), her name suggests Elizabeth's Latin motto *Semper Eadem* – a Latin phrase meaning 'Always the same', and a translation of an English motto 'Be always one' (Rosinger 1968, 13) – and she is similarly identified as a source of brightness. The first real test of Redcrosse's abilities is in his battle with Error, the monstrous hybrid-female serpent, where his "glistring armor" shines in the midst of the "darksome hole" which is her den and, with the help of Una, she is defeated.

Critics have noted that in Spenser's allegory Error represents not only a lack of moral rectitude but specifically Catholicism, the enemy of the one true religion: John M. Steadman noted that the books and papers spewed forth by Error "recall visual imagery from the anti-Catholic propaganda of the Reformation" (Steadman 1990, 252) and Richard Niccols identified Error's brood as the Jesuits and seminary priests sent to England by the Pope and the Spanish to agitate against Elizabeth and Protestantism (Niccols 1610, Fff6v). Another enemy of Redcrosse, and thus the enemy of Truth, is Duessa whose apparent beauty masks a degenerate interior. Her name signals her doubleness, and thus her deceitfulness, and she is aligned with the seductive and duplicitous nature of Catholicism. Error and Duessa are trials on the way to the object of Redcrosse's quest: defeating the dragon which holds Una's parents captive. As Douglas Brooks-Davies pointed out, the St George legend was well known in Elizabethan England, in both popular entertainment and Protestant religious propaganda, and while George stands for England and his princess and her lamb for the church, so the dragon specifically represents the papal Antichrist (Brooks-Davies 1990, 705). Josephine Waters Bennett similarly thought the fight with the dragon to be derived from the St George legend and "the significance of the whole allegory determined by contemporary interpretations of the Revelations" (Bennett 1942, 117) while Elizabeth Watson, acknowledging the Roman Counter-Reformation context, detected a more precise Catholic allusion to Pope Gregory 13th, pontiff from 1572 to 1585 (Watson 2000).

Kate M. Warren spoke for most critics when she found the allegory of Book 5 transparent: "It is chiefly historical, and the historical meaning, in its main outline, stands clearly forth" (1898, vii). Book 5 features rebellion in Ireland, the trial of Mary Queen of Scots, and the conflict in the Netherlands against Spain, all of which were regarded by English Protestants as the result of Catholic lawlessness. The main quest of Artegall, the knight of Justice and hero of Book 5, is to free "the faire Irena", the personification of Ireland, held prisoner by Grantorto, the giant who represents Catholic power. Traditionally Book 5, perhaps the most violent of the six complete Books, has made critics uncomfortable because of its less than opaque allusions to colonial activity in Ireland and its advocation of the violent treatment of transgressors. Ireland constitutes an important context for the unequivocal views put forward in Spenser's writings and, as we shall see in subsequent chapters, informs his desire to manipulate geographical reality so that the landscape might support, rather than hinder, the colonial project. Spenser was in Ireland in July 1577, possibly carrying letters from the Earl of Leicester to Sir Henry Sidney and Sir William Dury, and it was here that he witnessed the execution of Murrogh O'Brien in Limerick, an incident described in the *View*. In 1580 Spenser became secretary to the newly appointed Lord Deputy of Ireland, Arthur Grey de Wilton. He accompanied Grey on the military expedition against Papal forces at Smerwick which resulted in the massacre of around 600 Spanish and Italian soldiers who, it was rumoured, had previously been promised their lives by Grey, an allegation denied by Spenser in the *View*. According to Willy Maley, Petruccio Barducci, author of a subsequent account of the massacre, claimed that Spenser was among those who "profited from the massacre through ransoms for hostages" (Maley 1994, 14).

Spenser succeeded Lodowick Bryskett as clerk of the Faculties in the Court of Chancery in March 1581 and continued to accompany Grey on a number of military expeditions across Ireland. According to Bryskett's *Discourse of Civill Life*, published in 1606, Spenser was present at a meeting in Bryskett's house just outside Dublin in the spring of 1582 to discuss political and intellectual issues. Maley described those present as "a small clique of urbane young men, for the most part aged around thirty, predominantly Oxbridge-educated, and occupying a series of key posts in the New English colonial system" (Maley 1997, 69). Nicholas Canny claimed that those included in Bryskett's dialogue whose early careers can be traced were all closely associated with the Sidney/Leicester faction (Canny 2001, 3). At the end of August 1582 Grey was forced to return to England and Spenser's secretaryship came to an end. Spenser continued his work as a civil servant in Ireland and some time in 1588 occupied the Kilcolman estate, a ruined castle and 3000 acres of land confiscated by the crown from the defeated Earl of Desmond. In May 1589 he obtained official possession of the property, "paying around £20 annual rent" and establishing "a colony of six house-holders with their families" (Maley 1994, 50). In September 1598 Spenser was nominated for the post of sheriff of Cork and in October of that year the English planters in Munster were overthrown during the Irish rebellion led by Hugh O'Neill, the Earl of Tyrone. Kilcolman Castle was sacked and Spenser fled with his family to Cork.

A number of critics believe Book 5 to be the poetic exposition of Spenser's political opinions, articulated in the *View*, where Irenius insists on the moral necessity of political violence in order to subdue the indigenous population and those twelfth-century colonists who were accused of having 'gone native', the Old English. C. S. Lewis is typical of those critics who were disappointed by the Book's violence but he made efforts to distinguish between the sweet poet and the political pragmatist, claiming that "Spenser was the instrument of a detestable policy in Ireland, and in his fifth book the wickedness he had shared begins to corrupt his imagination" (Lewis 1936, 349). H.S.V. Jones claimed that Book 5 and the *View* "should always be studied together" for Book 5 "appears as a quite intelligible application of Spenser's moral philosophy" (Jones 1919, 13), and Kate M. Warren described Book 5 as "an apology and vindication for Lord Grey's rule in Ireland" (Spenser 1898, xiv). Similarly, Edwin Greenlaw claimed that Book 5 is Spenser's "exposition of a theory of government" (Greenlaw 1912, 351) and he specifically identified Artegall with Lord Grey. More recently Anne Fogarty and Richard McCabe noted the importance of considering the *View* not only in association with Book 5, and particularly the last two cantos of the Book, but with the entire poem. Anne Fogarty stated that the *View* and *The Faerie Queene* should be seen as "mutually defining intertexts" for both are inherently concerned with colonialism, and images of Otherness are central to both works (Fogarty 1989, 77).

Book 5 has never been a favourite amongst literary critics and some have sought to minimize the two-way traffic between Spenser's politics and his art. Jean Brink (1994) questioned Spenser's authorship of the *View*, indicating that evidence linking him to the text is weak, but the arguments put forward by her are less than convincing and are challenged in no uncertain terms by Willy Maley in 1997, 163-94. As Maley pointed out, Brink preferred to leave Book 5 of *The Faerie Queene* out of her discussion about authorship of the *View* "because of its inconvenient treatment of Ireland,

and because Irena does tend inevitably to lead to Irenius" (Maley 1997, 183). Maley also noted that "throughout her essay one has the feeling that Brink does not want the *View* to be by Spenser and that this colours her argument" (Maley 1997, 186).

Spenser lived in Ireland for nearly twenty years and his time there is traditionally viewed as a kind of exile that alienated him from the queen and court: a dedicatory sonnet by Spenser to the Earl of Ormond and Ossory in the 1590 edition of *The Faerie Queene* refers to Ireland as "saluage soyl ... Which being through long wars left almost waste, / With brutish barbarisme is ouerspredd", it is a land where "Not one Parnassus, nor one Helicone / [are] Left for sweet Muses to be harboured" (Spenser 1977, 742). As we have seen, Spenser has gained the reputation as an advocate of Elizabethan Protestant nationalism but this coexists, and indeed clashes, with his reputation as a sensitive and gentle poet. In order to illustrate the latter view of Spenser, Andrew Hadfield reported a story told by John Bailey to the English Association Conference in which a World War 1 English officer read *The Faerie Queene* to his men because, even though the soldiers did not understand what was being said, the poetry had a soothing effect (Hadfield 2001, 1). This is an especially notable anecdote because it emphasizes the inherent connections between notions of civility and ideas about what poetry is for. As Jeffrey Knapp pointed out, some Tudor writers characterized poets as particularly capable of promoting empire. Sidney claimed that poetry was the only way to civilize the barbarous Indians ("if ever learning come among them, it must be by having their hard dull wits softened and sharpened with the sweet delights of poetry" Sidney 1965, 98) and Knapp noted that for Sidney the story involving Orpheus, the first poet, who lulled savage beasts, "actually represents an historical truth disguised" since, as Sidney put it, Orpheus in fact moved "stony and beastly people" (Knapp 1992, 6; Sidney 1965, 96). Spenser was a poet and a colonist and his role in the colony of Ireland arguably explains some of the views expressed in his writing: like any colonist he was driven by the desire to control and shape the world around him, a desire evident in the topographical manipulation which dominated his imagination. To some extent, though, genre dictates Spenser's reputation as an opinionated advocate of English Protestant nationalism, an issue which will be considered more fully in the conclusion to this chapter. While Spenser is traditionally thought of as being specific to his time, an Elizabethan poet involved in the colonizing of sixteenth-century Ireland, Shakespeare has been conceived of in broader terms.

Shakespeare

In his commendatory poem prefacing *The First Folio* Ben Jonson said that Shakespeare "was not of an age, but for all time!" (Shakespeare 1968, 10) a phrase that voices what is perhaps the most commonly held belief about Shakespeare today, that his plays are universal and timeless. As Michael Dobson has shown, this view of Shakespeare emerged during the Enlightenment which saw the promotion of Shakespeare as England's national poet and the rise of what George Bernard Shaw termed 'bardolatry' (Dobson 1992, 1-16). In 1765 Samuel Johnson proclaimed:

> *Shakespeare* is above all writers, at least above all modern writers, the poet of nature; the poet that holds up to his readers a faithful mirrour of manners and of life. His characters are not modified by the customs of particular places, unpractised by the rest of the world; by the peculiarities of studies or professions, which can operate but upon small numbers; or by the accidents of transient fashions or temporary opinions: they are the genuine progeny of common humanity, such as the world will always supply, and observation will always find. His persons act and speak by the influence of those general passions and principles by which all minds are agitated, and the whole system of life is continued in motion. In the writings of other poets a character is too often an individual; in those of *Shakespeare* it is commonly a species. (Johnson 1765, viii-ix)

The notion that Shakespeare depicts the human condition was also common amongst the Romantics. Coleridge claimed that "In the plays of Shakespeare every man sees himself" (Coleridge 1960, 125) and Hazlitt praised the "generic quality" of his mind which "contained a universe of thought and feeling within itself" (Hazlitt 1908, 71-72). Matthew Arnold, in his poem "Shakespeare", emphasized the opaque quality which has commonly been attributed to Shakespeare: "Others abide our question. Thou are free. / We ask and ask: Thou smilest and art still, / Out-topping knowledge" (Arnold 1965, 49). The notion that the multivalent Shakespeare is all things to all people was voiced in the middle of the twentieth century by Harold C. Goddard:

Shakespeare is like life. There are almost as many ways of taking him as there are ways of living. From the child lost in one of his stories as retold by Charles and Mary Lamb, to the old man turning to his works for fortitude and vision, every age finds in them what it needs. Every new lover of them finds himself, as every generation, from the poet's to our own, has found itself. One by one all the philosophies have been discovered in Shakespeare's works, and he has been charged – both as virtue and weakness – with having no philosophy. The lawyer believes he must have been a lawyer, the musician a musician, the Catholic a Catholic, the Protestant a Protestant. Never was there a more protean genius. (Goddard 1951, 1)

The popular conception of "myriad-minded Shakespeare", as Coleridge called him (Coleridge 1907, 13), suggests that it is not clear where Shakespeare's political and religious loyalties lie because, unlike writers such as Spenser, he does not indicate his attitude toward these things in his writing. Undoubtedly the belief that Shakespeare is universal, timeless, and speaks for all is partly due to the indeterminacy of his writings. Where Spenser has been seen as a poet of firm opinions, a major force in the propagation of Elizabethan Protestant nationalism, Shakespeare has been characterized as a more subtle writer.

Shakespeare has traditionally been appropriated by the right and, as Alan Sinfield pointed out, the idea that the plays of Shakespeare embody universal truths has generally meant his work being used by the educational establishment to reinforce established practices in literary criticism and examinations. Sinfield also referred to a 1963 Ministry of Education report which emphasized the civilizing experience of contact with great literature (Sinfield 1985, 135), much as Sidney had done hundreds of years earlier. More recently, though, the Left have also claimed Shakespeare as theirs: the multivalency of his work facilitating oppressor and oppressed. Where Spenser is traditionally seen as 'Elizabeth's poet', Shakespeare did not respond to Henry Chettle's request to lament the death of Elizabeth and in *Englandes Mourning Garment* (1603) Chettle apparently rebukes Shakespeare for his silence:

> Nor doth the silver tonged *Melicert*,
> Drop from his honied muse one sable teare
> To mourne her death that graced his desert,
> And to his laies opend her Royall eare
> Shepheared remember our Elizabeth,

And sing her Rape, done by that Tarquin Death.
(Chettle 1603, D3r)

Additionally, where Spenser's career is read as distinctly Elizabethan, and
he a spokesperson for the Elizabethan age, Shakespeare was successful well
into the reign of James. Spenser advocated English Protestant militarism
but Shakespeare is considered more subtle in his approach to nationalism,
religion and politics. Spenser was a poet and colonist living for nearly
twenty years in Ireland but we do not know whether Shakespeare ever ven-
tured further afield than Stratford and London.

One explanation for Shakespeare's multivalency is that he was trying to
hide something. Critics have always been puzzled by what Shakespeare did
during the 'Lost Years', that period between 1585 (when Shakespeare's twins
Judith and Hamnet were baptised in Stratford) and 1592, when he surfaced
as an established playwright in London. In 1985 Ernst Honigmann set forth
a theory first proposed by Oliver Baker in 1937 and repeated in 1944 by E. K.
Chambers that Shakespeare spent some time during his early years in
Lancashire as a servant in Catholic households and that he was the player
'William Shakeshafte' kept by the Hoghton family near Preston in
Lancashire (Honigmann 1998). Chambers asserted that Shakespeare
might have adopted the variant 'Shakeshafte' as a player since his grand-
father "seems to be both Shakstaff and Shakeschafte, as well as Shakspere
... in the Snitterfield manor records"(quoted in Honigmann 1998, 4). A
'John Cottom' and a 'William Shakeshafte' were legatees in Alexander
Hoghton's will; he left his stock of theatre costumes and musical instru-
ments to his brother Thomas and requested that, if Thomas did not
choose to keep the players, his neighbour Sir Thomas Hesketh should
take care of Fulke Gillam and William Shakeshafte (Honigmann 1998,
3–6). As Honigmann pointed out, John Cottom, a Stratford schoolmaster
between 1579 and 1581, was a native of Lancashire who, around 1582,
returned to the area where his family owned property close to Lea where
the Hoghtons lived at this time (Honigmann 1998, 5). Chambers noted
that Sir Thomas Hesketh had connections with Henry Stanley, the fourth
Earl of Derby, and his son Ferdinando, Lord Strange, who probably took
over from his father's patronage of the theatre company Strange's Men
when he became the fifth Earl of Derby in 1593, and that "If William
Shakeshafte had passed from the service of Alexander Hoghton into that
of either Thomas Hoghton or Sir Thomas Hesketh, he might have had the

opportunity to gain access to the London theatrical world via Lord Strange" (quoted in Honigmann 1998, 4).

The theory that Shakespeare, assuming the name Shakeshafte, served in Catholic households between the years 1585 and 1592 reinforces the idea, long-held in some quarters, that Shakespeare was Catholic or harboured Catholic sympathies, an idea which, as we shall see in subsequent chapters, has important implications for the conceptual reshaping of land that occurs in his plays. Gary Taylor considered in detail the circumstantial evidence that might indicate Shakespeare's Catholicism: two seventeenth-century reports identify Shakespeare as a papist; he is "strongly associated with a number of known or suspected recusants" including his father and his daughter Susanna; his Stratford schoolmasters were Catholic; and his mother's family, the Ardens, had links with recusancy (Taylor 1994, 290–92). William's father had stopped attending church services apparently for "fear of process of debt" but Honigmann referred to research undertaken by D. L. Thomas and N. E. Evans which indicated that John Shakespeare was at this time much wealthier than hitherto assumed (Wilson 1997, 118), suggesting another reason for his absence from church. As Patrick Collinson pointed out, Stratford was slow to conform to the new religion and it is "probable that most of the members of this community were church papists" (Collinson 1985, 36). Richard Wilson claimed that Honigmann and others missed an important Catholic connection between Hoghton Tower and Stratford: the Jesuit mission which took place in the winter of 1580–81 (Wilson 1997, 11). Jesuit missionaries were known to have been operating in the vicinity of Stratford-upon-Avon by 1580, having come from the new seminary at Douai, founded by the Hoghtons on profits from their alum mines (Wilson 1997, 11). Simon Hunt, the master who taught Shakespeare from age seven to eleven, enrolled in Douai in 1575 and followed Robert Parsons as director of penance at the English college in Rome. Hunt's successor as a schoolteacher was another Catholic, John Cottom, the man named in Hoghton's will, and the 1580 mission under Parsons and Edmund Campion included Cottom's brother, Thomas. As Schoenbaum indicated, it has been suggested that it was during this mission that John Shakespeare signed his 'Spiritual Testament', a document asserting one's Catholic identity (Schoenbaum 1977, 50–54). The Testament, found in 1757 in the roof of the house in Stratford where Shakespeare was allegedly born, and now lost, was printed by Malone in 1790 and its authenticity allegedly established in 1923 with the discovery of the 1661 Spanish original. Wilson, among others, was convinced that the document was genuine but Schoenbaum urged caution: "Malone's paper has disappeared, and too many questions remain teasingly unanswered" (Schoenbaum 1977, 53).

Wilson asserted that when Campion went to Lancashire, accompanied by the young subseminarians whom he had recruited, one of the young men may have been Shakespeare. Campion stayed in Hoghton Tower which, with its great library, was the equivalent of "the secret college and headquarters of the English Counter-Reformation", and it was there that he wrote his *Ten Reasons* with arguments for Catholics to reject the Anglican Church. The authorities ordered the rooting out of seditious texts in Lancashire, the Privy Council ordered a search of Hoghton Tower for books used by Campion, and the Hoghtons were arrested. Stratford and Lancashire were centres of recusancy and Wilson claimed that Shakespeare's route, had things gone according to plan, "ought to have taken him from Stratford to Douai via the Jesuit clearing-house at Hoghton" (Wilson 1997, 12). Wilson responded to Peter Levi's objection that the talented Shakespeare would not have been attracted to obscure Lancashire by noting that in this period Lancashire was not obscure but, as Lawrence Stone pointed out, the centre of an important patronage network (Wilson 1997, 13). As Taylor noted, the idea that Shakespeare was Catholic goes back to the 17th century when John Speed denounced the playwright as a "papist" because of his scurrilous depiction of the Lollard martyr Sir John Oldcastle and Richard Davies, a chaplain at Oxford, recorded the testimony of surviving witnesses and wrote that Shakespeare "died a papist" (Taylor 1994, 290). But Wilson claimed to be the first to spot that the 1580 Jesuit crusade involving Shakespeare's recusant schoolmasters tied Stratford to Hoghton Tower and necessitated the adoption of aliases (Wilson 1997, 13), although Peter Milward criticized Wilson for ignoring earlier studies (including his own) which explored the trail from Stratford to Lancashire and Cottom's connections to the Lancashire gentry (Milward 1998).

Quite a few critics have argued that the Shakeshafte theory is flawed and their objections have been considered recently by Robert Bearman (Bearman 2002). In a note published in 1970 Douglas Hamer elaborated upon a point suggested by Mark Eccles in 1961 (*Shakespeare in Warwickshire*) and argued that the name Shakeshafte was a common one in late-sixteenth century Lancashire and thus it is not safe to assume that the Shakeshafte in Hoghton's will was the playwright. Hamer also noted that the Shakeshafte of the will would have been older than 17, Shakespeare's age when the will was written in 1581 (Bearman 2002, 84). Annuities took account of age or length of service and the William Shakeshafte named in the will received a substantial annuity compared with other servants which meant that he was probably older than those who received less, indicating that Shakeshafte and the playwright Shakespeare, aged only 17, were not the same man (Bearman 2002, 92). Bearman contributed to Hamer's objections to the Shakeshafte theory by considering evidence from Lancashire parish regis-ters, not easily available when Hamer was writing, and concluded that the name Shakeshafte "can be shown to be even more common than he demon-strated, with a particular concentration in the area where Hoghton family influence was pre-eminent" (Bearman 2002, 93). Bearman criticized those who claim a Lancashire connection which is "fuelled by the increasingly uncritical acceptance of the authenticity of a document known as John Shakespeare's 'Spiritual Testament', alleged to be roughly contemporary with the period in question" (Bearman 2002, 85n13).

Whatever the truth of claims for Shakespeare's Catholicism, the idea is attractive since it helps to explain his reputation as an indeterminate writer: if Shakespeare were hiding his belief in Catholicism when writing his plays this might account for the multivalency of his work. As Taylor pointed out, allusions in Shakespeare's work which indicate Catholic sym-pathies were "collected and examined by John Henry de Groot in *The Shakespeares and 'The Old Faith'* (1946), a work since polemically supple-mented by Peter Milward in *Shakespeare's Religious Background*" (1973) and augmented by some new allusions "which have only more recently come to light" (Taylor 1994, 293). Yet evidence of Shakespeare's Catholicism co-exists with evidence which appears to indicate his Protestant sympathies. According to Honigmann, the theory that Shakespeare was brought up Catholic and served Alexander Hoghton and Thomas Hesketh, "two very positively committed Catholics", is difficult to reconcile with the anti-Catholic tone of some of his early plays", for example the anti-Catholic bias toward Humphrey in *1 Henry 6* and *2 Henry 6* and in the rhetoric of *King John*. Honigmann suggested that this might be because Shakespeare's patron from around 1586, Lord Strange, was related to many Catholics and though he and his father were recusant-hunters, they might further demonstrate their loyalty by having Strange's Men produce plays with an anti-Catholic bias (Honigmann 1998, 118–19). Yet, as Honigmann noted, after *King John* Shakespeare wrote *Romeo and Juliet* where the friar "represents good sense and moderation" and *Hamlet* where "he relapsed into a Catholic view of purgatory" (Honigmann 1998, 122–23). Honigmann also detected an "insistent Catholicism" in *Measure for Measure*, an aspect of the play largely neglected by critics, and concluded that it "manages to present a Catholic point of view persuasively from the inside", carrying "Catholic ramifications" in Shakespeare's additions to the play's source so that it centres on a nun and a friar "who do *not* arouse the normal Protestant hysteria" (Honigmann 1998, 123). Gary Taylor has written about Shakespeare's lampooning of the Lollard martyr Sir John Oldcastle in *1 Henry 4*, considering the depiction an indication of Catholic sympathies (Taylor 1985, 99). He also observed Shakespeare's mockery of "the hypocrisy of Puritans" in *Measure for Measure*, his exploitation of "the Catholic belief in purgatory" in *Hamlet*, and noted Emrys Jones' assertion that Shakespeare exploited Catholic beliefs about All Souls' Eve in *Richard 3* (Taylor 1985, 99). Taylor further noted the 1609–1610 performances of *Pericles* and *King Lear* "by a band of recusant players with – in other respects – an obviously papist repertoire" (Taylor 1985, 99) although, as Stanley Wells pointed out, it is by no means certain whether the 'king Lere' they performed was Shakespeare's play or the anonymous source play *King Leir* which was also available in print (Shakespeare 2000b, 56). Like Honigmann, Taylor mentioned *Hamlet*, where "Shakespeare exploited the Catholic belief in purgatory" but, unlike Honigmann, emphasized evidence of Shakespeare's Catholic sympathies in *King John* since he removed most of the anti-Catholic polemic of his source (Taylor 1985, 99).

Samuel Harsnet's *A Declaration of Egregious Popish Impostures* (1603), a text which describes the activities of Catholic priests and their followers in the 1580s, some of whom had Lancashire connections, was first spotted as a source for the depiction of Edgar's difficulties in *King Lear* by the 18th century editor Lewis Theobald, and Kenneth Muir has explored Shakespeare's indebtedness to the text (Muir 1951, 11). Honigmann thought it likely that Shakespeare would have been interested to see who featured in the *Egregious Impostures* (Honigmann 1998, 124–25) and although curiosity does not necessarily indicate complicity, Gary Taylor's observation that

Shakespeare might have been indebted to a Catholic manuscript account of the same events makes Catholic sympathies more likely as does Taylor's point that "What Shakespeare's treatment ignores entirely is Harsnet's own contribution: his ceaseless mockery of the whole idea of demonic possession" (Taylor 1985, 99). Although Taylor acknowledged that "such internal evidence does not prove that Shakespeare was a secret Catholic" he claimed that "it does demonstrate, at the very least, his willingness to exploit a point of view which many of his contemporaries would have regarded as 'papist'" (Taylor 1985, 99). Honigmann considered Shakespeare a lapsed Catholic and found it "easier to imagine that a former Catholic might slip into this way of thinking than that a Protestant writer who had never been Catholic would do so" (Honigmann 1998, 123); although Shakespeare "normally wrote as one would expect from a committed Protestant ... he sometimes reverted to a Catholic viewpoint – which was most unusual in the drama of his day" (Honigmann 1998, 125). For Taylor the evidence indicated that "For much of his life – particularly in his first two decades in Stratford – he was almost certainly a church papist" (Taylor 1994, 298).

Richard Wilson, who also cited internal evidence for Shakespeare's Catholic sympathies, observed that the theory that Shakespeare was Catholic helps explain Shakespeare's unique position as the only Tudor and Stuart dramatist to come from outside London and the Universities:

> if Chambers and Honigmann are right, it was a detour to the recusant North that took Shakespeare in a clear opposite direction to the social logic of his professional field and constituted his freakish statistical difference. It was a Lancashire affiliation which made Shakespeare the outstanding example of the academic heretic, whose cultural power arises from marginality to the great metropolitan institutions. (Wilson 1997, 12)

Wilson detected a biographical component in the influence of Jesuit practice on Shakespeare's Edgar with recusancy in Lancashire forming a particularly appropriate context for what occurs in *King Lear*: "it is easy to see how Edgar's 'popish imposture' as Poor Tom might resonate in that country of secret tunnels, priest holes, and hidden chapels" (Wilson 1997, 12). Peter Milward also perceived a parallel between "the pitiful condition of Edgar" and the experiences of those Jesuit priests who engaged in 'the English mission':

The way he is obliged to leave his father's house, to put on disguise and change his name, to elude the 'guard and most unusual vigilance' set up against him, including the 'intelligence' given by spies and informers, in accordance with official 'proclamations', and so to 'lurk' in corners and even to pretend possession by an evil spirit (ii.3, iii.6) – all this is matched point by point with the experience of both the Jesuits and the seminary priests on the English mission. (Milward 1997, 114)

Milward quoted from a letter by Campion to the Jesuit General in 1580: "I cannot long escape the hands of the heretics; the enemy have so many eyes, so many tongues, so many scouts and crafts. I am in apparel to myself very ridiculous; I often change my name also ... Threatening edicts come forth against us daily (Milward 1997, 114–15). Gary Taylor likened Shakespeare's anonymity, his "self-erasure", with recusant secrecy: "the desire to protect yourself from those who would 'pluck out the heart' of your mystery is most understandable in adherents of a religion that was defined as treason" (Taylor 1994, 314). The connection made by Wilson, Milward, and Taylor between the persecution of recusants and the figure of Edgar suits Shakespeare's reputation for inscrutability, his tendency, unlike other dramatists, to remain hidden. As Julian Yates pointed out, it was the hidden nature of Catholic resistance that was particularly disconcerting for the recusant-hunter (Yates 1999, 68).

Although the theory that Shakespeare was Catholic helps explain the apparent indeterminacy of his writings, the issue of genre also has an important bearing upon the multivalency with which the author has become identified. Although Shakespeare is today regarded primarily as a dramatist, the Romantic notion of dramatic writing as poetry writ large dominated Shakespeare studies for many years and elided the crucial generic difference between Shakespeare and poets like Spenser. Charles Lamb thought that Shakespeare should be read rather than performed:

to see Lear acted, – to see an old man tottering about the stage with a walking-stick, turned out of doors by his daughters in a rainy night, has nothing in it but what is painful and disgusting. We want to take him into shelter and relieve him, – that is all the feeling which the acting of Lear ever produced in me. But the Lear of Shakespeare cannot be acted. The contemptible machinery, by which they mimic the storm which he goes out in, is not more inadequate to represent the horrors of the real elements than any actor can be to represent Lear; they might more easily propose to personate the Satan of Milton upon a stage, or one of Michael Angelo's terrible figures. The greatness of Lear is not in corporal dimension, but in intellectual ... .On the stage we see nothing but corporal infirmities and weakness, the impotence of rage; while we read it, we see not Lear but we are Lear, – we are in his mind, we are sustained by a grandeur which baffles the malice of daughters and storms. (Lamb 1891, 185–86)

Similarly Coleridge said that he "never saw any of Shakespeare's plays performed but with a degree of pain, disgust and indignation ... [and] was therefore not distressed at the enormous size and monopoly of the theatres, which drove Shakespeare from the stage to find his proper place in the heart and the closet, where he sits with Milton enthroned on a two-headed Parnassus" (Coleridge 1960, 230). That the Shakespeare scholar were better to stay locked in his study reading Shakespeare's plays rather than attending performances was also suggested by Matthew Arnold who claimed of his tragedies that "every speech has to be read two or three times before its meaning can be comprehended" (Arnold 1965, 602). Such ideas about performance were echoed by T. S. Eliot who thought Shakespeare should "be read rather than seen" and claimed to "rebel against" most performances of the play "because I want a direct relationship between the work of art and myself, and I want the performance to be such as will not interrupt or alter this relationship" (Eliot 1934, 14–15). These critics advocate a Shakespeare unsullied by the theatre, an emphasis on Shakespeare the poet over and above Shakespeare as a man of the theatre. The Romantics, and those who followed their view of Shakespeare the poet, would read Shakespeare's play alongside Spenser's *Faerie Queene* without concerning themselves about the generic distinction between drama, written for the stage, and poetry, written for private reading. The notion that Shakespeare's plays should be read as poems has been replaced by our stage-centred view of Shakespeare, a development which has its roots in the first half of the twentieth century.

  M.C. Bradbrook's *Elizabethan Stage Conditions*, published in 1932, triggered the rise in stage-centred thinking which would establish Shakespeare primarily as a dramatist rather than a poet. For Bradbrook the key to understanding Shakespeare was to understand the theatre industry within which he worked: "The business of getting to know an author is largely that of learning the implications of his personal code, his specialised uses of structure and words; and in the case of a dramatist, this will depend on his theatre and his audience" (Bradbrook 1968, 147–48). As though answering Matthew Arnold directly Bradbook went on:

> Continual and sensitive reading does much to assist the reader, but it cannot do everything to enable him to complete this essential task. The value of the study of Elizabethan stage conditions lies in this elucidation of the author's methods... . A study of his age will also discourage the purely personal and appreciative criticism which consists of the creation of an inferior kind of private poem. (Bradbrook 1968, 148)

For Bradbrook then, to privilege the reading of Shakespeare's plays over their performance is to ignore the creative conditions which gave rise to them and is in effect to misread drama as poetry; conversely, any attempt to dramatize Spenser's *Faerie Queene* would produce a very different creation to that intended by the poet and, one might say, an inferior kind of public play.

Bradbrook's work was hugely influential and encouraged the performance of Shakespeare's plays as a serious subject for academic study. The University of Bristol was the first in Britain to offer the study of drama at university level with the establishment of a drama department in 1947 by Glynne Wickham and, in 1951, The Shakespeare Institute, a postgraduate school of the University of Birmingham, was founded by the theatre historian Allardyce Nicoll who was its first director. Each of the Institute's subsequent directors, Terence Spencer, Philip Brockbank, Stanley Wells, Peter Holland and Russell Jackson have, along with the Institute's Fellows, emphasized a stage-centred study of Shakespeare's plays, something which is clear from their editing of various editions.

The Oxford Complete Works, published in 1986, was another important development in Shakespeare's plays being considered primarily in terms of performance rather than literature. The Oxford editors were not concerned with the plays as finally drafted by Shakespeare but rather with how they were first performed:

> The acknowledged genius of his work resides in its marriage of verbal and theatrical talents; if both powers operated in the initial phases of composition, both should also have operated in subsequent phases, and in practice multiple verbal and 'literary' variants always coexist with 'theatrical' variants affecting staging, pace, the shape of a scene, the character of an entrance or exit. One would hardly suppose that Shakespeare devoted less mental energy to theatrical problems the closer a play got to its first

performance; if anything, he might have become more concerned with that aspect of his craft as the realities of enactment drew nearer. (Wells et al. 1987, 19)

Apparently influenced by Jerome McGann's notion of the socialized text – which shifted emphasis away from authorial intention and toward those cultural and social factors which impacted upon the end product (McGann 1983) – the Oxford editors emphasized the role of numerous agents in the composition of Shakespeare's plays as they finally got performed.

Shakespeare was not a lone author whose plays were transmitted unaltered from head to pen to page to stage but, rather, many factors impacted upon the creation of the play text not least of which was the influence of the censor: "Most readers will, we feel sure, want to read Shakespeare in an unexpurgated and uncensored text; but anyone who wishes to consider Shakespeare's works as performed in his lifetime will need to take account of ways in which the political authorities influenced the object presented to the public" (Wells et al. 1987, 16). Economic pressures such as audience demand and competition with other theatres also influenced what got performed and undoubtedly Shakespeare's fellow actors contributed to the shaping of the script. As the Oxford editors pointed out, "Playwrights do, to varying degrees, lose control of their scripts once a play is handed over or sold to a theatre" and although it is unlikely that the views of Shakespeare, actor and shareholder in the company, were "lightly or consistently overruled by his colleagues or friends", there would have been a certain amount of negotiation in order to prepare the script for performance: "it seems reasonable to suppose that Shakespeare personally suggested many or most of the alterations made in rehearsal, and that he acquiesced in others" (Wells et al. 1987, 19). The implication is that, whatever his political or religious affiliations, Shakespeare had less freedom than poets such as Spenser to indulge in the role of literary creator, a role which allowed fantasies of geographical metamorphosis relatively free reign. Suggestions made by colleagues might explain Shakespeare's habit of revising his plays, something emphasized by the Oxford editors. In the case of *King Lear* we have two distinct versions, the *History of King Lear*, first published as a quarto in 1608 and the *Tragedy of King Lear*, first published in the 1623 Folio. The Oxford editors believed the latter to be a revision of the former and "a more obviously theatrical text" (Shakespeare 1988, 943). The variations:

streamline the play's action, removing some reflective passages, particularly at the ends of scenes. They affect the characterization of, especially,
Edgar, Albany, and Kent, and there are significant differences in the
play's closing passages. Structurally the principal differences lie in the
presentation of the military actions in the later part of the play; in the
Folio-based text Cordelia is more clearly in charge of the forces that come
to Lear's assistance, and they are less clearly a French invasion force.
(Shakespeare 1988, 943)

The Oxford editors believed these revisions "may have been dictated in
whole or in part by theatrical exigencies" or "may have emerged from
Shakespeare's own dissatisfaction with what he had first written"
(Shakespeare 1988, 943). Either explanation is contrary to the Romantic
notion of Shakespeare as a solitary genius: the Romantics would have
accepted the impulse to revision (Wordsworth regularly revised his work)
but they would have balked at revision being driven by the practicalities of
the theatre, an environment which they believed sullied Shakespeare's
work. That the two versions of *King Lear* were conflated since the early
eighteenth century is at best a desire to savour every scrap of Shakespeare
that we have but at worst a desire to conceal Shakespeare's participation in
the quite common theatrical practice of revision. At the very least, it mis-
represents his intellectual labour, for the two versions are, in important
details, mutually incompatible. In chapter 4 I will consider *The History of
King Lear* not least because, as the Oxford editors point out, it raises perti-
nent issues relating to national identity and power.

The Oxford editors also emphasized the collaborative nature of
Shakespeare's plays via his habit of working with other playwrights: with at
least two authors, one of whom was probably Thomas Nashe, on *1 Henry 6*;
with Thomas Middleton on *Timon of Athens*, with George Wilkins on
Pericles, and with John Fletcher on *The Two Noble Kinsmen* and *All is True*
(Wells et al. 1987, 217, 501, 557, 625 and 618). They considered it likely that
Measure for Measure and *Macbeth* were adapted by Middleton (Wells et al.
1987, 468 and 543) and also thought it possible that Shakespeare was one of
four authors who provided alterations and additions to the multi-authored
Thomas More (Wells et al. 1987, 461). More recently Brian Vickers outlined
the case for *Titus Andronicus* having been co-written with George Peele
(Vickers 2002, 148-243) and Jonathan Bate, editor of the Arden
Shakespeare edition of *Titus Andronicus* (1995), which assumed Shakespeare

to be sole author, found Vicker's argument convincing (Bate 2003, 3-4). The focus on Shakespeare's involvement in the process of revision and the collaborative nature of Shakespeare's plays, his participation in co- and multiple-authorship, presents us with a very different picture from that established by the Romantics who invested in the notion of Shakespeare as a lone genius.

The rise in stage-centred study of Shakespeare has alerted critics to the generic distinction between Shakespeare as dramatist and poets such as Spenser. Of course Shakespeare wrote poetry as poetry, and also wrote dramatic verse but, current thinking tells us, he was primarily concerned with dramatic production. Poets are traditionally considered to be univocal, solitary figures who, though also subject to the censure of the critics, have a greater degree of control over their product than dramatists. The latter must participate in the collaborative nature of the theatre industry and thus engage with actors, censors and economic pressures; as Bradbrook indicated, the stage and the audience for which the play was written were crucial components in the creation of the play text. Although poets might fall foul of the censor, drama is to a greater degree dependent on factors external to the author which impact upon the creative process. Shakespeare apparently relinquished sole control over his intellectual material, as evidenced by Terence Hawkes' suggestion that part of the Welsh scene in *1 Henry 4* "may have been written by Welsh-speaking actors working within the company" (Hawkes 2002, 30). Shakespeare's multivalency, his seemingly effortless ability to speak from all corners, has been used to suggest that he was Catholic but the realities of writing within the genre of drama undoubtedly forced his hand, apparently something not experienced by Spenser, writing in solitude in the remote corner of Ireland where he found himself.

In our time, then, Shakespeare and Spenser are apparently contrasting figures: whereas Spenser outlined what he intended his work to mean in his *Letter to Raleigh* and betrayed his political and religious views in other writings, there is a real sense amongst critics that our insight into Shakespeare is considerably further from his innermost mind and kept back by the medium as well as by his method. Where Spenser's allegiance to the Sidney/Leicester faction is likely and his religious views fairly transparent, Shakespeare's religious loyalties are harder to discern. Genre has traditionally had an important role to play in our view of both writers, yet Shakespeare, recently considered primarily a man of the theatre, was thought of as a poet by the Romantics and, as we shall see in the conclusion to this study, may have considered himself as such. Shakespeare and Spenser lived near the beginning of what Hawkes so memorably called "the Great Britain project". That this project has now come to an end indicates that this is a good time to re-visit the reputations which have shaped our view of both writers. It is in the context of the unravelling of the 'united kingdom' and via the phenomenon of characters imagining their power to reshape the world that the major works of both writers will be considered. As we shall see, topographical manipulation, fantasies about containing and altering the landscape, dominate in writing by Shakespeare and Spenser and, as the subsequent chapters will demonstrate, each author's approach to altering the landscape provides surprising as well as predictable insights.

CHAPTER 1

Pastoralism versus ruralism: Spenser's vision For Ireland

A S W E S A W I N the introduction to this study, genre has played an important part in the formation of traditional views of Shakespeare and Spenser. Although Spenser is remembered primarily as a poet, he also wrote a prose dialogue, *A View of the Present State of Ireland*, which juxtaposes an ideal, pastoral Ireland with its less-pleasing rural reality and outlines how best to subjugate the rebellious Irish in order to attain that ideal. Fantasies about containing and altering the landscape also dominate in Spenser's pastoral poetry, *The Shepheardes Calender*, *Colin Clouts Come Home Againe* and the pastoral episodes from Book 6 of *The Faerie Queene*. This chapter will consider Spenser's pastoral poetry alongside the *View*, which shares their urgent desire to reshape the landscape and to obliterate its peripheral dangers. Although the *View* was probably composed around 1596, 17 years after publication of *The Shepheardes Calender* and one year after *Colin Clouts Come Home Againe*, the opinions expressed therein provide a crucial retrospective lens through which to see Spenser's depiction of the landscape in his earlier visions of the pastoral.

A View of the Present State of Ireland

Spenser's prose dialogue *A View of the Present State of Ireland* is presented as a fiction, a conversation between two characters, Irenius and Eudoxus. Irenius is generally considered by critics to be Spenser's spokesman, as Alexander Judson put it, "Spenser's mouthpiece" (Judson 1945, 92), but genre demands that we treat Irenius as a character even if it is likely that he voices Spenser's opinions about how best to dominate the Irish and gain control of Ireland. As Ciaran Brady pointed out, Spenser probably wrote the *View* in dialogue form so as to disguise the crudity of his proposal from Elizabeth and her senior officials (Canny & Brady 1988, 202). The *View* begins with Eudoxus enquiring about Ireland from Irenius who has just returned from there: "But if that Countrie of Irelande, whence youe latelye come be so goodlie and Comodious a soyle as yee reporte I wonder that no course is taken for the turninge theareof to good vses, and reducinge that salvage nacion to better gouerment and Cyvilitye" (Spenser 1949, 1). This sets the tone for the attitude expressed by Irenius throughout the text: the landscape of Ireland is characterized as attractive and worthy of development but only in the right hands:

> And sure it is a moste bewtifull and swete Countrie as anye is vnder heaven, seamed thoroughe out with manye goodlye rivers replenished with all sortes of fishe moste aboundantlye sprinckled with manye swete Ilandes and goodlye lakes like little Inlande seas, that will carye even shipps vppon theire waters, adorned with goodly woodes fitte for buildinge of howsses and shipps so comodiously as that if some princes in the worlde had them they woulde sone hope to be Lordes of all the seas and ere long of all the worlde (Spenser 1949, 62)

Irenius begins by describing Ireland in paradisical terms but quickly shifts his focus onto the economic advantage to be had if that beauty were harnessed by "some princes in the worlde", presumably a nod towards Elizabeth who should heed the advice being offered by her loyal subject, Spenser. However the beautiful landscape harbours hidden dangers for those who would exploit it and Irenius outlines in detail what is required to achieve a pastoral idyll in Ireland: the clearing of dense woodland, the elimination of what he regards to be barbaric practices such as booleying (or transhumance) and, most importantly, the destruction of the indigenous populace who resist his vision of a "subdewed and reformed" nation (Spenser 1949, 227). Spenser's detailed plan to effect change, what Anne Fogarty called "his blueprint for an idealized Ireland" (Fogarty 1989, 88), proposes a physical rather than a conceptual reshaping of the landscape but this is complicated by the literary form of the dialogue and the literary dimensions of his proposals. As Julia Lupton put it, Spenser's fantasy is of "a blank land which can be inscribed upon like a map" (Lupton 1993, 98) but a more appropriate analogy in relation to the pastoral would be that of a blank page upon which can be inscribed the kind of pastoral idyll described in his poetry even if , as we shall see, the poetic idyll consistently falls short of the ideal.

Irenius proposes the opening up of the Irish landscape, in particular the woodland which is utilized by rebels as a refuge, and calls for a strong power of men to be sent into Ireland to subdue "all that Rebellious route of loose people which either doe now stande out in open armes, or in wandering Companies doe kepe the woodes spoilinge and infestinge the good subiecte" (Spenser 1949, 149). Irenius relates the Irish woodland to the Irish custom of wearing the mantle, a garment loathed by English officials because, like the woodland itself, it offered refuge and was an ideal disguise: the rebel uses the mantle "when he still flyethe from his foe and lurketh in the thicke woods and straighte passages, waytinge for Advantages it is his bedd yea and allmoste all his househoulde stuffe, for the wood is his house against all weathers and his mantle is his Cave to slepe in" (Spenser 1949, 101). Irish woodland, characterized as beautiful and full of potential, requires the imposition of English order and this can only be effected by alteration: "and firste I wishe that order weare taken for the Cuttinge downe and openinge of all places thoroughe wodes so that a wide waye of the space of C. [a hundred] yardes mighte be laide open in euerye of them for the safetie of trauellers which vse often in suche perillous places to be Robbed and sometimes murdered" (Spenser 1949, 224). Again Irenius emphasizes the intimate connection between woody or mountainous terrain in Ireland and the Irish who use it to their advantage, twice claiming that the Irish names 'Brin' (or 'Birne') and 'Toole' signify 'woody' and 'hilly' (Spenser 1949, 94, 170). As well as the desire to cut down woodland there is an emphasis on containment, having the land enclosed because "it is bothe a principall barre and empeachement vnto theves from stealinge of Cattle in the nighte and allsoe a gavle [gall] againste all Rebles And outlawes that shall rise vp in anie numbers againste that government" (Spenser 1949, 135). Irenius calls for bridges to be built on all rivers and gatehouses to be built on the bridges, for a fort to be built in all narrow passages and for highways to be fenced on both sides, for towns to be built by the highways and for them to be protected by gates that can be shut at night as in the English Pale (Spenser 1949, 224–25).

Reshaping the landscape in order to achieve a tactical advantage against Irish rebels and criminals is figured in medical and topographical terms:

Ireland is likened to a wicked person who is dangerously sick, needing the care of a physician and, before the true religion of Protestantism can be planted, reformation is required. Irenius thinks such a reformation should be begun "Even by the sworde. for all those evills muste firste be Cutt awaie by a stronge hande before anie good Cane be planted, like as the Corrupte braunches and vnholsome boughes are firste to be pruned and the foule mosse clensed and scraped awaye, before the tree cane bringe forthe anye good fruite" (Spenser 1949, 148). Irenius imagines annihilation before creating anew in what is a striking example of the vehemence with which he expresses his desire to purify the Irish landscape before asserting control. England in the time of King Alfred provides a model for the reformation of Ireland: "it is manifest by reporte of the Cronicles and other ancient writers that it was greatlie infested with Robbers and outlawes which lurk[ed] in woodes and faste places" with "euerie Corner havinge a Robin hoode in it that kepte the woodes and spoilled all passengers and inhabitantes as Irelande now hathe" (Spenser 1949, 201; 203). Again the notion of cleaning to eradicate and prevent disease is evident: the landscape of Ireland is currently infected with outlaws, as England once was, and these evils must be purged before English rule can take root.

In his desire to eradicate those rebels who dwell on the periphery Irenius advocates firstly containment by installing four garrisons about the country each holding 2000 soldiers and 200 horsemen. In imagining the consequences of his plan, calculation gives way to fevered fantasy:

> And these fowre garrisons issuinge forthe, at suche Convenient times as they shall haue intelligence or espiall vpon the enemye will soe drive him from one side to another, and tennys him amongest them, that he shall finde no wheare safe to kepe his crete [cattle], nor hide him selfe, but flyinge from the fire into the water and out of one daunger into another that is shorte space his Crete which is his moste sustenaunce shalbe wasted with prayinge or killed with drivinge or starued for wante of pasture in the woodes, and he him self broughte so lowe that he shall haue no harte nor habilitye to endure his wretchedness. The which will surelie come to passe in verye shorte time, for one winters well followinge of him will so plucke him on his knees that he will neuer be able to stand vp againe. (Spenser 1949, 154)

Here Irenius envisages turning the table on the Irish enemy whereby the English not only assert control but employ guerrilla tactics similar to those currently used by the Irish, implementing the element of surprise and taking advantage of shelter. Irenius urges a winter war:

> in Irelande the winter time yealdethe best services, for then the trees are bare and naked which vse bothe to Cloath and hide the kerne, the ground is Cold and wett which vseth to be his beddinge, the aire is sharp and bitter to blowe thoroughe his naked sides and legges, the kine are barren and without milke which vsethe to be his onelye foode. Neither if he kill them then will they yealde hime fleashe nor if he kepe them will they give him fode. besides then beinge all with Calfe for the moste parte they will thoroughe muche Chasinge and drivinge Cast all theire Calfes and lose theire milke which should relieve him the next sommer after. (Spenser 1949, 154)

In both passages the effects of preventing the Irish from keeping their cattle is elaborated upon in such detail that there is an overwhelming sense of vindictiveness and brutality. Elsewhere in the dialogue, Irenius speaks at length about the need to resist the temptation to pity the Irish.

The desire to reshape the Irish landscape in order to assert political control can be fulfilled by mimicking in Ulster what occurred in the Munster wars, a scorched earth policy:

> Allthoughe theare should none of them fall by the sworde nor be slaine by the soldiour, yeat thus beinge kepte from manuraunce, and theire Cattle from Comminge abroade by this hard restrainte they woulde quicklye Consume themselues and devour one another. The profe wheareof I saw sufficientlye ensampled in Those late warrs of mounster, for notwithstandinge that the same was a most ritche and plentifull Countrye full of Corne and Cattell that ye woulde haue thoughte they Coulde haue bene able to stande longe yeat ere one yeare and a haulfe they weare broughte to soe wonderfull wretchednes as that anie stonie harte would haue rewed the same. Out of eurie Corner of the woods and glinnes they Came Crepinge forthe vppon theire handes for theire Legges Coulde not beare them, they loked like Anotomies of deathe, they spake like ghostes Cryinge out of theire graues, they did eate of the dead Carrions, happie wheare they Could finde them, Yea and one another sone after, in so muche as the verye carkasses they spared not to scrape out of theire graves. And if they founde a plotte of water Cresses or Shamarocks theare they flocked as to a feaste for the time, yeat not able longe to Continve thearewithall, that in shorte space theare weare non allmoste lefte and a moste populous and plentifull Countrye sodenlye lefte voide of man or beaste, yeat sure in all that warr theare perished not manie by the sworde but all by the extreamitye of famyne which they themselves had wroughte. (Spenser 1949, 158)

Degeneration, something usually abhorred in Spenser's writings, is here considered necessary to starve the Irish into submission. In an effort to lay the country bare and gain control of it Irenius enthusiastically recommends displacement of the successfully subdued Irish. His policy is one of dividing in order to conquer, stipulating that the Irish should not come under the rule of one landlord but rather be separated from their acquaintances and scattered throughout the country: "ffor that is the evill which I nowe finde in all Irelande That the Irishe dwell alltogeather by theire septes and seuer- all nacions so as they maye practize or Conspire what they will wheares if theare weare Englishe shed amongest them and placed ouer them they should not be able once to sturr or to murmure but that it shoulde be knowne, and they shortened accordinge to theire demerrittes" (Spenser 1949, 179–80). As Clare Carroll pointed out, Cromwell's infamous 'to hell or Connaught' policy was modelled on the *View* (Carroll 1990, 176), an opinion with which Nicolas Canny recently concurred when he noted that those who imposed the Cromwellian settlement on Ireland "were consciously pursuing the course set by Spenser and his fellow reformers during the late sixteenth century, which had been occasionally invoked by their disciples during the first half of the seventeenth century" (Canny 2001, 552). It is not surprising that Richard McCabe should note a paral- lel between Lord Grey, whose brutal actions are heartily defended by Irenius in the *View*, and Cromwell since both Grey and Cromwell were particularly vicious in their treatment of the indigenous population (McCabe 1989, 119).

Throughout the *View* the emphasis on refiguring the landscape is focussed on the interior, those parts where the Irish enemy can remain unseen, and Irenius reiterates the need to lay Ireland and the Irish open to the 'view' of the English in order to establish English governance: "for the Irishemen I assure youe feares the gouernment no longer then he is within sighte or reache" (Spenser 1949, 189). For Irenius the organization of Irish society encourages degenerate behaviour, for example the Irish custom of booleying allows particular freedoms: "the people that live thus in these Bollies growe theareby the more Barbarous and live more licentiouslye then they Could in townes vsinge what meanes they liste and practisinge what mischiefs and villainies they will ... for theare they thinke them- selues haulfe exemted from lawe and obedience" (Spenser 1949, 98). He refers to the booleys again later: "for loke into all Countries that live in suche sorte by kepinge of Cattle, and youe shall finde that they are bothe verie Barbarous and vncivill and allsoe greatlye given to warr" (Spenser 1949, 217). Spenser believes that the Irish custom of booleying is a result of the Scythian origins of the Irish and thus proof of their barbarity. The spurious connection between the Scythians and the Irish, an alleged ancestry which makes them difficult to control, also provides a curious link between the Irish and wolves. Irenius notes that "the Scithians saide that they weare once euerie yeare turned into wolues and so it is written of the Irishe Thoughe mr *Camden* in a better sence do suppose it was a disease Called *lycanthropia* so named of the wolfe. And yeat some of the Irishe doe vse to mak the wolfe theire gossip" (Spenser 1949, 109). As Eileen McCracken pointed out, wolves, which had been exterminated in England before 1500, were plentiful in Ireland at this time (McCracken 1959, 288–89). Like the wolf with whom they are associated, the Irish have not yet been controlled but rather lurk on the periphery of civilized socie-ty ever ready to attack. In his description of the kerns, Irenius emphasizes their animal-like nature: they exhibit "the moste loathelye and barbarous tradicions of any people I thinke vnder heaven", they use "beastlye behavour that maye be The[y] oppress all men" and they "spoile ... steale they are Cruell and bloddye full of revenge and delightinge in deadlye execucion" (Spenser 1949, 123). Irenius allows that the kerns are "verye valiante and hardye" (Spenser 1949, 123) but this only serves to emphasize the need to bring them into check. Thomas Blenerhasset described the woodkern and the wolf as the most serious dangers confronting colonists in Ireland (Blenerhasset 1610, A3r-D1v), a view shared by Thomas Gainsford who noted that thieves and wolves were prevalent dangers (Gainsford 1618, 148).

Ireland is dangerous because it is strange, unknown, and unmapped. David J. Baker pointed out that the English did not have cartographic con-trol because in this period "A complete and detailed representation of Ireland did not exist" (Baker 1993, 82) and maps of Ireland by royal cartog-raphers "were often conjectural and muddled" (Baker 1993, 78). R. A. Butlin concurred that:

> In spite of the increase in surveying and cartography in the late sixteenth
> century, the English administrators still lacked the detailed geographical
> data necessary for a rational administrative framework, and thus relying

on an imperfect perception of the geography of Ireland failed to achieve
their objectives. (Butlin 1976, 167)

Bernhard Klein noted that in the Irish section of Laurence Nowell's *General
Description of England and Ireland* (1564–65) "Britain visibly curves west-
ward as if to bend over and encircle its neighbouring isle" which differs
from the medieval tradition of the "Gough" map where Britain is upright in
shape and Ireland is "an oddly-shaped smaller island that does not really
seem to belong there". Klein concurred with Michael Neill that alongside
the desire to keep the Irish at a distance was the need to incorporate Ireland
within England's borders for English national security. The pictorial
attempt at what Klein calls "geographical appropriation" is, however,
undermined in Nowell's map by the "Large clusters of green [which] suggest the intractability of a wild and barbaric landscape" with the viewer's
gaze drawn toward "the graphic irregularities and textual gaps of an 'unfinished' Ireland, acting as the constant reminder of the incomplete conquest"
(Klein 1998, paragraph 13).

In the *View* Irenius describes early modern Ireland as aesthetically and
economically attractive but also unpredictable and dangerous. On the
surface it is beautiful but terrors lurk within its woods and caves inhabited
by those who challenge English autonomy. In the *View* there is a desire to
reshape the land in order to reveal that which is hidden, to open up the
dense woods and secret places occupied by the rebellious and uncivilized
Irish. Irenius insists that the Irish landscape must be reorganized, laid bare
in order to be civilized and the political solution for the colonizer is to cut
through the landscape, rid it of rebellion and assert control upon a hostile
and unpredictable environment. In Spenser's *Shepheardes Calender* and
Colin Clouts Come Home Againe the tension between a pastoral idyll and a
rural reality is also evident and those enemies who threaten the peace in
colonial Ireland emerge from the shadows in poetry composed both before
and after 1580, the year Spenser took up his appointment as secretary to
Lord Grey in Ireland.

The Shepheardes Calender

Spenser's first major publication, and the one that would earn him the reputation of being a pastoral poet, was *The Shepheardes Calender*, published in

1579. Anticipating the *View*, the poem is multivocal and offers the reader several dialogues, not just one. Although Spenser was influenced by Virgil, whose poetic career began with pastoral verse, the calendar design is Spenser's innovation (Spenser 1989, 3). Richard McCabe characterized *The Shepheardes Calender* as "an exercise in courtly taste" where the word 'kerne' in the July eclogue carries none of the savage connotations evident in the *View* (McCabe 1993, 81). McCabe emphasized the gap between Spenser's early literary depiction of the pastoral existence and those writings, including the *View*, which followed his experiences in rural Ireland (McCabe 1993, 82), quoting W. B. Yeats to support his argument: "though he dreamed of Virgil's shepherds he wrote a book [the *View*] to advise ... the harrying of all that followed flocks upon the hills, and of all the wandering companies that keep the woods" (Yeats 1961, 373). McCabe concurred with Yeats that, having become a colonial politician, Spenser wanted to destroy the rural reality of what he had previously celebrated: the liberty of pastoral life. Although critics do not usually accord an Irish dimension to *The Shepheardes Calender* because the poem was published in 1579 and Spenser did not arrive in Ireland to take up his secretarial duties until August 1580, Willy Maley persuasively argued that Spenser "may have been steeped in Irish politics" earlier than previously thought, even as early as 1578 while serving under the Bishop of Rochester in Kent (Maley 1997, 30). Maley detected several "Irish elements" in *The Shepheardes Calender*, among them the possibility that E. K. is the Earl of Kildare and that a story by Richard Stanyhurst in Holinshed's *Chronicles* (1577) about the walling of New Ross in Cork is related to the 'widdowes daughter of the glenne' who betrays Colin Clout, the figure generally agreed to be Spenser's *alter ego*. He further proposed that Rosalinde, Colin Clout's object of desire, might represent Ireland, meaning that, contrary to what critics tend to believe, "Spenser's acquisition of an Irish estate represents the fulfilment of his youthful passion, not its displacement" (Maley 1997, 29).

Louis Montrose noted that in the early modern period figurative pastoralism borrowed from literal pastoralism but rejected the harsh reality of its labour. Literary pastoralism, which was dominated by aristocratic values and style even though most of its poets had humble origins, placed great emphasis on leisure in an attempt to mimic the leisure of the gentry who found manual labour unappealing. In pastoral literature the shepherd's toil is minimal and the manual labour required of other agrarian tasks is ignored. The main thrust of literary pastoralism was the imaginative creation of an elite society by a burgeoning middle class in an attempt to bring aristocratic values to the practice of shepherding (Montrose 1983). Yet although Spenser's shepherds enjoy the liberty of pastoral life (their toil is certainly minimal) the pastoral world created by Spenser in this early poem is not entirely idyllic. As Helen Cooper pointed out, "Much Renaissance pastoral writing, including Spenser's, concentrates more on the fallen world than the golden" (Cooper 1990, 530) and in *The Shepheardes Calender* Spenser is particularly alert to the ambivalences of the pastoral existence; far from presenting his reader with a golden world, the pastoral environment of *The Shepheardes Calender* is tinged with sadness, disillusionment and, above all, an ever-present peripheral threat to the community of shepherds which suggests an Irish colonial dimension to the poem. But, curiously, this coexists with a sense of optimism and the notion that the natural world can be supportive if properly managed.

In the January eclogue Colin perceives a parallel between his feelings of unrequited love for Rosalinde and the winter landscape:

> Thou barrein ground, whome winters wrath hath wasted,
> Art made a myrrhour, to behold my plight:
> Whilome thy fresh spring flowrd, and after hasted
> Thy sommer prowde with Daffadillies dight.
> And now is come thy wynters stormy state,
> Thy mantle mard, wherein thou maskedst late.
> (*The Shepheardes Calender* January, 19–24)

Critics concur that the January eclogue is primarily amatory and Colin's pipe-breaking at the end of the eclogue is a demonstration of romantic despair, but Lin Kelsey and Richard S. Peterson suggested that the pipe-breaking is a sign of discontent over patronage. They further remarked that Spenser's consideration of "the Ovidian reed" may indicate the identity of Rosalind since both 'reed' and 'roseau', the French word for 'reed' or pipe, might allude to Queen Elizabeth, both words incorporating "puns on the slender, red-haired queen's emblem, the red (and white) Tudor rose" (Kelsey & Peterson 2000, 255). The possible allusion to Elizabeth and a political rather than a wholly romantic context becomes more likely if we consider the implication of the marred mantle, an image which recurs in the November eclogue where the mantle is again mentioned in the context of waste:

Ay me that dreerie death should strike so mortall stroke,
That can vndoe Dame natures kindly course:
The faded lockes fall from the loftie oke,
The flouds do gaspe, for dryed is theyr sourse,
And flouds of teares flowe in theyr stead perforse.
The mantled medowes mourne,
Theyr sondry colours tourne.
O heauie herse,
The heauens doe melt in teares without remorse.
O carefull verse.
(*The Shepheardes Calender* November, 123–132)

Just as Colin imagined the natural world to be reflecting his plight in the January eclogue so here the natural world responds to the death of Dido and the "mantled medowes" are considered to be in mourning. In both eclogues the mantle evokes degeneration and loss. In the *View*, as we saw above, Irenius abhors the Irish custom of wearing the mantle which he considers "a fitt howsse for an outlawe, a mete bedd for a Rebell and an Apte cloake for a thefe" (Spenser 1949, 100). Eudoxus notes that the mantle is an ancient garment worn by, amongst others, the Greeks and Romans (Spenser 1949, 99), but Irenius emphasizes the Irish misuse of it, thus associating the mantle with degeneration and, as in the January and November eclogues, the mantle of Summer, the garment worn by ancient peoples, has been marred by the uses to which it is put in Ireland.

The February eclogue features a debate between a young and old man and in the fable of the old oak and the young briar ambition is shown to be self-destructive. The eclogue provides comment on the conflict between inexperience and wisdom but of particular interest is the fable told by Thenot, "an olde shepheard", to Cuddie, "an unhappy Heardmans boye", where manipulation of the landscape results in an unforeseen and undesirable outcome. In the fable "an aged Tree" that was once "a goodly Oake" is reproved by "a bragging brere" for what the briar perceives to be the oak's uselessness and detrimental effect on his beauty. The briar complains to the husbandman who then chops down the tree but the result is not what the briar expected; instead of being made more attractive by the absence of the tree the briar suffers from the harsh effects of the winter weather "For nowe no succoure was seene him nere" (228) and is effectively destroyed: "That nowe vpright he can stand no more: / And being downe, is trodde in the durt / Of cattell, and brouzed, and sorely hurt" (234–236). The argument notes that the eclogue "is rather morall and generall, then bent to any secrete of particular purpose" but critics have sought to identify a specifically religious allegory, for example Edwin Greenlaw noted that "The fall of Catholicism in England was often compared to the fall of a great tree, or reformers were urged to cut down the tree of Catholicism" (Spenser 1943, 261) while L. S. Friedland suggested that "The Oak may represent not the Roman Church, but the Anglican Church engendered by narrow, strident, scratchy dissenters" (Spenser 1943, 262). But the fable also suggests a specifically Irish context: the role of woodland in the colony.

Spenser's comment on the damaging effects of ambition, with a likely nod towards the court, provides a curious analogue to his focus on trees and woodland in the *View* and *The Faerie Queene*. Irenius champions "the Cuttinge downe and opening of all places throughe wodes" in order to assure "the safetie of trauellers" (Spenser 1949, 224) and Guyon performs such an action in the Bower of Bliss when "Their groues he feld, their gardins did deface" (2.12.83.6). Thenot remarks that the "spitefull brere ... / Causlesse complained" (147–148) and the narrative is weighed in favour of the tree but the reader is presented with a particular difficulty: since the tree protects the briar which is "puffed up with pryde and vaine pleasaunce" it is presumably to the greater good that the tree should be cut down. In the *View* Irenius describes Ireland as "a most beautiful and sweet country as any is under heaven ... adorned with goodly woods" but the woods provide protection to the country's rebels and, besides, the country's beauty comes second to the economic use to which the woods can be put since they are "fit for building of houses and ships" (Spenser 1970, 18–19). The ambivalence felt by Spenser toward the Irish landscape in the *View* – it is both beautiful and dangerous, aesthetically pleasing in its current state but useful when cut down – can be detected in February's fable since the tree is both benevolent, protecting the briar from the harsh winter weather, and harmful, sustaining its pride and vanity. The checking of pride that results from the destruction of the oak appears to prefigure the vehemence with which Guyon destroys Acrasia's bower and the enthusiasm with which Irenius advocates the cutting down of Ireland's woodland.

The April eclogue contains a song composed by Colin and praising Eliza in Petrarchan terms: she is a goddess and should be adorned with flowers by virgins; but before the song is sung by Hobbinoll, Thenot questions the reasons for Hobbinoll's sadness:

TEll me good Hobbinoll, what garres thee greete?
What? hath some Wolfe thy tender Lambes ytorne?
Or is thy Bagpype broke, that soundes so sweete?
Or art thou of thy loued lasse forlorne?
(*The Shepheardes Calender* April, 1–4)

The reference to lamb-tearing wolves alerts the reader to the dark under-side of the pastoral existence and, fundamentally, to that which the shep-herds cannot control: those violent forces which lurk on the edge of their otherwise idyllic environment. Louis Montrose noted that celebrations of the pastoral usually emphasize a life of ease, yet here Hobbinoll announces himself to be Eliza's "shepherds swayne, / Albee forswonck and forswatt I am": he is her servant even though tired with work and sweaty (97–99). While we never actually read about the shepherds working, this report of industry and the threat from wolves contradicts the notion that, as Montrose put it, "the literary shepherd's day is typically occupied by singing, piping, wooing and the other quaint indulgences of the pastoral life" (Montrose 1983, 427–28).

Wolves are both literal and metaphorical in *The Shepheardes Calender*, representing a mortal threat to shepherds and lambs and also the threat posed by corrupt clergy. In the May eclogue, the first of three ecclesiastical eclogues, Piers denounces greed and ambition, describing how "under colour of shepeheards... /... crept in wolves, ful of fraude and guile, / that often devoured their own sheepe" (126–8). This attack on degenerate clergy denounces papists as "faitors" (imposters), comparing them to the fox who will disguise himself as a poor pedlar in order to trick true Christians by bringing "bells, and babes, and glasses in hys packe" (240) which E. K. (the contemporary and anonymous annotator of the poem) glosses as "the reliques and ragges of popish supersition, which put no smal religion in Belles: and Babies .s. Idoles: and glasses .s. Paxes, and such lyke trumperies", meaning by "Babies" 'dolls', by "Paxes" 'plates showing Crucifixion images to be kissed during mass', and by "trumperies" 'deceits' (Spenser 1989, 104n240). In the September eclogue Diggon reports on the countries he has visited abroad where shepherds are either lazy or false, the sheep "wander at wil" and some have been eaten by wolves (141–148). Similarly in the July eclogue Thomalin denounces those shepherds in Rome who mistreat their sheep, referring to them as wealthy "wisards" who keep "fat kernes" (197; 199). Richard McCabe's assertion that this use of the word 'kerne' carries none of the savage connotations evident in the *View* (McCabe

1993, 81) does not take into account the extent to which these fat kernes and the Irish foot-soldiers discussed in the *View*, if not equally savage, are both morally corrupt. In the September eclogue Hobbinoll corrects Diggon, remarking that foxes have replaced wolves and Diggon reports that these creatures dress in sheep's clothing and fear "the great hunt" (159), perhaps an allusion to the Reformation, before proceeding to tell a story about Roffynn's dog and how cunning wolves can be (180–225).

Spenser's eclogues form part of a literary tradition considered by Barbara Brumbaugh in the context of a speech by Philip Sidney made at an Ambassadorial dinner in 1577 and recorded for posterity by Philip Camerarius, a Protestant scholar with whom Sidney had spoken about forming a Protestant league (Brumbaugh 2000, 273). Critics have hitherto assumed the subject of Sidney's speech, the elimination of wolves from England, to be a straightforward historical account of the animals' expulsion, but Brumbaugh argued that it also alludes to the established Protestant literary convention of satiric 'hunting' dialogues which figure Catholics, particularly the clergy obedient to the pope, as wolves who prey upon faithful Christians. The Christians, or sheep, can be protected by particularly outspoken Protestant clergy, or loudly barking dogs (Brumbaugh 2000, 274–80). Brumbaugh emphasized the dog/clergy analogy, but dogs as guardians of the True Church, a metaphor applied by Sidney in his *Defence of Poetry* (Brumbaugh 2000, 281), may extend to other guardians of the faith, in particular those rhetoricians who contribute to the fight against Catholicism. Brumbaugh noted that in his *Defence* Sidney links pastoral and allegory, claiming that "under the pretty tales of wolves and sheep" can lurk "considerations of wrong-doing and patience" (Brumbaugh 2000, 278) and in his allegories as well as in the *View* Spenser can certainly be regarded as a loud barker.

In the June eclogue Colin laments that Rosalind, who accepted his love for a time, has now forsaken him and loves Menaclas, another shepherd. Unlike Colin, Hobbinoll has found happiness in beautiful surroundings and Colin admires his situation:

> O happy *Hobbinoll*, I blesse thy state,
> That Paradise hast found, whych *Adam* lost.
> Here wander may thy flock early or late,
> Withouten dreade of Wolves to bene ytost:
> Thy lovely layes here mayst thou freely boste.

> But I unhappy man, whom cruell fate,
> And angry Gods persue from coste to coste,
> Can nowhere fynd, to shroude my lucklesse pate.
> (*The Shepheardes Calender* June, 9–16)

Hobbinoll advises Colin to "forsake the soyle, that so doth thee bewitch" (18) and leave "those hilles", contrasting Colin's home with his own in the dales which he characterizes as a pastoral idyll:

> Here no night Rauens lodge more blacke then pitche,
> Nor eluish ghosts, nor gastly owles doe flee.

> But frendly Faeries, met with many Graces,
> And lightfote Nymphes can chace the lingring night,
> With Heydeguyes, and trimly trodden traces,
> Whilst systers nyne, which dwell on *Parnasse* hight,
> Doe make them musick, for their more delight:
> And *Pan* himselfe to kisse their christall faces,
> Such pierlesse pleasures haue we in these places.
> (*The Shepheardes Calender* June, 23–32)

That Colin lives amongst hills and wolves might suggest the dangers of climbing upwards (the hills representing ambition) but also that he feels the influence of sinister and malevolent forces (represented by wolves) and has neglected his music because of grief resulting from his unrequited love for Rosalind. In the August eclogue the environment is more benevolent and the sad song written by Colin about Rosalind and sung by Cuddie addresses the natural world:

> YE wastefull woodes beare witnesse of my woe,
> Wherein my plaints did oftentimes resound:
> Ye carelesse byrds are privie to my cryes,
> Which in your songs were wont to make a part:
> Thou pleasaunt spring hast luld me oft a sleepe,
> Whose streames my tricklinge teares did ofte augment.
> Resort of people doth my greefs augment,
> The walled townes do worke my greater woe:
> The forest wide is fitter to resound
> The hollow Echo of my carefull cryes,
> I hate the house, since thence my loue did part,
> Whose waylefull want debarres myne eyes from sleepe.
> (*The Shepheardes Calender* August, 151-163)

Colin's complaints have echoed through the woodland and he believes not only that the natural world empathizes with his grief but that he has begun to merge into that world, his words forming part of its bird-song and his tears forming part of its waters. The connections made by Judith Owens between Spenser's "reformist" designs for Ireland in the *View* and his intentions for his bride in the *Epithalamion*, the poem published in 1595 which celebrates his second marriage, are illuminating also for *The Shepheardes Calender*. The refrain in the marriage poem, variations on 'The woods shall to me answer and my Eccho ring', can signify harmony but has been read by some critics as a source of disturbance and Owens claimed that the woods around Kilcolman give the refrain social and political significance. As we have seen, Spenser thought that deforestation was a necessary prerequisite for the subjugation of Ireland and Owens made a connection between the title of his prose dialogue, the *View*, and his desire "to see this country and its people" who literally hide from sight and remain hidden in the sense of not being known (Owens 2000, 42). Owen stated that in the *Epithalamion* Spenser desires "to make the woods answer" to his song and thus subject both the country and his bride to "English ways" and that in the opening stanza of the *Epithalamion* Spenser looks back to England and the classical world in order to "find the order and vision" into which he "at least initially wishes to place his bride and thus Ireland"; the praising of his bride will edify her and Ireland since an Ireland "resonating with his exemplary love" with woods echoing his song "would be an Ireland reformed by his poetic vision and so rendered intelligible" (Owens 2000, 45). In *The Shepheardes Calender* the woods also echo with the poet's words but rather than looking back to England and the classical world Spenser looks forward, presumably anticipating his next project, the epic *Faerie Queene* and perhaps, as Maley suggested, the fulfilment of his youthful passion in Ireland. Although the subject matter of the August eclogue is sad, the natural world is supportive and there is a sense of optimism that, despite the threat from wolves in the earlier eclogues, nature can assist the shepherds if properly manipulated, managed according to what Owens termed "English ways".

In the December eclogue Colin sings to Pan of his life, which he compares to the seasons of the year. When youthful in spring he feared no danger: "I went the wastefull woodes and forest wyde, / Withouten dreade-of Wolves to bene espyed" (23–24). Colin thought the spring would last forever but summer brought manhood and unrestrained love "(For love then in the Lyons house did dwell) / The raging fyre, that kindled at his ray" (57–58). This was also a time spent close to nature and Colin describes the natural world experienced during the summer of his life as sinister but with the potential for benevolence:

> The bush my bedde, the bramble was my bowre,
> The Woodes can witnesse many a wofull stowre.
>
> Where I was wont to seeke the honey Bee,
> Working her formall rowmes in Wexen frame:
> The grieslie Todestool growne there mought I se
> And loathed Paddocks lording on the same.
> And where the chaunting birds luld me a sleepe,
> The ghastlie Owle her grieuous ynne doth keepe.
> (*The Shepheardes Calender* December, 65–72)

Although Colin is looking back over his long life, the poet Spenser has only just begun his career and is perhaps anticipating spending the summer of his life in Ireland. The "stowre" or conflict in the woods might refer to Colin's emotional anguish at unrequited love or allude to the armed conflict between colonizers and rebels in the woods of Ireland, a place where one cannot go "Withouten dreade of Wolves". Yet in Ireland the "grieslie", "loathed", and "ghastlie" coexists with the potential delights of the honey bee. Colin has learnt practical skills during the summer of his life such as the making of "timber cotes ... as might save my sheepe and me fro shame" (77–78) and he describes having learnt to understand the landscape:

> The sodain rysing of the raging seas:
> The soothe of byrds by beating of their wings,
> The power of herbs, both which can hurt and ease:
> And which be wont tenrage the restlesse sheepe,
> And which be wont to worke eternall sleepe.
> (*The Shepheardes Calender* December, 86–90)

The natural environment is potentially malevolent, harbouring unpredictable dangers but at the same time offering curative herbs. Although Colin, Spenser's *alter ego*, is bidding farewell to his "little Lambes and loved sheepe" and "Woodes that oft my witnesse were", Spenser is perhaps looking forward to residing in a land which, if properly altered, will offer all of nature's plenty including honey bees and benevolent herbs.

The dark underside to the pastoral existence present in *The Shepheardes Calender* is consistent with the representation of Ireland in the *View*: although Ireland is physically and economically attractive, the society of shepherds (Spenser's fellow colonizers) is undermined by those malevolent forces which lurk on its periphery. What is remarkable is that the sense of optimism present in *The Shepheardes Calender*, written at the beginning of Spenser's literary career, had not been entirely extinguished by the time he came to write the *View*. Both texts concentrate on that which undermines the pastoral idyll but are also characterized by a sense of hope and present a fantasy that topographical manipulation will bring about the dreamed-of pastoral idyll. As we shall see, this sense of optimism, the notion that real change is possible, is also a feature of *Colin Clouts Come Home Againe*.

Colin Clouts Come Home Againe

Colin Clouts Come Home Againe, published in 1595, was dedicated to Spenser's fellow-colonizer Walter Raleigh and in the dedication Spenser thanked him for "your singular favours and sundrie good turnes shewed to me at my late being in England" (Spenser 1989, 526). The poem's title is ambiguous – does it refer to a poem written by Colin Clout called "Come Home Againe"? Does 'home' refer to England, the place where Colin has just been or Ireland, the place to which he has just returned? What is the meaning of 'againe'? Has Colin been home before? That the opening of the poem coincides with his return suggests that its title refers to the present, not the past, and thus home is Ireland, the place to which Colin has returned because he is unhappy with the corruption and competition of life at court. At the beginning of the poem Hobbinoll tells Colin that he has been sorely missed by the Shepherds, by himself in particular, and by the natural world which has suffered greatly in his absence:

> Whilest thou wast hence, all dead in dole did lie:
> The woods were heard to waile full many a sythe,
> And all their birds with silence to complaine:
> The fields with faded flowers did seem to mourne,
> And all thier flocks from feeding to refraine:
> The running waters wept for thy returne,.
> And all their fish with languour did lament:
> (*Colin Clouts Come Home Againe* 22–28)

Now that Colin has returned, the shepherds consider themselves to be "blessed and so blythe" and the natural world has sprung to new life: "But now both woods and field, and floods revive, / Sith thou art come, their cause of meriment, / That us late dead, hast made againe alive" (29–31). Colin's music is ostensibly the reason for rejuvenation and rejoicing but also apparent is the notion that Spenser wants his readers to consider the influence he holds in Ireland and that Hobbinoll's celebration of Colin's return constitutes a kind of poetic wish-fulfilment: the shepherds need the poet Colin but at the same time Ireland needs Spenser, perhaps in the combined role of poet and servant of the state.

Colin's presence exerts a powerful influence on his companions and on the world around him but he is preoccupied with memories of meeting Cynthia (a familiar name for Elizabeth) at court:

> And since I saw that Angels blessed eie,
> Her worlds bright sun, her heavens fairest light,
> My mind full of my thoughts satietie,
> Doth feed on sweet contentment of that sight:
> Since that same day in nought I take delight,
> Ne feeling have in any earthly pleasure,
> But in remembrance of that glorious bright
> My lifes sole blisse, my hearts eternall threasure.
> (*Colin Clouts Come Home Againe* 40–47)

Although Colin has returned home because the court was corrupt, his thoughts remain at court and it is this ambivalence about here and there, home and court, which is a marked feature of the poem. Another important feature of the poem is the ambivalence with which each particular location is regarded: home is both safe and potentially hostile, the court is both glorious and corrupt. As we have already seen, in the *View* Ireland is figured worthy of praise, "a moste bewtifull and swete Countrie" (Spenser 1949, 62), but is at the same time a hostile environment full of dense "wodes" and "perillous places" (Spenser 1949, 224). At the behest of Hobbinoll, Colin describes how he came to be at court and the role of the Shepheard of the Ocean (Raleigh) in encouraging him to leave his home to visit Cynthia. Colin first meets the Shepheard of the Ocean while sitting "Under the foote of *Mole* that mountaine hore, / Keeping my sheepe amongst the cooly shade, / Of the greene alders by the *Mullaes* shore" (57–59) and their encounter is typically pastoral:

> He pip'd, I sung; and when he sung, I piped,
> By chaunge of turnes, each making other mery,
> Neither envying other, nor envied,
> So piped we, untill we both were weary.
> (*Colin Clouts Come Home Againe* 76–79)

The pleasant nature and mutuality of their friendship appears at least partly conditioned by the nature of the environment within which they play, which Colin in his song describes as a "pleasant vale" (107), the same environment which causes little concern to the shepherds who listen to Colin's story since "their flocks devoyd of dangers feare, / Did round about them feed at libertie" (lines 54–55). Yet there is a darker undercurrent in the songs of Colin and the Shepheard of the Ocean indicating that this pastoral world is not immune to hostility. Although Colin relates that the tunes made both men merry, both songs feature deceit and punishment and Colin notes that the Shepheard of the Ocean sang "a lamentable lay" (164). Furthermore, the Shepherd of the Ocean, who has come "far from the main-sea deepe" (67) suddenly speaks with harshness about Colin's home:

> He gan to cast great lyking to my lore,
> And great dislyking to my lucklesse lot:
> That banisht had my selfte, like wight forlore,
> Into that waste, where I was quite forgot.
> (*Colin Clouts Come Home Againe* 180–183)

The description of Colin's home as a "waste" is unexpected, particularly given earlier descriptions of its "cooly shade" and "greene alders by the *Mullaes* shore" (58–59). Although the Shepherd of the Ocean may be referring to the land as merely sparsely inhabited and uncultivated (OED 'waste' *sb* 1.a) the sense is overwhelmingly negative since this is a place where Colin has been "forgot". Colin compares the home to which he has returned, Ireland, to life in that place from which he has just returned, England:

> Both heaven and heavenly graces do much more
> (Quoth he) abound in that same land, then this.
> For there all happie peace and plenteous store
> Conspire in one to make contented blisse:
> No wayling there nor wretchednesse is heard,
> No bloodie issues nor no leprosies,
> No griesly famine, nor no raging sweard,
> No nightly bodrags, nor no hue and cries,
> The Shepheards there abroad may safely lie,
> On hills and downes, withouten dread or daunger:
> No ravenous wolves the good mans hope destroy,
> Nor outlawes fell affray the forest raunger.
> (*Colin Clouts Come Home Againe* 308–319)

Thestylis wonders why Colin has left "that happie place" (654) in order to return to "this barrein soyle / Where cold and care and penury do dwell: / Here to keep sheepe, with hunger and with toyle" (656–658). As in *The Shepheardes Calender* this reference to hard work, even though we never actually see any work done, emphasizes the darker underside of the pastoral existence. Colin describes how in England the arts are considered valuable with "poets wits ... had in peerlesse price" (321) and there is an abundance of virtue and grace, but he prefers the familiarity of the imperfect pastoral existence to the court's "unknowen wayes" where a man must "trust the guile of fortunes blandishment" (670–671). When describing his journey from Ireland to England Colin refers to the land he is leaving as "our mother" (226), a curiously affectionate term to use about Ireland (especially if we agree that Colin is Spenser's *alter ego*) unless he considered it 'home'. As the land disappears there is a focus on the vastness and danger of the sea which serves to emphasize the geographical distance between the two land masses and perhaps alludes to the cultural distance between them also. The court has its benefits but there is a caveat accompanying the praise:

> For end, all good, all grace there freely growes,
> Had people grace it gratefully to use:
> For God his gifts there plenteously bestowes,
> But graceless men them greatly do abuse.
> (*Colin Clouts Come Home Againe* 324–327)

Colin's censure of Irish society is countered by his desire to return there and the acknowledgement that England lacks grace. Ironically, Colin's claim that in England "poets wits are had in peerlesse price" is also true of poets in Ireland. In the *View* Irenius denigrates the Celtic poets, or bards, claiming that "so far from instructing young men in moral discipline ... whomsoever they find to be most licentious of life most bold and lawless in his doings, most dangerous and desperate in all parts of disobedience and rebellious disposition, him they set up and glorify in their rhymes, him they praise to the people, and to young men make an example to follow" (Spenser 1970, 73). But, as Richard McCabe pointed out, it is clear that Spenser also envied the bards who enjoyed an influence and prestige which exceeded that of their English counterparts. Indeed Spenser noted that they "are had in so high regard and estimation amongst them that none dare displease them for fear to run into reproach through their offence" (Spenser 1970, 72). As a poet Spenser presumably felt drawn to the esteem in which the Irish held their bards even if he rejected the uses to which they put their poetry.

Like the "lamentable lay" sung by the Shepherd of the Ocean, Colin's song is concerned with punishment. Yet while the Shepherd of the Ocean claims his punishment is unwarranted, he was "faultlesse" (167), Colin sings of the betrayal of the river Mole by the deceitful Bregog ("So hight because of his deceitfull traine", 118). Mole had forbidden any love between his daughter Mulla and her brother Bregog but in order to deceive him Bregog divided himself and, whilst Mole watched one course, secretly slid into Mulla (141–144). Mole learned of the deceit and punished Bregog by showering him with rocks "So of a River, which he was of old, / He none was made, but scattred all to nought" (152–153). Mole is Spenser's name for the Ballyhowra Hills in Munster to the north of his estate in Kilcolman and Mulla his name for the river Awbeg which bordered his estates to the south and west. His renaming of the Irish rivers betrays a desire to assert ownership, to put his stamp on the savage landscape, while the destruction of Bregog, of which he claims ownership (referring to it as "my river" [92]), suggests a fantasy of absolute control over the landscape where deceit is met with violence. In the *View* Irenius asserts the need to respond to Irish deception with violence: "wheare no other remedye maie be devized nor no hope of recouerie had theare muste neds this violente meanes be vsed" (Spenser 1949, 148) and the punishment of Bregog similarly suggests that obliteration is necessary to assert control. As we shall see in the next chapter, deceit is also met with violence in *The Faerie Queene* where villains are utterly destroyed in an effort to assert control over the landscape.

Colin declares that he will inscribe Cynthia's name in the landscape:

> Her name recorded I will leaue for ever.
> Her name in every tree I will endosse,
> That as the trees do grow, her name may grow:
> And in the ground each where will it engrosse,
> And fill with stones, that all men may it know.
> The speaking woods and murmuring waters fall,
> Her name Ile teach in knowen termes to frame:
> And eke my lambs when for their dams they call,
> Ile teach to call for *Cynthia* by name.
> (*Colin Clouts Come Home Againe* 631–639)

Spenser imagines an Irish landscape where the name of Elizabeth will grow, its dissemination being actively encouraged by the Irish landscape, which currently impedes the establishment of English rule. The landscape as an active participant in the poet's agenda is also explored in the next chapter

[47]

which considers fantasies of containment and control in *The Faerie Queene*.

Spenser further imagines his praise of Elizabeth being adopted and rehearsed by the local populace:

> And long while after I am dead and rotten:
> Amongst the shepheards daughters dancing rownd,
> My layes made of her shall not be forgotten,
> But sung by them with flowry gyrlonds crownd.
> And ye, who so ye be, that shall survive:
> When as ye heare her memory renewed,
> Be witnesse of her bounty here alive,
> Which she to *Colin* her poore shepheard shewed.
> (*Colin Clouts Come Home Againe* 640–647)

Spenser foresees English success in Ireland when, many years after his death, the name of Elizabeth will be praised by the firmly established community of shepheards. This constitutes a double-fantasy: that Elizabeth's influence shall prevail in Ireland and that his poetry "shall not be forgotten" – he will posthumously enjoy the kind of success experienced by the Irish bards. It may also however suggest veiled criticism of the queen: Elizabeth has hitherto not made her mark sufficiently in Ireland and therefore he must make it for her.

Elizabeth also figures in *The Mutabilitie Cantos*, possibly part of the unfinished Book 7 of *The Faerie Queene*, where Mulla's sister, the nymph Molanna, betrays the goddess Diana by arranging for the God Faunus to catch a glimpse of her bathing naked. Before Molanna's betrayal Ireland "florished in fame / Of wealths and goodnesse, far aboue the rest / Of all that beare the *British* Islands name" and was a favourite haunt of the gods including Cynthia "that is soueraine Queene profest / Of woods and forrests, which therein abound, / Sprinkled with wholsom waters, more then most on ground" (7.6.38.1–9). As a result of Molanna's betrayal Ireland has become degenerate: "*Arlo* through *Dianaes* spights / (Beeing of old the best and fairest Hill / That was in all this holy-Islands hights) / Was made the most vnpleasant, and most ill" (7.6.37.5–9). Molanna's betrayal has led to Diana's departure from Ireland: she has "abandond" the brook, and "quite forsooke" the forests and countryside:

> Them all, and all that she so deare did way,
> Thence-forth she left; and parting from the place,
> There-on an heauy haplesse curse did lay,
> To weet, that Wolues, where she was wont to space,

> Should harbour'd be, and all those Woods deface,
> And Thieues should rob and spoile that Coast around.
> Since which, those Woods, and all that goodly Chase,
> Doth to this day with Wolues and Thieues abound:
> Which too-too true that lands in-dwellers since haue found.
> (*The Faerie Queene* 7.6.55.1–9)

This is 'the present state of Ireland' and it requires the attention of Elizabeth, urged on by men like Spenser. Ireland suffered greatly under Colin's absence and if Elizabeth's name, or the English control that it represents, is to flourish the country requires direction and control.

The Faerie Queene Book 6

In *The Faerie Queene* pastoralism is most fully considered in Book 6, the poem's last complete Book, which was first published along with Books 4 and 5 and a reprint of Books 1–3 in 1596. Calidore, the hero of Book 6, has been absent from much of the action that takes place in the Book's central cantos, having apparently abandoned his lady Serena in canto 5 (6.5.3–6). In canto 9 the narrator explains what Calidore has been up to while absent from the poem:

> Great trauell hath the gentle *Calidore*
> And toyle endured, sith I left him last
> Sewing the *Blatant beast*, which I forbore
> To finish then, for other present hast.
> Full many pathes and perils he hath past,
> Through hils, through dales, throgh forests, & throgh plaines
> In that same quest which Fortune on him cast,
> Which he atchieued to his owne great gaines,
> Reaping eternall glorie of his restlesse paines.
> (*The Faerie Queene* 6.9.2.1–9)

This canto is typical of a recurrent feature of *The Faerie Queene*: the notion that action goes on in real time and is not arrested by the act of narrating, a feature which alerts us to the fact that the action is not entirely under the narrator's control. Calidore has not yet caught the beast and it is in the middle of his pursuit that he comes across some shepherds:

> Playing on pypes, and caroling apace,
> The whyles their beasts there in the budded broomes

> Beside them fed, and nipt the tender bloomes:
> For other worldly wealth they cared nought.
> (*The Faerie Queene* 6.9.5.3–6)

Although he enquires after the Blatant Beast, Calidore is soon distracted from the task in hand by his hospitable hosts who "Offred him drinke, to quench his thirstie heat, / And if he hungry were, him offred eke to eat" (6.9.6.8–9) and by the strikingly beautiful Pastorella who is "full fayre of face, / And perfectly well shapt in every lim" (6.9.9.1–2).

Apparently this is an idyllic life and later, in conversation with Pastorella's father, Meliboe, Calidore announces that he is impressed by "the happie life, / Which Shepheards lead, without debate or bitter strife" (6.9.18.8–9). Calidore admires the freedom of pastoral life – "How much (sayd he) more happie is the state, / In which ye father here doe dwell at ease, / Leading a life so free and fortunate" (6.9.19.1–3) – but Meliboe's response is qualified:

> If happie, then it is in this intent,
> That hauing small, yet doe I not complaine
> Of want, ne wish for more it to augment,
> But doe my self, with that I haue, content;
> So taught of nature, which doth litle need
> Of forreine helpes to lifes due nourishment:
> The fields my food, my flocke my rayment breed;
> No better doe I weare, no better doe I feed.
> (*The Faerie Queene* 6.9.20.2–9)

As in *The Shepheardes Calender* and *Colin Clouts Come Home Againe*, the pastoral world is not entirely idyllic and it is clear that Meliboe has some cause to complain were he not resolved to make do with "hauing small", suggesting that this is not necessarily a life of ease. Meliboe continues:

> Therefore I doe not any one enuy,
> Nor am enuyde of any one therefore;
> They that haue much, feare much to loose thereby,
> And store of cares doth follow riches store.
> The litle that I haue, growes dayly more
> Without my care, but onely to attend it;
> My lambes doe euery yeare increase their score,
> And my flockes father daily doth amend it.
> What haue I, but to praise th'Almighty, that doth send it?
> (*The Faerie Queene* 6.9.21.1–9)

Again the praise of pastoral life is qualified, with the second "therefore" suggesting that Meliboe is not envied by others specifically because he does not envy them, not because envy is not possible. Meliboe repeats the assertion that he possesses little and although he claims a daily increase, his assertion that this is "Without my care" is subsequently contradicted by his claim that he must "attend it", that is, he must work by tending his sheep in order to guarantee their increase. Most significantly, Meliboe's assertion that "all the night in siluer sleepe I spend, / And all the day, to what I list, I doe attend", which suggests a life of pastoral ease, is undermined by his responsibilities:

> Sometimes I hunt the Fox, the vowed foe
> Vnto my Lambes, and him dislodge away;
> Sometime the fawne I practise from the Doe,
> Or from the Goat her kidde how to conuay;
> Another while I baytes and nets display,
> The birds to catch, or fishes to beguyle:
> And when I wearie am, I downe doe lay
> My limbes in euery shade, to rest from toyle,
> And drinke of euery brooke, when thirst my throte doth boyle.
> (*The Faerie Queene* 6.9.23.1–9)

As in *The Shepheardes Calender* and *Colin Clouts Come Home Againe*, the peace of the pastoral world is threatened by wild animals and it is suggested that Meliboe must hunt in order to live; like Hobbinoll in the April eclogue, who announces himself to be Eliza's servant even though tired with work and sweaty (97–99), Meliboe is tired from manual labour. Meliboe's references to hard work and the threat to his sheep from wild animals undermines Calidore's estimation of the pastoral existence as a "safe retyre" where Meliboe is "Fearlesse of foes, or fortunes wrackfull yre" (6.9.27). Calidore may have "with greedy eare / Hong still vpon his melting mouth attent" (6.9.26.1–2) but we get the impression that he has not really been listening to what Meliboe has said.

When praising the existence enjoyed by Meliboe and his fellow shepherds Calidore describes the life led by other men who are forced to endure:

> all the tempests of these worldly seas,
> Which tosse the rest in daungerous disease;
> Where warres, and wreckes, and wicked enmitie
> Doe them afflict, which no man can appease
> (*The Faerie Queene* 6.9.19.4–7)

Calidore himself is clearly the victim of such unrest since he envies Meliboe's life: "And wish my lot were plast in such felicitie" (6.9.19). Waldo F. McNeir and Andrew Hadfield independently have made a connection between Calidore and Artegall, the knight of Justice who is commonly thought to represent Elizabeth's Lord Deputy, Arthur Grey de Wilton, under whom Spenser served in Ireland. McNeir noted that "all the heroes of *The Faerie Queene* are in a sense dispensers of justice, human or divine, and Calidore together with some of his doubles such as Calepine continues this special function of Artegall" (McNeir 1969, 151). Hadfield claimed that Calidore's failure to complete his quest is related to the ending of Book 5 "where the Blatant Beast is unleashed as a direct result of Artegall's inability to make Ireland governable". According to Hadfield, the allegory of the Blatant Beast indicates the spread of chaos through Britain because Elizabeth has refused to take the opportunity presented to her by the knight of Justice to impose order upon Ireland and courtesy cannot exist without the imposition of justice (Hadfield 1997b, 173). Spenser's use of nautical imagery in the context of unrest occurs also in the *View* where Ireland is compared to a ship which has been "rente and torne a sunder" but which Grey manages to control "like a moste wise pilott" who has "helde her moste stongelye even againste those roringe billowes" of rebellion, and "safely broughte her out of all" (Spenser 1949, 63). Calidore again uses nautical imagery when elaborating upon his description of the troubled world from which he has come:

> Giue leaue awhyle, good father, in this shore
> To rest my barcke, which hath bene beaten late
> With stormes of fortune and tempestuous fate,
> In seas of troubles and of toylesome paine,
> That whether quite from them for to retrate
> I shal resolue, or backe to turne againe,
> I may here with your selfe some small repose obtaine.
> (*The Faerie Queene* 6.9.31.3–9)

The society of shepherds, although not ideal, provides a refuge from the more hostile environment which lies beyond the society's environs and with which Calidore is familiar, a world which contains the Blatant Beast. As Anne Fogarty pointed out, one of the roots of 'blatant' is an earlier form of the word 'to bleat' and so the monster can be read as "a monstrous antitype of the pastoral, arcadian world" (Fogarty 1989, 99). In her view, far from being a neglect of duty, Calidore's sojourn with the shepherds:

allows the poet to establish a heterotopic sphere from which the problems of the court may be reviewed. Just as Ireland in the *View* functions as the place of difference in which the lineaments of order may be traced, so too Calidore's sojourn amongst the shepherds serves to consolidate and redefine the virtue of courtesie. (Fogarty 1989, 99)

Calidore joins the society of shepherds in much the same way that Spenser and his associates joined the society of new English in Ireland which was impeded from achieving a pastoral idyll not only by the beasts which lay on the edge of their society, wolves and the wolf-like kern, but by the resistance and criticism of the English court here figured in the shape of the Blatant Beast.

The idyll desired by Spenser for Ireland, and outlined in detail in the *View*, is temporarily realized in the dance of the Graces on Mount Acidale, a location which is described by the narrator as paradisical:

> ... a place, whose pleasaunce did appere
> To passe all others, on the earth which were:
> For all that euer was by natures skill
> Deuized to worke delight, was gathered there,
> And there by her were poured forth at fill,
> As if this to adorne, she all the rest did pill.
> (*The Faerie Queene* 6.10.5.4–9)

The hill is surrounded by woodland "Of matchlesse hight, that seem'd th'earth to disdaine" and is protected by "a gentle flud" which is "Vnmard with ragged mosse or filthy mud" (6.10.6). This environment bears little relation to the rural reality outlined in the *View* where woodland harbours dangerous beasts and water provides the rebel with protection: here "Ne mote wylde beastes, ne mote the ruder clowne / Thereto approch, ne filth mote therein drowne" (6.5.7.4–5). The dance itself is beautiful and harmonious:

> All they without were raunged in a ring,
> And daunced round ; but in the midst of them
> Three other Ladies did both daunce and sing,
> The whilest the rest them round about did hemme,
> And like a girlond did in compasse stemme:
> And in the middest of those same three, was placed
> Another Damzell, as a precious gemme,
> Amidst a ring most richly well enchaced,
> That with her goodly presence all the rest much graced.
> (*The Faerie Queene* 6.10.12.1–9)

The vision is disrupted by Calidore, an incident described by the narrator as a "mishap" (6.10.18.8) and by Calidore himself as "my ill fortune" (6.10.20.7). Although arguably Calidore's voyeurism and curiosity are evidence of moral weakness, the action which causes the disappearance of the dancers is motivated by the admirable desire to uncover the truth:

> Much wondred *Calidore* at this straunge sight,
> Whose like before his eye had neuer seene,
> And standing long astonished in spright,
> And rapt with pleasaunce, wist not what to weene;
> Whether it were the traine of beauties Queene,
> Or Nymphes, or Faeries, or enchaunted show,
> With which his eyes mote haue deluded beene.
> Therefore resoluing, what it was, to know,
> Out of the wood he rose, and toward them did go.
> (*The Faerie Queene* 6.10.17.1–9)

For Humphrey Tonkin, Mount Acidale represents "a world of perfect order ... a vision of order which transcends both court and country" and the episode is "the concretization of an idea lurking in the back of Spenser's mind throughout the *Faerie Queene* – poetry as order, the true poet as the orderer and shaper of a universe" (Tonkin 1972, 293). If Calidore can be identified with Artegall, and thus Grey, then perhaps Spenser's vision of a new order for the society of shepherds, evident both here and in the *View*, has been disrupted by the "ill fortune" or recall of Grey. The graces are described as "daughters of delight, / Handmaides of Venus" who "to men all gifts of grace do graunt" (6.10.15.1, 4) and whereas grace is said to be absent from the English court in *Colin Clouts Come Home Againe*, Spenser's vision of their dance on Mount Acidale reveals the possibility of their presence in a re-ordered Ireland despite the temporary setback, or disruption, of Grey's recall.

In *The Shepheardes Calender* the threat from wolves remains peripheral but in the episode featuring Calidore's pastoral sojourn Brigants, who live on the edge of the pastoral world, invade and destroy the peaceful society of shepherds. The invasion by the Brigants is prefigured by the appearance of a tiger, a beast whose presence indicates an escalation in the threat which peripheral savagery presents to Meliboe and his companions. The tiger appears from nowhere when Calidore is out walking with Pastorella and Coridon (6.10.34.1–6) and threatens Pastorella, who may represent the

New English colonist untouched by Irish influences as well as the economically desirable potential of the land itself (Fitzpatrick 2000, 116–21). Coridon runs from the scene and will later be entirely rejected by Pastorella for his cowardice (6.10.37.3–4) but Calidore reacts bravely:

> He had no weapon, but his shepheards hooke,
> To serue the vengeaunce of his wrathfull will;
> With which so sternely he the monster strooke,
> That to the ground astonished he fell;
> Whence ere he could recou'r, he did him quell,
> And hewing off his head, [he] it presented
> Before the feete of the faire *Pastorell*;
> Who scarcely yet from former feare exempted,
> A thousand times him thankt, that had her death preuented.
> (*The Faerie Queene* 6.10.36.1–9)

That Calidore represents the New English settler is indicated by his ability to deal with both these incidents. If Pastorella does represent Ireland then it is clear that Calidore is better able to deal with the realities of rural life than the native Coridon. Although it is unlikely that Coridon represents the native Irish, who are figured in the more violent and capable Brigants, he may carry a more general signification and symbolize those who advocated a less aggressive approach to the situation in Ireland than Spenser would in the *View*.

The depiction of the Brigants is informed by the conventions of Greek romance – the pirates and warriors of Heliodorus and Longus – but they clearly also represent Irish rebels who act with violence against the community of shepherds:

> A lawlesse people, *Brigants* hight of yore,
> That neuer vsde to liue by plough nor spade,
> But fed on spoile and booty, which they made
> Vpon their neighbours, which did nigh them border,
> The dwelling of these shepheards did inuade,
> And spoyld their houses, and them selues did murder;
> And droue away their flocks, with other much disorder.
> (*The Faerie Queene* 6.10.39.3–9)

That the Brigants represent Irish rebels was recognized by M. M. Gray (1930, 420) and H. C. Chang (1955, 129–35) and further evidence that the Brigants are Irish is the description of where they live – "a little Island ...

Couered with shrubby woods, in which no way / Appeard for people in nor out to pas" (6.10.41.6–8) – which Andrew Hadfield noted resembles a crannog, or fortified lake dwelling, as used by Hugh O'Neill in the Nine Years War (Hadfield 1997b, 184). The depiction of the Brigants may also be informed by the tradition of the Wild Man who, like the wood-dwelling Irish, lives dangerously close to the civilized community; as Hayden White put it, "He is just out of sight, over the horizon, in the nearby forest, desert, mountains, or hills" (White 1972, 20). In the *View* Irenius proposes the destruction of the Irish landscape and Irish customs in order to impose English rule and thus achieve a pastoral idyll for the community of shepherds, but here the destruction of a way of life is depicted as barbaric and the Brigants are characterized only by the "disorder" and destruction they cause. Some communities are more valuable than others. Woodland dominates the environment inhabited by the Brigants and the emphasis is on concealment: they live "vnderneath the ground" in "hollow caues" hidden by "thick shrubs" and consumed by "darknesse dred" (6.10.42.1–5). As Humphrey Tonkin pointed out, the Brigants plunge the "inhabitants of a green and sunlit world, into the wintry darkness of their anti-society beneath the earth" and the episode constitutes "a kind of infernal parody" of the pastoral existence (Tonkin 1972, 143–44). Similarly, John Erskine Hankins noted that "the cave suggests the absence of light, the presence of spiritual darkness, the 'abyss' of Chaos, and the descent to hell" (1971, 74), but it may also emphasize the New English desire to literally enlighten, to see or 'view' clearly, as Spenser proposed, the unnatural Irish environment, something which can only be done via alteration. Calidore draws the Brigants into the light to fight – much like the New English could if Ireland's landscape were altered – and rescues Pastorella, bringing her forth "to the ioyous light" (6.9.50.4), something that might be achieved for the New English colonists if Ireland's rebels were obliterated.

The invasion by the Brigants destroys the peace enjoyed by Meliboe and his adopted daughter Pastorella and in the subsequent story featuring Pastorella's biological parents, Claribell and Bellamoure, boundaries and borders, darkened prisons and the symbolic force of light recur. Like Pastorella, Claribell resists union with a Celtic foreigner, undermining her father's desire that she marry "the Prince of *Picteland* bordering nere" (6.12.4.6). As punishment for her disobedience, Claribell's father "them in dongeon deepe / Without compassion cruelly he threw" (6.12.5.6–7). Just as Calidore rescues Pastorella, bringing her forth "to the ioyous light" (6.9.50.4), so baby Pastorella, conceived in the darkness of the dungeon, is brought forth into the light by Claribell's servant:

> The trustie damzell bearing it abrode
> Into the emptie fields, where liuing wight
> Mote not bewray the secret of her lode,
> She forth gan lay vnto the open light
> The litle babe, to take thereof a sight.
> (*The Faerie Queene* 6.12.7.1–5)

Pastorella is herself associated with the light – the mole, or pattern on her skin being "christall bright" – and the story of her parents who, like her, have suffered as a result of Celtic intrusion, provides closure to the former pastoral episode. However, the stories of Claribell and Bellamoure, read in conjunction with that of Pastorella, may also constitute a fantasy on the part of Spenser that the strict observation of boundaries and resistance to Celtic violence will eventually be rewarded.

Spenser's prose dialogue and his pastoral poetry focus on those peripheral threats which undermine the existence of an idyllic society of shepherds. We saw earlier that a recurrent feature of *The Faerie Queene* is the notion that the poem's action is not entirely under the narrator's control but the desire to control, to shape the landscape and its inhabitants, is nevertheless a recurring feature of Spenser's writing. That the *View* was not published during Spenser's lifetime confronts the reader with a peculiar irony: Irenius's passionate plea for topographical manipulation in the 'present' (it is *A View of the 'Present' State of Ireland*), his efforts to engage with Elizabethan reality in a timely manner, was not successful. The next chapter will further consider Spenser's efforts to control and contain subversive elements in the landscape of Fairyland and, in particular, fantasies that involve topographical co-operation in the containment and destruction of said elements.

CHAPTER 2

⤸

Marrying waterways and resolving conflict in
The Faerie Queene

A S W E S A W I N the previous chapter, in the *View* Spenser advocates the literal reshaping of the Irish landscape in order to assert
control upon the land and its people, an impulse also evident in the
conceptual reshaping which occurs in the shorter pastoral poems and pastoral episodes from *The Faerie Queene*. This chapter will further consider
Spenser's preoccupation with topographical manipulation as a means to
assert control over the landscape by considering a neglected episode from
Book 4 of *The Faerie Queene*, the marriage of the Thames and the Medway,
and a series of episodes involving the obliteration of villains with the active
participation of a landscape that had hitherto supported their evil deeds. It
will become apparent that most of these episodes occur in Book 5 of the
poem which, as the introduction noted, critics have read as the poetic exposition of Spenser's political opinions articulated in the *View*.

In April 1580 Edmund Spenser wrote a letter to his old Cambridge
friend Gabriel Harvey telling him about a literary project he intended to
undertake in the near future:

> I minde shortely at conuenient leysure, to sette forth a Booke . . . whyche I
> entitle, *Epithalamion Thamesis*, whyche Booke I dare vndertake wil be very
> profitable for the knowledge, and rare for the Inuention, and manner of
> handling. For in setting forth the marriage of the Thames: I shewe his first
> beginning, and offspring, and all the Countrey, that he passeth thorough,
> and also describe all the Riuers throughout Englande, whyche came to
> this Wedding, and their righte names, and right passage, etc. A worke
> beleeue me, of much labour, wherein notwithstanding Master *Holinshed*
> hath muche furthered and aduantaged me, who therein hath bestowed

[58]

singular paines, in searching oute their first heades, and sourses: and also in tracing, and dogging oute all their Course, til they fall into the Sea. (Spenser 1949, 17)

We do not know what became of Spenser's project; he may have abandoned it – perhaps because it was too ambitious – or it may simply have been lost. The Variorum edition identified six critics who thought that the marriage of the Thames and the Medway, which occurs in Book 4 canto 11 of *The Faerie Queene*, completes the intention announced in Spenser's letter to Harvey concerning Epithalamion Thamesis, with just one dissenting voice (Spenser 1949, 266).

The marriage of the rivers mirrors the betrothal of Britomart and Artegall (4.6.40–41) and, as in Book 3, the history of the partners and their relationship to each other is a continuation of the central concern of the chronicles in Book 2 which highlight the importance of English history, the place of the house of Tudor within it, and the function of Britomart and Elizabeth as part of the Tudor family. The rivers' lineage mirrors that of Britomart's progeny, which is said to come from the Trojan kings who claimed to be related to the immortal and royal classical gods. Neptune appears with his queen Amphitrite and there is a focus on her physical beauty:

> And by his side his Queene with coronall,
> Faire *Amphitrite*, most diuinely faire,
> Whose yuorie shoulders weren couered all,
> As with a robe, with her owne siluer haire,
> And deckt with pearles, which th'Indian seas for her prepaire.
> (*The Faerie Queene* 4.11.11.5–9)

The description of Amphitrite is consistent with contemporary Petrarchan descriptions of Elizabeth, with an emphasis on precious materials: ivory, silver and pearls, the last being particularly associated with the queen (Yates 1947, 74–75). The same Petrarchan motifs are utilized in the depiction of the bride (Medway), her handmaids, and the nymphs, whose beauty is described in terms of precious metals, long hair, flowers and pale skin (4.11.45–51). But more is at work here than mere encomium of Elizabeth. The physical description of Amphitrite also alludes to English colonial expansion with the notion that the Indian seas serve the queen, prepare pearls especially for her, and so are willing aquatic subjects. The colonial allusion is particularly clear in the narrator's description of the royal issue: first the seventeen sea gods who govern the waves, then the nine founders of Nations who control the world (4.11.13–16). This emphasis on nationhood and the governance of waters mirrors contemporary conflicts over the ownership and governance of land and, most importantly, urges action. Travel abroad to new and economically rewarding lands is highlighted when the narrator lists famous rivers of the world including "Rich Oranochy, though but knowen late; / And that huge Riuer, which doth beare his name / Of warlike Amazons, which doe possesse the same" (4.11.21.7–9). Spenser's reference is topical: Raleigh refers to the Orinoco throughout his *Discovery of Guiana,* which was first published in 1596, the same year as Books 4–6 of *The Faerie Queene.* The narrator then refers to the "warlike Amazons" who live in the region between the Orinoco and the Amazon and makes a plea for the colonization of Guyana:

> Ioy on those warlike women, which so long
> Can from all men so rich a kingdome hold;
> And shame on you, O men, which boast your strong
> And valiant hearts, in thoughts lesse hard and bold,
> Yet quaile in conquest of that land of gold.
> But this to you, O Britons, most pertaines,
> To whom the right hereof it selfe hath sold;
> The which for sparing litle cost or paines,
> Loose so immortall glory, and so endless gaines.
> (*The Faerie Queene* 4.11.22.1–9)

Men who allow themselves to be ruled by women, even strong "warlike" women, are weak and the emasculation of Britons who "quaile in conquest of that land of gold" will reach its epitome in the gender inversion which takes place in Book 5: the feminization of Artegall at the hands of the Amazon, Radigund. When Britomart takes control of the city of Radegone from Radigund she shares power with Artegall; unlike Elizabeth she does not rule alone and, unlike Elizabeth, she gracefully accepts advice from men.

The exhortation to colonize Guyana (4.11.22) emphasizes the benefits of exploiting the landscape and thus prefigures the lengthy advice relating to Ireland that will be offered in the *View.* Simon Shepherd detected in the exhortation Spenser's backing for the policies of the militant Protestant faction of Raleigh and Essex in the 1590s and his support for Raleigh's call to colonize the Americas:

The Amazons of South America are an invitation to British men to act out the policies of international Protestantism. They are an incitement to Raleigh to prove himself a hero of the faction, a modern day Theseus, by conquering the Amazons, by colonising South America. (Shepherd 1981, 28)

The passage itself also alludes to Ireland and Elizabeth's reluctance to spend money in the Irish wars ("The which for sparing litle cost or paines, / Loose so immortall glory, and so endless gaines"). As we saw in the previous chapter Irenius believed money to have been misspent and mismanaged, a problem exacerbated by Elizabeth's habit of providing money in several small amounts rather than a lump sum.

Ireland is explicitly referred to in the lengthy description of the Irish rivers which attend the marriage of the Thames and the Medway (4.11.40–44), many of which Spenser names along with others "whose names no tongue can tell" (4.11.44.6). Apparently this constitutes a shift in focus since Spenser, in his letter to Harvey, wrote of his intention to describe "all the Riuers throughout Englande, whyche came to this Wedding" (Spenser 1949, 17), making no mention of Ireland at all. After a brief flurry of interest in the 1960s (Fowler 1964, 170–75; Roche 1964, 167–84; and Oruch 1967), Spenser's marriage of the Thames and the Medway has attracted little critical comment. The marriage of the rivers occurs in Book 4, the one devoted to the praise of 'friendship', which critics have increasingly referred to in terms of 'concord' or, more specifically, *discordia concors*: the birth of concord from discord. Concord carries the interpersonal sense of harmony and agreement but it has political and public dimensions too. Appropriately enough, this public display of concord, the marriage, occurs in one of the series of Books of *The Faerie Queene* (4–6) concerned with public virtues and published together in 1596. The river-marriage canto focuses on the landscape and so it is significant that 'concord' should also have a topographical sense, for it is also recorded as a legal term pertaining to land: "An agreement made in court respecting the conveyance of a fine of lands; also, an agreement made between two or more upon a trespass committed" (OED concord *sb*. 3).

In the July eclogue of *The Shepheardes Calender* Spenser refers to "The salt Medway, that trickling stremis / adowne the dales of Kent: / Till with his elder brother Themis / his brackish waues be meynt" (81–84). In Book 4 of *The Faerie Queene*, published seventeen years later, Spenser has changed the sex of the Medway with the effect that the rivers are transformed from brothers to betrothed. That the rivers should become lovers is hinted at in *The Shepheardes Calender* by reference to the Medway's "brackish waues" which are "meynt" , that is 'mingled', with those of his brother. Calling the Thames the elder brother in the earlier poem appears to make the relationship hierarchical but not if Spenser was thinking of the Irish inheritance practice of gavelkind (whereby land was distributed equally among sons) rather than the English law of primogeniture. Even if we do consider the relationship in *The Shepheardes Calender* to be hierarchical it is so in a different way from that presented in *The Faerie Queene* in that the shift from brothers to lovers is primarily significant in terms of gender, not rank. It might be objected that allowing the rivers to remain an image of platonic male friendship would have been more fitting for a Book devoted to friendship but, on the other hand, changing the sex of the Medway allows Spenser to bring the rivers together in a public celebration, an event that would hardly be possible were the rivers to remain brothers or even male (it seems unlikely that Spenser would entertain the notion of gay marriage). That the merging of the rivers should be presented as a marriage, a legal contract which describes a relationship which is both public and private, alerts us to Spenser's preoccupation in his river poetry with the sexual act and its consequences and the way in which the private sexual union is related to public, indeed political, life.

A.M. Buchan and Alastair Fowler detected political and national dimensions in the union of the rivers in Book 4, particularly in Spenser's choice of the Medway as a marriage partner for the Thames. Fowler claimed that the Medway was by no means an obvious partner for the Thames and, in fact, Spenser was the first to write about the marriage of these two rivers (Fowler 1964, 171). He also objected to Buchan's assertion, following John Upton, that the Medway was chosen by Spenser as a compliment to Philip Sidney whose home, Penhurst, was in Kent. According to Fowler, the Thames is representative of England as a whole and the Medway in Kent was chosen as spouse for the Thames because of its associations with Elizabeth, whose royal palace was in Kent and who could be considered the most appropriate spouse for England (Fowler 1964, 172). The whole canto, is, according to Fowler, "a festival piece, celebrating a visionary England – and Ireland – united in friendly alliance, and married to a sovereign whose policy promises a strong and prosperous peace" (Fowler 1964, 174–75). Fowler summed up the relationship between England and Ireland in the canto as one of "friendly alliance", suggesting partnership and equality, the ideal humanist marriage, one might say.

Fowler's easy reading of the river-marriage canto is inadequate because it makes no attempt to consider the strained effect of Ireland's presence at this celebration which takes place in England. If we consider the relationship between England and Ireland as a marriage then we must conclude that the relationship is not governed by mutuality. Fowler's notion of the relationship as a "mutual" marriage is fine in terms of Spenser's poetic reality but is naive in terms of political reality ignoring as it does the history of the relationship between the two countries. The reality of England's relation to Ireland is that of a powerful entity which dominated and exploited despite resistance; if the marriage metaphor is appropriate then surely England, the husband, has been guilty of sexual violence, as Seamus Heaney pointed out in his poem "Act of Union" which depicts colonized Ireland as a victim of rape (Heaney 1975, 49). This violent reality is avoided by both Fowler and Spenser in favour of an illusion of conviviality. Despite the great lengths Spenser goes to in order to conjure up an image of "friendly alliance", might he at some level be aware that the picture he paints is somewhat forced?

Certainly the Irish rivers are among the guests celebrating the wedding of the Thames and the Medway: "Ne thence the Irish Riuers absent were, / Sith no lesse famous then the rest they bee, / And ioyne in neighbourhood of kingdome nere" (4.11.40.1–3). But the narrator is somewhat defensive about their inclusion: "Why should they not likewise in loue agree, / And ioy likewise this solemne day to see? (4.11.40.4–5). The question anticipates criticism about the Irish presence which the narrator justifies by reference to their fame and proximity. There are many Irish rivers attending the ceremony but the narrator does not list them all: "I them all according their degree, / Cannot recount, nor tell their hidden race, / Nor read the saluage cuntreis, thorough which they pace" (4.11.40). Whether the narrator "cannot" give us this information because he does not know it or whether he is prevented from disclosing it is unclear but in a literary work we have to treat the narrator's drawing attention to this absence in the account as itself significant. The fact is that the history of the rivers named and their relation to the Irish landscape remains unstated. As Andrew Hadfield noted, the Irish rivers are guests "only on the condition that much of the history they carry with them is hidden from view" (Hadfield 1997b, 144). But why include the Irish rivers at all if their history must be suppressed? Of all the histories that might be suppressed in this account, surely the one which most urgently calls out for elision is that of England's role in Ireland's violent past? Spenser envisages a peaceful celebration which includes Ireland's waterways but from which Ireland itself – its history, and its people – are excluded. Yet they are not entirely concealed, for Spenser's reference to the river's "hidden race" and "saluage cuntreis" alerts us to what he desires to keep hidden, with the word 'saluage' carrying overtones of violence, thus allowing us a glimpse of the darker underside of Ireland. Whether Spenser accidentally or deliberately allows us this glimpse is difficult to ascertain but if accidental then it seems likely to be an effort on his part to control the savage island.

The impulse to control and contain the landscape and its truths is evident in Spenser's habit of renaming Ireland's topographical features. This poetic idiosyncrasy reflects English legal attempts to control naming, an example of which is An "Act for the English Order, Habit, and Language" (1537):

> And be it enacted that every person or persons, the King's true subjects, inhabiting this land of Ireland, of what estate, condition or degree he or they be, or shall be, to the uttermost of their power, cunning and knowledge, shall use and speak commonly the English tongue and language ... [and] shall bring up ... his ... children in such places, where they shall or may have occasion to learn the English tongue, language, order and condition. (Maxwell 1923, 113)

Perhaps the most significant renaming in Spenser's river-marriage canto is that of "Mulla" for the river Awbeg: "And Mulla mine, whose waues I whilom taught to weep" (4.11.41.9) being a reference to Spenser's earlier use of the fictive name in *Colin Clouts Come Home Again*, published in 1595. In renaming the river, Spenser claims ownership, control and authority: "Mulla *mine*". Claiming possession of this river in the context of a marriage ceremony is significant: the male poet has imagined the river female in its former poetic creation and in his river-marriage canto becomes a husband-figure taking possession of the female by renaming. In the same way that a woman loses her name in marriage so the Awbeg has been renamed by Spenser, the implication in both cases being that identity is negated and he who controls language controls that which he names.

Just as glimpses of Ireland's hidden history darken the joyful proceedings underway in Proteus's hall, so too do the stories of sexual violence which frame the narrative. It is disturbing that the marriage of the Thames and the Medway should be celebrated in Proteus's hall while Florimell suffers at the hands of Proteus. A victim of his sexual aggression, she has been held captive in his dungeon for seven months (4.11.4). It is even more disturbing that the narrator should first remind the reader of Florimell's predicament and then leave her there during his description of the joyous event going on above her prison:

> Bvt ah for pittie that I haue thus long
> Left a fayre Ladie languishing in payne:
> Now well away, that I haue doen such wrong,
> To let faire *Florimell* in bands remayne,
> In bands of loue, and in sad thraldomes chayne;
> From which vnlesse some heauenly powre her free
> By miracle, not yet appearing playne,
> She lenger yet is like captiu'd to bee:
> That euen to thinke thereof, it inly pitties mee.
> (*The Faerie Queene* 4.11.1)

We might well ask what other function a narrator performs if it is not one comparable to that of a "heauenly powre" that might free Florimell but, as we saw in the previous chapter, the notion that action goes on in real time and is not arrested by the act of narrating is a recurrent feature of *The Faerie Queene*; again we are alerted to the fact that the action is not entirely under the narrator's control. Another instance of sexual violence is evident in Spenser's account of the rape of the nymph Rheusa by Blomius, resulting in the creation of three Irish rivers (4.9.42). It is perhaps ironic that the marriage of the Thames and the Medway should be celebrated amidst such feminine reluctance: not only is Florimell held against her will by the lustful Proteus and Rheusa subjected to rape, but the bride herself, the Medway, has taken much persuading:

> Long had the *Thames* (as we in records reed)
> Before that day her wooed to his bed;
> But the proud Nymph would for no worldly meed,
> Nor no entreatie to his loue be led;
> Till now at last relenting, she to him was wed.
> (*The Faerie Queene* 4.9.8.5–9)

That Proteus's sexual violence should mar the peaceful celebration of sexual love that takes place in his house suggests a broader political reference. Florimell's prison is "wall'd with waues" (4.11.3.6), and therefore an island. The aggression to which Florimell is subjected and the close proximity of the place in which she is threatened to the site of peace and order evokes Irish aggression against English peace, suggesting either the threat to England from Ireland or the threat within Ireland itself. If we focus on the latter suggestion then the peace threatened is contained within an island and so the violence alluded to is against either the Pale or against Ireland's principal towns. Security was a priority in Elizabethan Ireland. As R. A. Butlin pointed out, the city of Cork was situated on an island accessible only by bridges (Butlin 1976, 159) and its walls were "ten feet thick in places and fifty feet high" with the gates "continually guarded" against Irish outlaws (Butlin 1976, 160).

Spenser's desire to contain the Irish landscape by renaming and claiming ownership ("Mulla mine"), mirrors the act of marriage as a means of containing female sexuality. But his efforts at containment are not entirely successful and Ireland's violent reality can be glimpsed. The celebration of the marriage of the Thames and the Medway is framed and interrupted by stories of sexual aggression disruptive to the celebration of friendship and equality in marriage.

As well as being an attempt to control naming, the "Act for the English Order, Habit, and Language" (1537) insisted that the Irish conform to English social practices: the "rude and ignorant" Irish should have "a conformity, concordance, and familiarity in ... manners, order and apparel, with them that be civil people, and do profess and acknowledge Christ's religion, and civil and politic orders, laws and directions ..." (Maxwell 1923, 112–13). Aside from the demand that the Irish speak and teach their children English, the act denounced Irish fashions regarding hair and articles of clothing, and demanded that the Irish "use and keep their houses and house–holds ... according to the English order, condition and manner..." (Maxwell 1923, 113–14). Spenser's preoccupation with sexual and topographical containment mirrors the desire of English commentators in this period to control what they perceived as general Irish incontinence. In *A New Description of Ireland*, Barnaby Rich wrote that the Irish "had rather stil retaine themselues in their sluttishnesse, in their vncleanlinesse, in their rudenesse, and in their inhumane loathsomnes, then they would take any example from the English, either of ciuility, humanity, or any manner of Decencie" (Rich 1610, D4v). Similarly John Davies in *A Discoverie of the True Causes why Ireland was never Entirely Subdued* referred to "their promiscuous generation of Children; their neglect of lawfull Matrimony; their vncleannesse in Apparrell, Diet, & Lodging; and their contempt and scorne of all thinges necessary for the Ciuill life of man" (Davies 1612, Aa2r). Spenser's reference to the "saluage cuntreis" through which the Irish rivers flow suggests that Ireland is uncultivated but also that its people are barbaric. It might also, given Spenser's preoccupation with chastity, nod towards dangerous female sexuality, evoking as it does the bawdy Elizabethan pun on "countrey" (Montrose 1993, 188).

Just as the mention of Ireland's "hidden race" and "saluage cuntreis" allows us to glimpse a darker Ireland, so too does Spenser's reference to the "balefull Oure, late staind with English blood", thought by P.W. Joyce and A.C. Hamilton to allude to the defeat of Lord Grey on the banks of the Avonbeg at Glenmalure in 1580 (Spenser 1935, 271; Spenser 1977, 516). The poetic implications of the river stained with blood are multiple: it suggests that despite attempts by the narrator to hide Irish history its savagery pollutes the very land and its waters. Also evident is the sense that there has been an undesirable mixture of Irish fluids and English blood whereby English blood spilled on the Irish landscape and absorbed by Irish rivers becomes a metaphor for miscegenation. The defeat of the English cannot be forgotten because their blood has made an indelible mark on the Irish water. There is a significant parallel between Spenser's Oure, in which Irish fluids and English blood are mixed, and the Severn in Shakespeare's *1 Henry 4*, where the blood of the Welsh Glyndŵr and the English Mortimer is mingled:

> Three times they breathed and three times did they drink,
> Upon agreement, of swift Severn's flood,
> Who, then affrighted with their bloody looks,
> Ran fearfully among the trembling reeds,
> And hid his crisp head in the hollow bank,
> Bloodstainèd with these valiant combatants.
> (*1 Henry 4* 1.3.101–106)

As in Spenser's river-marriage canto, this blood-mingling is linked to miscegenation. As Philip Schwyzer noted, Mortimer "unites his blood with Owain Glyndŵr's not once but twice – first literally, and with potent symbolism, in the waters of the Severn as they do battle on its banks (1.3.102–7), and then in marriage with Glyndŵr's daughter" (Schwyzer 1997, 36). Terence Hawkes claimed that Mortimer's enrapture with his Welsh wife is feminine, narcotic, sensual. The seduction is centred on her voice and "Holinshed's sparse reference to her, 'daughter of the said Owen', is expanded in the play to create a far more disturbing figure who, Circe-like, seems easily able to subvert Mortimer's English manhood" (Hawkes 1998, 123). However, as we shall see in chapter 5, Mortimer's relationship with the Welsh landscape also has an important role to play in his transformation.

Some of the rivers that converge upon the marriage celebration of the Thames and the Medway in Spenser's allegory are confluent in geographical reality and the reader might easily suppose that confluence will be a metaphor for the unification enacted in marriage. But Spenser disrupts this conceit by bringing to the marriage rivers from across England and Ireland (indeed the wider world) which have no confluence with the Thames or Medway. Rhonda Lemke Sanford argued that Spenser's description of the world's rivers which "seems to set no limits on which rivers are included or on the level of detail he will employ in his representation" constitutes the translation of early modern and antique maps into ecphrastic poetry with the aim of warning Elizabeth and England that they must expand the horizons of their empire further than those represented by their predecessors (Sanford 2002, 40–45). Although the geography of united rivers motivates Spenser's allegory, he appears to deliberately exceed his physical metaphor in order to assert that unity is ultimately a conceptual, not a physical, reality. Acknowledging that the British Isles are indeed an archipelago, Spenser offers a fantasy of unification which asserts the primacy of human achievement – economic interdependence and political integration – over geographical reality.

Spenser's desire for a psychologically united kingdom, which involves Ireland's rivers in an English celebration, is hindered by the violent reality of Irish history: rivers stained with blood, a hidden race and savage lands impinge upon the festivities. It becomes clear to the reader that Spenser's notion of concord, what Fowler called being "united in friendly alliance", can only be achieved through selective amnesia. Spenser can only have his united kingdom by denying Ireland's political reality and it is the knowledge of this reality which explains his defensiveness when justifying the presence of the Irish rivers at the marriage of the Thames and the Medway.

Recalling that *Epithalamion Thamesis* remained unfinished, it is perhaps not too fanciful to suggest that Spenser's intentions to produce a work with a particularly English focus became modified by his experiences in Ireland. Spenser mentioned *Epithalamion Thamesis* in a letter to Gabriel Harvey dated April 1580. As we saw in the introduction, later that year Spenser became secretary to Lord Grey and was probably present at the siege of Smerwick in Munster that November when Grey slaughtered hundreds of Italian and Spanish troops. In the *View* Irenius praises Grey's actions at Smerwick and advocates for Ulster the kind of famine that successfully subdued the population in Munster (Spenser 1949, 156–59). Spenser benefited from the consequences of such aggression in Ireland: as Andrew Hadfield put it, "... the land which was confiscated as a result of the Desmond Rebellion (1579–83) – of which the massacre at Smerwick was a significant incident – went to establish the Munster Plantation after 1584, where Spenser made his fortune ..." (Hadfield 1997b, 18). Given the intense violence of everyday life in Ireland and Spenser's role in that violence, it is not at all surprising that while living there his priorities changed and a more exciting series of ideas and connections occurred to him, encouraging a shift in focus. A project focussing on English rivers thus evolved into a project alert to Ireland's relationship with England and Ireland's bloody history.

In Book 4 of *The Faerie Queene* Irish rivers come together "in order seemly good" to attend the wedding of the Thames and the Medway, "To doe their duefull seruice, as to them befell" (4.11.44.9). Although they come from "saluage cuntreis" the rivers are respectful, subservient even, in fulfilling what the narrator regards as their duty. The Irish rivers have been extracted from their usual environment, and have thus left behind their savage context in order to celebrate this English union. We might wonder whether Spenser wants us to think of the rivers leaving their Irish beds and flowing in English beds, or whether they take with them their native soil which gives them their identity. Whichever is the case, it is clear that Spenser presents his reader with a fantasy of topographical manipulation wherein the character of a place has been transformed in much the same way that the dance of the Graces on Mount Acidale in Book 6 of *The Faerie Queene* transforms the rural reality of Ireland as described in the *View* into a pastoral idyll, "a place, whose pleasaunce did appere / To passe all others" (6.10.5.4–5).

The description of the marriage of the Thames and the Medway is a celebration of English nationhood and the governance of waters. Here Spenser presents us with a fantasy whereby Irish rivers have been absorbed into the English landscape. Given Spenser's denunciation of the degeneration of the Old English in the *View* (Spenser 1949, 113, 117), we might expect this cartographic miscegenation to be disturbing but there is little trace here of any malevolent Irish influence. This is because the process of absorption has been inverted and Englishness absorbs Irishness rather than the other way round. Most importantly, there is no indication that the presence of the Irish rivers will spoil the joyful celebrations. The episode serves as a model for the attempted resolution in poetry of competing territorial claims and makes explicit Spenser's perception of the importance of landscape within the political, historical and social concerns of the poem. The celebratory tone of the episode belies its function as a fantastical, selective and imaginative reshaping of landscape which subordinates geographical reality to an ideological ideal.

In Spenser's imagination the Irish rivers are altered by being extracted from their usual environment and, with their savage history suppressed, they can safely join in the celebration taking place in England. This kind of radical manipulation of the landscape is apparent in other episodes from *The Faerie Queene* where a landscape which has previously supported rebellion shifts allegiance and actively supports the colonial project. In Book 2 of *The Faerie Queene* a villainous mob, captained by Maleger, lays siege to Alma's House of Temperance. There are so many of them that they obliterate all signs of the landscape: "So huge and infinite their numbers were, / That all the land they vnder them did hide" (2.11.5.7). Earlier in the episode Maleger and his men, rather than concealing the landscape, used the landscape as a hiding place from which to launch their attack:

> A thousand villeins round about them swarmd
> Out of the rockes and caues adioyning nye,
> Vile caytiue wretches, ragged, rude, deformd,
> All threatning death, all in straunge manner armd,
> Some with vnweldy clubs, some with long speares,
> Some rusty kniues, some staues in fire warmd.
> (*The Faerie Queene* 2.9.13.2–7)

The landscape of Fairyland – its rocks and caves, as well as its woodland – harbours those who wish to attack the virtuous. Maleger, the captain of the mob that attacks the home of temperance, is a corpse-like figure:

> As pale and wan as ashes was his looke,
> His bodie leane and meagre as a rake,
> And skin all withered like a dryed rooke,
> Thereto as cold and drery as a Snake,
> That seem'd to tremble euermore, and quake:
> All in a canuas thin he was bedight,
> And girded with a belt of twisted brake,
> Vpon his head he wore an Helmet light,
> Made of a dead mans skull, that seem'd a ghastly sight.
> (*The Faerie Queene* 2.11.22.1–9)

Critics tend to agree that Maleger represents sickness, the most likely etymological explanation of his name being *male* "badly" + *aeger* "diseased, sick". His sickness is physical and spiritual and perhaps even mental and psychic (Osgood 1931, 504–06; Hankins 1971, 84–86; Rollinson 1990). The battle between Maleger and Arthur closely resembles the battle between Hercules and Antaeus in Greek myth. Like Antaeus, Maleger is revived by contact with the earth and, just as Hercules strangled Antaeus by holding him aloft, so Arthur defeats Maleger by lifting him above the ground and squeezing him to death in a violent embrace. Spenser's story, however, takes the myth a step further. In order to ensure Maleger's demise Arthur:

> Vpon his shoulders carried him perforse
> Aboue three furlongs, taking his full course,
> Vntill he came vnto a standing lake;
> Him thereinto he threw without remorse,
> Ne stird, till hope of life did him forsake;
> So end of that Carles dayes, and his owne paines did make
> (*The Faerie Queene* 2.11.46.4–9)

What is most striking about this action is that the landscape which revived Maleger now contributes to his decay and, crucially, the element that once enabled him to fight (earth) has been replaced by water, an element alien to him and perhaps suggestive of baptismal water (Woodhouse 1950, 222).

While Arthur's battle with Maleger is undoubtedly influenced by the myth of Hercules and Antaeus, it is difficult to read Spenser's description of

Maleger without thinking of the by now famous description in the *View* of the starving Irish as "Anotomies of deathe" (Spenser 1949, 158). In an important early paper tracing the influence of Spenser's Irish experience on *The Faerie Queene*, M. M. Gray claimed that in the depiction of the siege of Alma's castle Spenser was alluding to the Munster rebellion and that the figure of Maleger is "perhaps in some particulars like the starving rebel leaders" (Gray 1930, 416). Maleger's resilience, suggested Gray, is a comment upon the resilience of the Irish rebels because "Just the same disconcerting vitality characterized rebellion in Ireland" (Gray 1930, 416). Suppose we allow that Maleger has an Irish dimension, what might the manner of his death tell us about Spenser's feelings toward the Irish landscape, and what are the wider implications of those feelings? If we return to the episode in Book 4 featuring the Irish rivers, we begin to see a pattern emerging: in the description of the Irish rivers and the death of Maleger the landscape has been transformed from a source of danger and uncertainty to an instrument of benevolence. In the river-marriage canto the Irish rivers are separated from their savage history and so too in the Maleger episode the landscape shifts from being a supporter of violence to an agent of virtue which is finally responsible for the destruction of an arch-villain. As we shall see in Chapter 5, similar fantasies existed about the demise of the Welsh rebel Owain Glyndŵr: Holinshed, amongst other English historians, claimed that the landscape which had previously facilitated his rebellion finally participated in his demise.

Like Maleger, the figure of Malengin, also named Guile, who appears in Book 5 of *The Faerie Queene*, initially gains strength from his environment. The virtuous Samient tells Artegall that Malegin's "wylie wit ... / And eke the fastnesse of his dwelling place, / Both vnassaylabe, gaue him great ayde" (5.9.5.1–3). As Andrew Hadfield noted, critics have recognized that the description of Malengin echoes Spenser's depictions of Irish rebels in the *View* (Hadfield 1997b, 161n46). When pursued by Artegall, Malengin flees into the landscape "Vp to the rocke he ran, and thereon flew / Like a wyld Gote, leaping from hill to hill, / and dauncing on the craggy cliffes at will" (5.9.15.3–5). Protean Malengin changes from a fox to a bush, from a bush to a bird, from a bird to a stone, from a stone to a hedgehog. As his metamorphoses into a bush and a stone demonstrate, Malengin can not only become an animal of the kind that inhabits the landscape but can also become part of the landscape itself. Malengin's crossing of the division between the animate and the inanimate world prefigures his fate at the hands of Talus:

> But when as he would to a snake againe
> Haue turn'd himselfe, he with his yron flayle
> Gan driue at him, with so huge might and maine,
> That all his bones, as small as sandy grayle
> He broke, and did his bowels disentrayle;
> Crying in vaine for helpe, when helpe was past.
> So did deceipt the selfe deceiuer fayle,
> There they him left a carrion outcast;
> For beasts and foules to feede vpon for their repast.
> (*The Faerie Queene* 5.9.19.1–9)

Hadfield claimed that Malengin's absorption into the landscape makes his presence more frightening: "… the implication is that Malengin, like Error, has been destroyed only for his legacy to become even more ghostly and terrifying as it becomes part of the very landscape and, hence, virtually invisible and even more protean than the 'human' figure" (Hadfield 1997b, 163). But there is little to suggest that Malengin has ever been or ever becomes "ghostly". Although the description of his "hollow eyes deepe pent" (5.9.10.5) might suggest the spectral, it could just as easily suggest hunger which, given his resemblance to the Irish, seems more likely. When fleeing from Artegall he transforms himself into substantial, solid forms and there is no reason to believe that Malengin's spirit remains when his bones are ground into tiny pieces by Talus. Hadfield's earlier comment that "Talus can neither contain Malengin nor keep him at bay, and his only recourse is absolute destruction …" (Hadfield 1997b, 163) is closer to the mark. In a sense the landscape colludes with Talus, absorbing the dust of Malengin's malevolent body in order to leave little trace of him behind. That the remains of Malengin are left to become food for scavengers need not imply that he continues to be a threat. In Shakespeare's *Titus Andronicus*, probably first performed sometime between 1592 and 1594 (Wells et al. 1987, 113–14), the "barbarous Tamora" suffers a similar fate on the order of Lucius:

> As for that ravenous tiger, Tamora,
> No funeral rite, nor man in mourning weed,
> No mournful bell shall ring her burial;
> But throw her forth to beasts and birds to prey.

> Her life was beastly and devoid of pity,
> And being dead, let birds on her take pity.
> (*Titus Andronicus* 5.3.194–199)

This speech concludes the play and apparently constitutes closure. Certainly Tamora is incorporated into the natural world via the birds that will inevitably consume her, what James L. Calderwood called an "anti-Ovidian metamorphosis" (Calderwood 1971, 23), but it seems unlikely that Shakespeare expected his audience to consider the defeated queen to remain a threatening presence.

Abandoning the bodies of wrongdoers in the open air without burial rites is a traditional occurrence and a common feature of *The Faerie Queene*. Having defeated their foes the knights of Fairyland usually move on to another adventure, leaving the bodies of their enemies where they fell. Presumably we are to suppose that these corpses become food for the animal occupants of Fairyland and are thus absorbed into the natural world and there is little doubt that the villains concerned have been successfully eliminated. Figures do continue to be a threat after they have been defeated, but only if they survive in a bodily form. Hadfield is right to suggest that Adicia continues to be a threat but this is because, like Duessa in Book 1, she has been allowed to escape (Hadfield 1997b, 160–61). Unlike Malengin, Adicia is not crushed. When Spenser wants to suggest that malevolent figures are still a threat he allows them to remain alive: at the end of Book 1 Duessa flees into the wilderness but she has not been eradicated and so we expect her to return. Similarly Grille remains a troubling presence because the source of his degeneration, Acrasia, is captured but not destroyed and he himself is not annihilated: "Let Grille be Grille, and haue his hoggish mind" (2.12.87.8). The figures who are destroyed bodily represent, for that moment at least, a small victory against the influence of vice in Fairyland.

Many critics have recognized Malengin as representing the rebel Irish (Hadfield 1997b, 161n46) yet although Ireland is a central part of the allegory of Book 5, Catholic Spain and the threat it represents also figure. Malengin's fate is not unique; the bodies of other recognisably Catholic wrong-doers are similarly smashed to pieces. The Souldan, a pagan tyrant, is generally recognized as alluding to Philip 2 of Spain and his death to the defeat of the Spanish (Spenser 1977, 585–87; Hardin 1990, 7; Hadfield 1997b, 157). In his confrontation with Arthur, the Souldan is tossed from his own runaway chariot and killed by it:

> the pagan hound
> Amongst the yron hookes and graples keene,
> [was] Torne all to rags, and rent with many a wound,
> That no whole peece of him was to be seene,
> But scattred all about, and storw'd vpon the greene.
> (*The Faerie Queene* 5.8.42.5–9)

In order to emphasize that the Souldan presents no further danger, the narrator announces that the tyrant has been "rapt and all to rent, / That of his shape appear'd no litle moniment" (5.8.43.8–9). Only his battered shield and armour remain and, just as Pollente's head was stuck on a pole, so they are hung on a tree by Arthur to warn against evil. Although the Souldan is recognisably Spanish, he is associated with all Catholics, including the Irish, when he is referred to as a pagan who "neither hath religion nor Fay, / But makes his God of his ungodly pelf, / And Idols serues" (5.8.19.7–9). In the *View* Irenius denounces the Irish as "all Papistes by theire profession but in the same so blindelye and brutishly enformed for the moste parte as that ye woulde rather thinke them *Atheists* or infidles" (Spenser 1949, 136). For Spenser non-Protestants, be they Muslims or Catholics, merge together to form an undifferentiated religious enemy. As Richard McCabe put it, "The Christian/Paynim dichotomy provides Spenser with a means of organising his political allegory. The 'pagans' of romance fiction are the Catholics of reformed politics" (McCabe 1989, 112).

The Souldan's improper veneration of idols is echoed in Geryoneo's idol, another symbol of Catholic power in Book 5. The utter destruction of Geryoneo which apparently constitutes the liberation of Belge (the Low Countries) from Geryoneo's grip (that is, the grip of Catholic Spain) is reinforced when Arthur smashes Geryoneo's idol in front of Belge:

> Then in he brought her, and her shewed there
> The present of his paines, that Monsters spoyle,
> And eke that Idoll deem'd so costly dere;
> Whom he did all to peeces breake and foyle
> In filthy durt, and left so in the loathely soyle.
> (*The Faerie Queene* 5.11.33.5–9)

The idol is trodden into the soil by Arthur and there is no indication that its influence remains, something reinforced by the celebrations that follow his success:

> Then all the people, which beheld that day,
> Gan shout aloud, that vnto heauen it rong;
> And all the damzels of that towne in ray,
> Came dauncing forth, and ioyous carrols song:
> So him they led through all their streetes along,
> Crowned with girlonds of immortall baies,
> And all the vulgar did about them throng,
> To see the man, whose euerlasting praise
> They all were bound to all posterities to raise.
> (*The Faerie Queene* 5.11.34.1–9)

The biblical allusion to Exodus in Arthur's destruction of the idol is certainly unequivocal about the finality of its demolition: "Thou shalt not bowe downe to their gods ... but vtterly ouerthrowe them, and breake in pieces their images" (Anon. 1560, Exodus 23:24).

The bodily disintegration suffered by Malengin and the Souldan is not unique to Book 5. In the first Book of the poem Kirkrapine is torn to pieces by Una's lion, a symbol of royal power (Aptekar 1969, 58–69). Una represents the one true religion of Protestantism, the figure of Elizabeth, and perhaps an idealized Ireland (Fitzpatrick 1998, 13–16). Given that Una's lion defends the truth of Protestantism, it might constitute a specific reference to Henry 8, as noted by James Nohrnberg (1976, 218). Kirkrapine is a robber of the church and although, as Mary Robert Falls pointed out, he might be an allusion to Protestant ecclesiastical abuses (Falls 1953), the context of the episode suggests that Kirkrapine is a symbol of the cupidity of the Roman Catholic church in England. Although Hamilton allowed that the reference extends to any religious greed, including the corruption of post–Reformation English bishops, he acknowledged that "The primary reference [is] to the greed of Rome, by which the English Church was pillaged ..." (Spenser 1977, 59). Kirkrapine is not only torn into pieces but, like Maleger, is also consumed by the landscape:

> Him booteth not resist, nor succour call,
> His bleeding hart is in the vengers hand,
> Who streight him rent in thousand peeces small,
> And quite dismembred hath: the thirstie land
> Drunke vp his life; his corse left on the strand.
> (*The Faerie Queene* 1.3.20.1–5)

Again it seems that the land has actively co–operated with a villain's demise and the disintegration of his body has rendered him harmless. As in the river-marriage canto English national interests dominate and any trace of malevolent influence disappears via a fantastical representation of the allegiance of territory; the land is apparently enthusiastic in the role it plays since it thirstily guzzles the villain's blood, as though from physical need, rather than merely absorbing it.

Malengin is killed in Book 5 of *The Faerie Queene*, the one that critics generally agree contains the most obvious allusions to Ireland. If Malengin is symbolic of one of the numerous Irish rebels who threaten the colonising project, then Grantorto is a leader of such men, although he does resemble an Irish Kern (a foot soldier, not a leader of men) in his confrontation with Artegall (Spenser 1977, 615). Whether he represents Philip of Spain or the Pope is less important than his role in the overall thrust of the allegory as a Catholic miscreant with an interest in Ireland. When Artegall kills Grantorto the villain is said to eat the earth: "He did him smite with all his might and maine, / That falling on his mother earth he fed" (5.12.23.6–7), which is an inversion of what has happened to Maleger, Malengin, and Kirkrapine. The action of gnawing the earth is either the involuntary effect of a heavy fall or a final act of defiance, an unnatural attack upon the source of life itself. It also recalls the biblical curse upon the serpent, that it shall eat dust (Spenser 1977, 537). Significantly, the land, Irena or Ireland, takes the side of Artegall, or Lord Grey, against Grantorto. She and her people, presumably the Irish, rejoice at this defeat of the representative of Catholic power in a scene which resembles the celebrations following the defeat of Geryoneo's idol:

> Which when the people round about him saw,
> They shouted all for ioy of his successe,
> Glad to be quit from that proud Tyrants awe,
> Which with strong powre did them long time oppresse;
> And running all with greedie ioyfulnesse
> To faire *Irena*, at her feet did fall,
> And her adored with due humblenesse,
> As their true Liege and Princesse naturall;
> And eke her champions glorie sounded ouer all.
> (*The Faerie Queene* 5.12.24.1–9)

Spenser's fantasy that English Protestant strength is welcome and appreciated in the colony is obviously a denial of the political reality all around him just as in the river-marriage canto he denies geographical reality even if he cannot wholly ignore the rivers' "hidden race" and the "saluage cuntreis" through which they run.

Another malevolent figure in Book 5 who literally "bites the dust" is Pollente. He has been recognized by Pauline Henley as a representative of Spanish might and of Sir John of Desmond, who was beheaded during Grey's campaign of 1581. Henley claimed that "Pollente begins as the power of Spain, and ends as Sir John of Desmond" (Henley 1928, 139–40) while Andrew Hadfield made the plausible suggestion that Spenser might have been thinking of another rebel because what happens to Pollente's head "resembles the description given of the fate of Rory Oge O'More in John Derricke's *The Image of Ireland* (1581), a work which Spenser may well have known" (Hadfield 1997b, 159). The fight between Artegall and Pollente takes place in the river which flows beneath Pollente's toll-bridge. When Pollente attempts to leave the river he is decapitated:

> But *Artegall* pursewd him still so neare,
> With bright Chrysaor in his cruell hand,
> That as his head he gan a litle reare
> Aboue the brinke, to tread vpon the land,
> He smote it off, that tumbling on the strand
> It bit the earth for very fell despight,
> And gnashed with his teeth, as if he band
> High God, whose goodnesse he despaired quight,
> Or curst the hand, which did that vengeance on him dight.
> (*The Faerie Queene* 5.2.18.1–9)

Pollente not only consumes the earth but is also consumed by its waters when "His corps was carried downe along the Lee, / Whose waters with his filthy bloud it stayned" (5.2.19.1–2). The Lee, a river in Cork, actively transports Pollente's body away from the site of his sins and his resistance, in effect colluding with Artegall in his punishment. If, as Henley believed, Pollente represents Desmond or if, as Hadfield suggested, he represents Oge O'More, then the spillage of his blood into Irish water is a fitting redress for the English blood previously spilled into the Irish river Oure detailed in the river-marriage canto (4.11.44.5). John Erskine Hankins claimed that Spenser's source for Pollente's river and bridge is Rodomonte's river in Ariosto's *Orlando Furioso* and that the battle between Artegall and Pollente is based on the first two of Rodomonte's battles of the bridge. Hankins also noted that Spenser departs from his source when, unlike the villain Rodomonte, Pollente is killed in his own river (Hankins 1971, 91–92). Spenser's decision to deviate from his source suggests a desire to implicate Pollente's river in his punishment. Pollente used the landscape to make attacks upon his victims more effective but ultimately the landscape colludes in his destruction and the disposal of his bloody corpse. That the water remains bloody after Pollente's demise might act as a warning to future transgressors of the fate that awaits them.

As we saw in Chapter 2, Irenius in the *View* comments on the natural beauty and economic potential of the Irish landscape:

> And sure it is, a moste bewtifull and swete Countrie as anye is vnder heaven, seamed thoroughe out with manye goodlye rivers replenished with all sortes of fishe moste aboundantlye sprinckled with manye swete Ilandes and goodlye lakes like little Inlande seas, that will carye even shipps vppon theire waters, adorned with goodly woodes fitte for buildinge of howsses and shipps so comodiously as that if some princes in the worlde had them they woulde sone hope to be Lordes of all the seas and ere long of all the worlde (Spenser 1949, 62)

Richard McCabe's response to the above passage from the *View* acknowledged its covert resentment toward the Catholic inhabitants of Ireland who do not make good use of the raw materials surrounding them:

> This is an extraordinary passage. Aesthetic appreciation of natural beauty gradually modulates, through plans for its commercial exploitation, into fantasies of world empire as beauty, money and power coalesce. Ideally the countryside should serve the court. As matters stand, however, Ireland's "commodious" landscape is wasted upon "idle" pastoral inhabitants who choose to leave it, contrary to the English practice, unenclosed and therefore "wyld" and "desart" (McCabe 1993, 83).

Particular episodes in *The Faerie Queene* enact a kind of imaginative enclosure whereby a landscape that has been wild is finally brought to order. Initially the landscape has acted to sustain its villainous inhabitants but when they are defeated the landscape colludes with the virtuous to enact revenge upon them. The role of the landscape in suppressing those inhabitants who resist law and order is evident throughout *The Faerie Queene* but is particularly marked in Book 5 which is appropriate, given its references to Ireland. Just as the Irish rivers attending the marriage of the Thames and the Medway have abandoned their savage context in order to celebrate an English union, so the Irish landscape appears to bow to the will of the colonist and join with him in ridding its woods, caves and waterways of rebels.

The episodes discussed above constitute moments of resolution in *The Faerie Queene* where we can identify clear winners and losers in the fight between vice and virtue. There is, as it were, a provisional finality when a particular enemy has been bodily annihilated, victories which tend to be signalled by the bodily disintegration of the enemy. The repeated destruction of recognisably Catholic villains suggests an almost neurotic desire to cleanse the landscape of their influence. That the landscape co-operates in this process makes the result all the more satisfying for the frustrated colonist.

My phrase "provisional finality" has, of course, a latent contradiction, a sense of unfinished business. I fully intend both sides of this contradiction: it is over, for now. Post-colonial thinking about *The Faerie Queene* and Ireland tends to privilege the non-closure of colonial projects, the failure to resolve tensions, and especially the disruption of identity which colonialism entails. Influenced by theoretical ideas, particularly those of Jacques Derrida and Homi Bhabha, critics have recognized that traditional dichotomies such as English versus Irish or colonizer versus colonized are inadequate. Stephen Greenblatt's explanation of Guyon's aggression in the Bower of Bliss (*The Faerie Queene* 2.12.83) focused upon colonial efforts to avoid the "threat of absorption" that colonized cultures presented to the colonizer, that is the threat of the constructed binaries of Self and Other, civilized and uncivilized, collapsing into each other (Greenblatt 1980, 172). As Andrew Hadfield put it, nationhood cannot be considered in terms of polarities because no identity – colonizer or native – is pure but rather both groups will be altered by contact (Hadfield 1997b, 1–4). However, these ambivalences should not blind us to the historical victories of the colonizers. Evidenced in the Irish rivers leaving their home and coming to England in the river-marriage canto and in the ambivalent landscape discussed here, we have reason to suppose that Spenser wanted us to consider the degree to which soil itself gives or effaces identity.

Willy Maley referred to "the genocidal actions of English forces" in Munster between 1580 and 1583. During these years approximately thirty thousand people living in the Munster area were eradicated in order to make way for around four thousand New English settlers. Maley commented: "The English euphemism for the settlement which followed in the wake of this act of genocide, 'repeopling', hardly begins to tell the story of that horrific depopulation" (Maley 1997, 61). Like the English forces in Munster, the heroes in Fairyland clear the landscape of their enemies and thus open the way for its reclamation by the virtuous. They effectively enact the annihilation before creating anew that Irenius so painstakingly outlined as necessary in the *View*. The participation of the landscape in this destruction constitutes a New English fantasy but perhaps also represents the worst imaginings of those people who could find no escape from massacre in Munster and who perhaps considered the very land itself to have conspired against them in their suffering.

CHAPTER 3

⌒

Internal insurrection and foreign invasion: Richard 2, Cymbeline *and* The History of King Lear

WHEREAS WE CAN identify Spenser's geographical location during the composition of *The Faerie Queen* – he was in Ireland on his Kilcolman estate – we know little of Shakespeare's movements and cannot say for sure whether he wrote his plays in London, Stratford on Avon, or elsewhere. As Stanley Wells recently pointed out, critics are mistaken to believe that Shakespeare necessarily lived in London during his professional life since he may have commuted from Stratford, a relatively peaceful location in which to write (Wells 2002, 27–38). It is not possible, then, to understand Shakespeare's works in relation to personal concerns about place and cultural identity using biographical knowledge for we do not know enough about his life. As we saw in the Introduction, however, recent work on his possible Catholicism has closed some of the gaps in our knowledge. Nonetheless Shakespeare's works do disclose a similar interest in place, identity and power as Spenser, albeit in a far less overt form and apparently focusing rather more on the internal politics of the more easterly of the two main islands that comprise the north-east Atlantic archipelago.

For Irenius in the *View* the degeneration of the Old English in Ireland should act as a warning to a new generation of English settlers to resist the Irish influence which would taint the civility they have acquired. *Richard 2, Cymbeline,* and *The History of King Lear* share Spenser's preoccupation with national identity and inevitably English and British identity are informed by their opposites. In *Richard 2* what it means to be English and the centre's relationship with its borderlands is explored while in *Cymbeline* and *The*

History of King Lear ancient Britain and foreign invasion form a context for considering issues closer to home. Although Britain and, more specifically England, form the focus of these plays, Ireland also constitutes an oblique presence, as we shall see. In *Richard 2* and *Cymbeline* the king is figured in terms of the landscape itself, prophecy dominates, and a curious botanical allegory serves to explicate issues of governance. In *The History of King Lear*, the landscape undergoes manipulation at the hands of its most powerful inhabitant, the king, and its least powerful inhabitant, Poor Tom of Bedlam (the fictional character created by Edgar), both of whom can be said to have doubtful motives. These plays present England and ancient Britain subject to internal factions and under siege from foreign powers; they share a pre-occupation with topographical fantasies involving external powers which threaten political autonomy.

Richard 2

As we saw in the previous chapters, Spenser's prose dialogue and his pastoral poetry focus on those peripheral threats which undermine his vision of a pastoral idyll. Shakespeare's *Richard 2*, written entirely in verse, is also informed by the disruption of a ruling elite but in this play disorder comes from within in the shape of Bolingbroke's rebellion as well as the peripheral threat from Ireland. In the opening scene of *Richard 2* the concepts of Englishness, the English landscape, and geographical distance from England are introduced when Bolingbroke accuses Mowbray of treason and Mowbray responds:

> I do defy him, and I spit at him,
> Call him a slanderous coward and a villain;
> Which to maintain I would allow him odds,
> And meet him, were I tied to run afoot
> Even to the frozen ridges of the Alps,
> Or any other ground inhabitable,
> Wherever Englishman durst set his foot.
> (*Richard 2* 1.1.60–66)

In his indignant response to Bolingbroke's accusations Mowbray alerts the audience to his nationality, reminding them that he is an Englishman who would traverse desolate landscapes far from England in order to prove his innocence. Bolingbroke picks up on the nationally charged rhetoric and asserts that all the treasons "survey'd by English eye" and "Complotted and contrived in this land" (1.1.94–96) originate with Mowbray. Furthermore, claims Bolingbroke, Mowbray is responsible for plotting the death of the duke of Gloucester, whose blood "like sacrificing Abel's, cries / Even from the tongueless caverns of the earth / To me for justice and rough chastisement" (1.1.104–106), the implication being that the landscape, irrevocably stained with Gloucester's blood, calls upon the morally honourable man, Bolingbroke, to take action. Although both men refer to their lineage, Bolingbroke asserts himself as a more noble Englishman than Mowbray when he swears "by the glorious worth of my descent" to avenge Gloucester's murder. Richard claims that his motive for banishing Bolingbroke and Mowbray is to prevent the spillage of English blood on English soil: "For that our kingdom's earth should not be soiled / With that dear blood which it hath fostered" (1.3.125–6), an ironic assertion given Bolingbroke's reference to Gloucester's blood which seeks justice and the fact that blood will become a recurring motif in the relationship between Bolingbroke and Richard.

The banishment of Bolingbroke and Mowbray applies to "our territories" rather than to England specifically and the reaction of each man to banishment is very different. Bolingbroke is brief and to the point, making no explicit reference to England or Englishness: "Your will be done. This must my comfort be: / That sun that warms you here shall shine on me, / And those his golden beams to you here lent / Shall point on me and gild my banishment." (1.3.144–147). As with Richard's reference to the shedding of blood there is a suggestion here of future events since Bolingbroke implies that the sun's golden beams have only been lent to Richard; just as Bolingbroke will feel the heat of the sun outside England he will soon possess the sun of kingship. In the notion that the sun shines in other places besides England Bolingbroke presents himself as an internationalist, unlike the insular Mowbray who, having been given "a heavier doom" (1.3.148) than his rival emphasizes at great length his allegiance to England and the English language (1.3.154–173). That Bolingbroke takes comfort from the natural world rather than English nature in particular is especially striking in the context of the heartfelt lament from Mowbray who cannot regard banishment from England into "the common air" (1.3.157) as anything other than torture: "What is thy sentence then but speechless death, / Which robs my tongue from breathing native breath? (1.3.172–73). Having been rebuked by Richard for his efforts to solicit pity ("It boots thee not to be compassionate. / After our sentence plaining comes too late", 1.3.174–175), Mowbray again makes reference to the distinction between England and other countries in what seems to be a pointed reply to Bolingbroke's response to banishment: "Then thus I turn me from my country's light / To dwell in solemn shades of endless night" (1.3.176–177).

Whilst the point of 1.3 may be to demonstrate Bolingbroke's fortitude in the face of adversity it also suggests that, unlike Mowbray, he is aware that excessive recourse to the imagination cannot change his situation and may actually cause harm. Bolingbroke imagines that the sun will shine upon him in banishment but, unlike Mowbray, he does not lose control of his imagination and provoke further rebuke from Richard. It is not that Bolingbroke is indifferent to banishment but he astutely observes the futility of pleading with Richard. He speaks later with passion about his banishment but in private, with his father John of Gaunt. In this conversation Gaunt advocates fantasy as a palliative for the pain of exile but Bolingbroke rejects his suggestions and again shows himself to be a realist, a man who denies the power of the imagination to bring relief. He is the pragmatic man of action who cannot "cloy the hungry edge of appetite / By bare imagination of a feast" (1.3.296–297). Rather than act upon Gaunt's suggestions to imagine his banishment "a travel that thou takest for pleasure" (1.3.262) Bolingbroke insists on calling it "an enforced pilgrimage" (1.3.264) and utters his affectionate but brief and firm farewell to England: "sweet soil, adieu" (1.3.306).

The theories of Elizabethan culture developed by "old" historicists such as E. M. W. Tillyard and Lily B. Campbell read *Richard 2* in the context of the Tudor myth as an orthodox condemnation of regicide and they dichotomized the figures of Richard and Bolingbroke. As Graham Holderness pointed out, for such critics "The general Elizabethan philosophy of 'order' is regarded as the basic structure of all fifteenth/sixteenth-century historiographical writing: the metaphysical dialectic of 'order' and 'disorder' was observed in the process of English history, and explained in terms of the ruling idea of providence" (Holderness 1985, 195). More recently the feminist critics Jean Howard and Phyllis Rackin maintained that Bolingbroke's nationalistic masculinity can be contrasted with Richard's effeminacy: for Bolingbroke England is a "mother" and "nurse" and he is "a trueborn Englishman" (1.3.307–9) whereas "Richard's language effeminizes him as a mother and infantilizes the land as his child" (Howard & Rackin 1997, 151). Howard and Rackin further argued that Bolingbroke's "bare imagination" in his rejection of "the effeminate pleasures of the court and the feminine pleasures of the imagination" in 1.3 can be contrasted with Richard's fertile imagination in his cell soliloquy in 5.5 where he conceives of his female brain and male soul uniting in the "androgynous fertility" of his imagination (Howard & Rackin 1997, 153). R. Morgan Griffin argued persuasively against the traditional dichotomising of Bolingbroke and Richard and was particularly critical of Jean Howard and Phyllis Rackin for their "fairly orthodox estimation of Richard's character" (Griffin 1999, 25).

What Howard and Rackin overlooked was the contrast between Bolingbroke and Gaunt. Certainly in the early part of the play this contrast between father and son is more marked than that between monarch and subject. In suggesting that Bolingbroke use fantasy as a remedy for exile in 1.3 Gaunt speaks of particularly effeminate courtly pleasures: "musicians", "fair ladies", "the delightful measure of a dance" and it is these pleasures – the effeminate pleasures of the court and the imagination conjured by his father, not the king – that Bolingbroke rejects. These lines appear only in the 1597 Quarto not the Folio, and the Oxford editors suggest that Shakespeare may have deleted them as part of his revisions to the text (Wells et al. 1987, 306–07). Whatever the reason for their exclusion from the Folio, the effect of their presence in the Quarto is to make more overt the dichotomy between Bolingbroke and Gaunt. Although there is little evidence that Bolingbroke is necessarily antagonistic to the imagination, he denies its power to alter the particular situation in which he finds himself. Griffin has suggested that Bolingbroke rejects his father's advice not because he is incapable of being imaginative but because "Gaunt is giving ridiculous advice" (Griffin 1999, 26). In 1.3 it is Gaunt rather than Richard who is firmly aligned with the feminine in juxtaposition to Bolingbroke's masculinity and whose effeminate expression, entirely inappropriate in the circumstances, causes him to be rejected by Bolingbroke.

Gaunt privileges the power of the imagination again, in the nationalistic speech for which he is most famous. This once-great warrior is an inactive old man, forced to assert himself as a man of words. Gaunt's verbally eloquent fantasies, rooted in the land, are nationalistic but also geographically erroneous. His famous encomium of England as a "precious stone set in the silver sea" (2.1.46) imagines the country to be "bound in with the triumphant sea" (2.1.61), conveniently obliterating the troublesome regions of Wales and Scotland. Gaunt's notion of England as an island protected from "the envy of less happier lands" is a fiction which ignores the unsettling presence of other regions beyond its borders, particularly Ireland, which proves pivotal in relation to the future of Richard, England's king. For Shakespeare's audience it would be clear that "the silver sea" between England and Ireland was not necessarily adequate defence against Irish rebellion (with perhaps Spanish involvement) since repeated efforts were made during the early modern period to subdue uprisings in that country. The idea of England as an island is also evident in Spenser's conception of Britain in *The Faerie Queene* where, as Nicholas Canny pointed out, "pseudo histories and genealogies" explain how "Wales and Scotland, like the various regions of England, came to be part of a single British inheritance" (Canny 2001, 24–25) with the result that the island incorporating England, Scotland and Wales is redefined in the poem as "England writ large" (Canny 2001, 26).

After his famous speech about England as an island, Gaunt puns on his own name: "Gaunt am I for the grave, gaunt as a grave, / Whose hollow womb inherits naught but bones", a verbal link to his earlier reference to England as "This blessed plot, this earth, this realm, this England, / This nurse, this teeming womb of royal kings". As Julia Reinhard Lupton pointed out in relation to Spenser's *View*, 'plot' could also mean policy or strategy or map (Lupton 1993). Spenser's prose dialogue was written to influence Elizabethan's policy on Ireland and Gaunt's reference to England as a "blessed plot" and his mapping out of the England of his imagination is similarly an effort to influence royal behaviour even though, ironically, he speaks his prophecy too soon, before Richard is present to hear it. Gaunt's manipulation of geographical reality, the obliteration of regions that lie on England's borders, may extend to a manipulation of historical reality in an attempt to control his own reputation. Harry Berger Junior noted the controlling impulse behind Gaunt's famous speech: "an *ars moriendi* by which he strives to reduce himself to the self-representation he wishes to impose on himself, his son, and the future. The death he chooses is that of the wise, good and unheeded elder, the prophetic speaker of painful truth ..." (Berger Junior 1999, 239). 'Plot' can also mean grave and for Gaunt the prospect of his grave, or plot, allows him licence to fantasize that his re-birth as "a prophet new-inspired" will afford him an honourable reputation after death. Holinshed characterized Gaunt as "a turbulent and self-seeking magnate" (Shakespeare 1961, xxxiv) and certainly Shakespeare appears to be suggesting the egotistical aspect of his nature. Gaunt fantasizes about the influence his imagination can assert upon the governance of England and hopes that posterity will remember him not as "agèd Gaunt" but as a man of influence. In Gaunt's fantasy his illness and decrepitude are projected onto the youthful Richard, despite Richard's protestations:

> JOHN OF GAUNT: O no: thou diest, though I the sicker be.
> KING RICHARD: I am in health; I breathe, and see thee ill.
> JOHN OF GAUNT: Now He that made me knows I see thee ill:
> Ill in myself to see, and in thee seeing ill.
> Thy deathbed is no lesser than thy land,
> Wherein thou liest in reputation sick;
> (*Richard 2* 2.1.91–96)

The notion of England as a deathbed and the king sick and dying as a result of a damaged reputation is very powerful but the momentum cannot be sustained, ironically due to the very frailty that Gaunt has used as a rhetorical weapon against Richard. Toward the end of the dialogue and just a few lines before his final exit, Gaunt runs out of steam and, prefiguring the gardening metaphors that abound in 3.4, dares Richard to continue his attacks upon Edward's sons and "crop at once a too-long withered flower" (2.1.134). The verbal parallel between Gaunt as "a too-long withered flower" in this scene and England's traitors as "too fast-growing sprays" in 3.4 emphasizes the notion of an appropriate rate of growth: Gaunt has outlived his usefulness and the traitors should never have been allowed to flourish.

Gaunt's conceptual reshaping of the land, with its omission of Scotland and Wales, is an obvious manipulation of geographical reality; another substantial omission occurs in the play. As Peter Ure pointed out, Shakespeare did not include "the whole of Holinshed's long account of Richard's campaign in Ireland" (Shakespeare 1961, xxxii). We might conclude that Ireland only gets a brief mention despite its pivotal role in the fate of the English monarch because it was a dangerous subject for writers in Elizabethan England. Andrew Hadfield pointed out that hardly anything obviously dealing with Ireland was entered in the Stationers' Register or published during Elizabeth's reign; nothing appears in the 1560s, the records for the 1570s are lost and between 1580 and 1603 there are only twelve Stationers' Register entries relating to Ireland (Hadfield 1994, 461). 253 surviving works containing the word "Ireland" (or words beginning with those letters, such as "Ireland's") were printed between 1580 and 1620 but this does not necessarily tell us anything about content since the word was part of the monarch's title (Pollard & Redgrave 1976). In *1 Henry 4* Ireland is mentioned three times: Northumberland recalls that Richard proclaimed Mortimer his heir before his expedition to Ireland (1.3.145–150); Hotspur recalls Bolingbroke's rebellion when Richard "was personal in the Irish war" (4.3.84–90); and Worcester criticizes Henry for taking advantage of "the contrarious winds / that held the King / So long in his unlucky Irish wars" (5.1.49–57), "unlucky" because Richard's absence from England afforded Bolingbroke the opportunity to rise against him. What is striking about these references to Ireland is that the country is associated not with Irish rebellion, as it is in *Richard 2*, but with Bolingbroke's rebellion in England.

In the opening scene of *Henry 5* the King urges caution against invading France without first guarding against the invasion of England by the Scots (1.2.136–154) but Richard II is not so careful of his kingdom: English rebellion occurs because Richard is absent from England and it is a neat irony that he is absent in a place which itself lacks a firm presence in early modern English culture. As we saw in chapter 2, the English did not have cartographic control of Ireland in this period because, as David J. Baker pointed out, "A complete and detailed representation of Ireland did not exist" (Baker 1993, 82) and maps of Ireland by royal cartographers "were often conjectural and muddled" (Baker 1993, 78). Bernhard Klein claimed that the inability to fully delineate Ireland in maps of the period corresponded to the way in which Ireland was represented on the Elizabethan stage where it "is rarely more than a shadowy and indistinct background of the dramatic scenery, always only partially coming into view" (Klein 1998, paragraph 5). Klein considered the way in which a number of plays from the Shakespeare canon including *Richard 2* "invest to different degrees in the image of a nebulous territory beyond the porous borders of the national sphere, at once confirming, and posing a threat to, England's cultural integrity" (Klein 1998, paragraph 6). Shakespeare's decision to omit Holinshed's account of Richard's campaign in Ireland does to the history of *Richard 2* what Gaunt does to the cartography of England, that is it manipulates reality in order to create a particular imaginative effect and one that has a distinctly political edge.

When Richard returns from Ireland he immediately attends to the soil from which he has absented himself and, curiously, imbues it with the potential for the same kind of malevolence toward Bolingbroke that he sought to quell in Ireland:

> Feed not thy sovereign's foe, my gentle earth,
> Nor with thy sweets comfort his ravenous sense;
> But let thy spiders that suck up thy venom
> And heavy-gaited toads lie in their way,
> Doing annoyance to the treacherous feet
> Which with usurping steps do trample thee.
> (*Richard 2* 3.2.12–17)

The gentleness of Richard's motherly affection for the soil, which Howard and Rackin considered effeminate, sits uneasily with his desire that the soil take upon itself an Irish-like venomous quality, the call that its "lurking adder" cause death to his enemies apparently inspired by recent contact with the Irish rebels, the "rough rug-headed kerns, / Which live like venom where no venom else" (2.1.157–8). That Richard, having just returned from Ireland, should call upon Welsh soil to protect his kingship does not bode well given that the Welsh army, believing Richard to be dead, will not stay and fight. Although Salisbury appeals to the Welshman's loyalty – "Stay yet another day, thou trusty Welshman. / The King reposeth all his confidence in thee"(2.4.5–6) – his pleading cannot prevail in the face of Welsh superstition which believes that natural omens: withered bay trees, meteors, and a bloody moon, indicate "fearful change" (2.4.8–11). That Richard should lose Welsh support as a result of their faith in natural omens (a faith echoed by Owain Glyndŵr in *1 Henry 4*) undercuts the faith Richard places in the natural world upon landing in Wales.

Christopher Highley noted that in the public imagination of the early modern period Ireland, Scotland, and Wales were "inextricably intertwined and could even be constructed as a single territorial and economic zone with a common linguistic and cultural heritage" (Highley 1997, 6). Preconceived ideas about the Irish "were readily transferrable to the Welsh and Scots" but Scotland "having emerged as an independent kingdom within the British isles, represented in political terms a different case from Wales and was thus not useful to English observers in thinking about Ireland" (Highley 1997, 6–7). The Welsh had once been as rebellious as the Irish, went the argument, but after the subjugation of Wales in the late-thirteenth century and its formal union with England in 1536 it could offer a "model colony" which English colonizers could look toward in order to "vindicate the wisdom and blessings of English expansionism" (Highley 1997, 70). But Wales was also a centre of Catholic dissent; in 1597 a Spanish observer noted that Milford Haven contained many Catholics who were hostile to the English and in 1599 a group of Welsh gentry informed the Privy Council that local people proclaimed the Earl of Tyrone prince of Wales and king of Ireland, believing him to be descended from Owain Glyndŵr (Highley 1997, 86–87). Richard's allusion to Irish venom and his faith in Welsh soil are unlikely contexts for English fortitude and, ironically, it is the Irish rebellion from which he draws strength which has facilitated Bolingbroke's rebellion brewing in his absence. Richard's influence over the natural world has already been shown to be weak when, having gone to Ireland to assert his authority, he is prevented from quelling the more pressing rebellion in England by "the contrarious winds" which stall his return journey. Gaunt's fantasy that the natural world is on the side of England might be read two ways in relation to these ill winds that stay Richard: as a blatant fantasy or, if we are to suppose that the natural world takes an interest in English government, as an expression of preference for Bolingbroke.

Howard and Rackin considered Richard to be feminized whereas Bolingbroke asserts his masculinity and Englishness, but they overlooked the similarities between the men and the significance, in terms of gender, of both being characterized as part of the landscape. Throughout the play those around Richard identify him with the natural world and he and Bolingbroke alternate between thinking of themselves as the land itself and the land's maintainer. That matters of political governance are couched in horticultural terms is most clearly evident in the garden scene, 3.4. Within earshot of Richard's queen, the gardener tells one of his men to "like an exe-cutioner / Cut off the heads of too fast-growing sprays / That look too lofty in our commonwealth" because "All must be even in our government" (3.4.33–36). This order provokes open discussion of the affairs of state:

> [FIRST] MAN Why should we, in the compass of a pale,
> Keep law and form and due proportion,
> Showing as in a model our firm estate,
> When our sea-wallèd garden, the whole land,
> Is full of weeds, her fairest flowers choked up,

Her fruit trees all unpruned, her hedges ruined,
Her knots disordered, and her wholesome herbs
Swarming with caterpillars?
(*Richard 2* 3.4.41–48)

Like Gaunt, who spoke of the land as "bound in with the triumphant sea" (2.1.61), the First Man compares the small garden in which he works, and which lies "within the compass of a pale", to the wider commonwealth, "our sea-wallèd garden", but for him this larger unit seems to be the island of Britain, "the whole land" (3.4.44), not specifically England. This may signal that although the gardener and his men speak in metaphors, imagination has little place in the practical labour with which they are involved and with which England should be governed; unlike Gaunt, the gardener and his men are geographically precise. The garden of Britain is ruined because weeds choke flowers and fruit trees are left unpruned but also because hedges have not been maintained. The idea that Britain's boundaries require maintenance alerts us to the issue of England's dangerous border-lands and, given Richard's efforts at quashing Irish rebellion, the gardener's reference to "a pale" may glance at the Pale in Ireland (that district around Dublin which maintained direct contact with England and in which English influences prevailed) and raise questions about the validity of Richard's attempts to impose order beyond the natural limit of Richard's "sea-wallèd garden", that is, Britain.

The metaphor of neglected land for disordered government is a preoccupation of texts overtly concerned with Irish rebellion. As we saw in chapter 2, Irenius in Spenser's *View* stresses the need for reformation in Ireland before laws can be enforced: "all those evils must first be cut away with a strong hand before any good can be planted ... before the tree can bring forth any good fruit" (Spenser 1970, 94–95). The political impetus of the gardening metaphor is also evident in Spenser's *Faerie Queene*, a text which is preoccupied with Ireland and Irish rebellion (Fitzpatrick 2000) and where, as Nicholas Canny pointed out, Spenser likened the task of his knights to that of the pruning gardener (Canny 2001, 23). The importance of implementing and maintaining boundaries in Ireland was also stressed in Luke Gernon's *A Discourse of Ireland* (1620) in which a subdued Ireland is figured as a young maiden who requires a husband (Falkiner 1904, 349–50). Alexander Leggatt noted that a "general sense of ruin" pervades *Richard 2*: the perception by the Duke of York that Richard is less noble than was

Edward the Black Prince, the offices left empty after Gloucester's murder, and the withered trees that foretell Richard's fall (Leggatt 1988a, 56–57). This sense of ruin extends to the land itself and the boundaries neglected under Richard's rule. The Queen's address to the Gardener as "old Adam's likeness" (3.4.73) recalls Gaunt's reference to England as "This other Eden" (2.1.42) but insult takes the place of encomium when she denounces him as being a "little better thing than earth" (3.4.78). Associating the gardener who clearly denounces Richard's governance of England with the earth has the overall effect of making the earth itself appear to demand Richard's deposition. Whilst Gaunt and the Gardener are associated with paradise, Richard has made efforts to co-opt serpents in the defence of his kingdom (3.2.4–25) thus reminding us of Eve's role in humanity's fall from grace.

Richard is described as a neglectful gardener who "hath suffered this disordered spring" (3.4.49) and simultaneously as the garden which has "met with the fall of leaf" (3.4.50) whilst Bolingbroke is the active, even violent, gardener who is responsible for weeds being "plucked up, root and all" (3.4.53). The image of the king as garden is later revived by Bolingbroke who says he is sorrowful that Richard's blood "should sprinkle me to make me grow" (5.6.46). Bad management by Richard leads to a kind of re-colonization of England by Bolingbroke and although it is not true to say that Richard is feminized throughout the play he is finally feminized by his disempowerment. When in 3.3 Bolingbroke likens himself to water and Richard to fire he is apparently humble, "yielding" to the king, but the comparison is well chosen for Bolingbroke's element penetrates the earth (with which Richard is identified) and thus becomes part of it. Bolingbroke's surprising accusation against Bushy and Green – that they have made Richard "unhappied and disfigured clean" and "with your sinful hours / Made a divorce betwixt his queen and him" (3.1.10–12) – prepares us for a sexually compromised figure. In penetrating Richard, Bolingbroke has effectively inhabited Richard's role and thus asserted his right to rule and maintain England. Richard's blood becomes a recurring motif and references to his blood as a stain upon the land and blood as manure (4.4.128) are invoked as though to suggest violent penetration of his person.

Bolingbroke's possession of England is also a mastering of Richard, a process which has distinctly sexual overtones. The principle of feminine land (for which the figure of Richard stands) requiring masculine intervention and governance (something achieved by Bolingbroke) is a recurring

theme in the early modern period. The trope of the colonizer as husbandman and the reference to enclosure in Luke Gernon's *Discourse of Ireland*,
puns on the cure of a 'husband' and 'husbandry' as a synonym for farming
and careful management, something that could be achieved by adequate
hedging or 'embracing' (Falkiner 1904, 349–50). The fusion of ruler and
land to be ruled was made explicit in the naming of the colony of Virginia,
first settled in 1607, which identified the land with the 'Virgin Queen',
Elizabeth, and simultaneously asserted her right to govern it. Indeed,
Elizabeth's motto *Semper Eadem* – which, as we saw in the Introduction, is a
Latin phrase meaning 'Always the same', and a translation of an English
motto 'Be always one' (Rosinger 1968, 13) – implied fusion in her royal body
of the separate and typically gendered identities of land as female and
monarch as male ruler of that land (Fitzpatrick 2000, 22). The Virginia
colony was thus constructed in terms of colonial penetration whilst at the
same time signifying the power of Elizabeth, the Virgin Queen. In *Richard 2*
the colonial model differs since Richard, clearly identified with the land, is
finally feminized and husbanded by Bolingbroke.

It seems clear that Richard is indeed finally feminized not because, as
Howard and Rackin put it, he "prefers words to deeds, has no taste for
battle, and is addicted to luxurious pleasures" (Howard & Rackin 1997, 143)
but because of his loss of power. Richard acknowledges this loss of power
and the resultant degradation in 5.5 in conversation with the groom who
enters his cell. Having told Richard that Bolingbroke rode Richard's horse
Barbary through London and that the horse was proud to carry him,
Richard rails on the animal before retracting his complaints:

> Forgiveness, horse! Why do I rail on thee,
> Since thou, created to be awed by man,
> Wast born to bear? I was not made a horse,
> And yet I bear a burden like an ass,
> Spurred, galled, and tired by jauncing Bolingbroke.
> (*Richard 2* 5.5.90–94)

Being ridden, and made sore ("galled"), by Bolingbroke carries strong
sexual connotations with Richard imagining himself an effeminate figure
forced to submit to his aggressor's 'spurring'. In his earlier soliloquy
Richard considers that being "unkinged" by Bolingbroke has made him
"nothing" (5.5.38), a word that in the early modern period connoted the
vagina and thus would have suggested both his own sense of worthlessness

and his current state of effeminacy (Williams 1994, 960–61). Richard's physical efforts to prevent further degradation are halted with the violation of his person by Exton's knife, a violation desired, though not requested by Bolingbroke. Richard's royal person has been penetrated and possessed by Bolingbroke and it is perhaps inevitable that his body is literally penetrated by someone loyal to Bolingbroke.

For a contemporary audience the death of a feminized king would presumably carry echoes of the sodomitical act that kills the king at the end of Marlowe's *Edward 2*. Charles R. Forker listed the numerous parallels between *Richard 2* and Marlowe's play (Shakespeare 2002, 159–64) and although, as he pointed out, Shakespeare avoided "the degradation and extremes of cruelty and terror of Marlowe's death scene" (Shakespeare 2002, 160) the notion of penetration and blood is still evident, albeit in a less overt manner. Exton's actions prompt an equivocal statement on kingship and landownership from Richard: "Exton, thy fierce hand / Hath with the King's blood stained the King's own land" (5.5.109–110). In this moment of strong armed resistance Richard still regards himself as king but it is not clear to whom the land belongs. That Richard considers the land "stained" with his blood may indicate his desire to become a lasting reminder to Bolingbroke of his sin, just as the staining of Pollente's river in Book 5 of *The Faerie Queene* (an episode discussed in Chapter 3) might act as a warning to future transgressors of the fate that awaits them. Things have come full-circle since Gloucester's blood cried "Even from the tongueless caverns of the earth ... for justice and rough chastisement" (1.1.105–106); it is now Bolingbroke the King who is guilty of bloodshed and Richard the subject who is a victim of murder and whose blood has been absorbed into the earth.

In *Richard 2* both claimants to the throne of England's "other Eden" are figured simultaneously as gardener and garden. The principle of gendered land requiring masculine intervention and governance is a recurring theme in this period but the gendered dichotomy which critics have identified in this play emerges only after the crisis of usurpation. In the sexualized "undecking" of the king, the ideological naturalization of power performed by aristocratic nomenclature and ritual is exposed, leaving Richard feminized by his disempowerment. Richard, his eyes "full of tears" having stripped himself of Royal adornment, considers himself to be without an identity: "I have no name, no title, / No, not that name was given me at the font, / But 'tis usurped" (4.1.254–256) and proclaims to "know not now what name to call myself!" (4.1.249). Having been feminized, made 'nothing', by disempowerment, Richard fantasizes that he might disappear altogether:

> O, that I were a mockery king of snow,
> Standing before the sun of Bolingbroke
> To melt myself away in water-drops!
> (*Richard 2* 4.1.259–261)

Like John of Gaunt (but unlike Bolingbroke) Richard turns to fantasy in a crisis and, as with Gaunt's suggestion that fantasy act as a palliative for the pain of exile and the abuse of princes, his imaginings are firmly rooted in the landscape. Ultimately, however, fantasies centred on the landscape are ineffectual and in Richard's deposition is writ large the notion that imagination is a poor substitute for the political pragmatism that will make for successful governance of the garden of England and the colony of Ireland.

Cymbeline

In *Richard 2* John of Gaunt fantasizes that England is a "sceptred isle", a "little world", a "precious stone set in the silver sea, / which serves it in the office of a wall" (2.1.40–47), his imagination obliterating those lands which are adjacent to England's borders: Wales, Scotland, and Ireland. In *Cymbeline* the Queen delivers a similar encomium of the island in which she lives although her praise is of a land where "Britons", not specifically Englanders, "strut with courage". She advises Cymbeline to ignore Roman demands for tribute and urges him to:

> Remember, sir, my liege,
> The kings your ancestors, together with
> The natural bravery of your isle, which stands
> As Neptune's park, ribbed and paled in
> With banks unscalable and roaring waters,
> With sands that will not bear your enemies' boats,
> But suck them up to th' topmast. A kind of conquest
> Caesar made here, but made not here his brag
> Of "came and saw and overcame".
> (*Cymbeline* 3.1.16–24)

The Queen's choice of metaphor is curious since "Neptune's park" connects the British landscape with the Roman God of the sea, an ironic connection because it suggests Roman ownership of Britain in the context of denying the Romans tribute and, moreover, an entirely inappropriate metaphor since he who governs the sea is being invoked to describe the land. Her use of this Roman God prefigures the key role played by Jupiter in the play with his prophecy on the future state of Britain:

> Whenas a lion's whelp shall, to himself unknown, without seeking find, and be embraced by a piece of tender air; and when from a stately cedar shall be lopped branches which, being dead many years, shall after revive, be jointed to the old stock, and freshly grow; then shall Posthumus end his miseries, Britain be fortunate and flourish in peace and plenty. (*Cymbeline* 5.3.232–238)

We might wonder why the Queen's rejection of tribute payment and her encomium of Britain are couched in terms of Roman ownership and, moreover, why this great display of nationalistic pride should come from the mouth of a villainous female protagonist. Jodi Mikalachki considered *Cymbeline* in the context of early modern attempts to recover English national origins and the tension between efforts "to establish historical precedent and continuity" and "to exorcise a primitive savagery" which could be "declare[d] obsolete" (Mikalachki 1995, 302). In Book 2 of *The Faerie Queene* Guyon reads from a chronicle of Briton Kings which describes the civilizing influence of Brutus on ancient Britain; before the coming of Brutus the land was a "saluage wildernesse, Vnpeopled, vnmanurd, vnprou'd, vnpraysd" (2.10.5.3–4). Mikalachki noted that "powerful and rebellious females in native historiography threatened the establishment of a stable, masculine identity for the early modern nation" and that Jacobean dramas set in Roman Britain often conclude with a renewed relationship between Britain and Rome, what Mikalachki called "a masculine embrace" which "depend[s] on the prior death of the female character who has advocated or led the British resistance to Rome" (Mikalachki 1995, 303). If Cymbeline's Queen represents a feminized savage resistance to the masculinized civilization represented by Rome this may explain why she is such a caricature of female evil. She is a type rather than a fully realized protagonist and her function is to disrupt the bonding between Britain and Rome. The debt that Cymbeline owes the emperor is figured in terms of familial relationships and male honour:

LUCIUS: When Julius Caesar – whose remembrance yet
Lives in men's eyes, and will to ears and tongues
Be theme and hearing ever – was in this Britain
And conquered it, Cassibelan, thine uncle,
Famous in Caesar's praises no whit less
Than in his feats deserving it, for him
And his succession granted Rome a tribute,
Yearly three thousand pounds, which by thee lately
Is left untendered.
(*Cymbeline* 3.1.2–10)

The powerful memory of Julius Caesar and his relationship with Cassibelan prefigures and thus takes precedence over the Queen's demand that he "remember" British kings, something reinforced when, despite his refusal to pay tribute, Cymbeline acknowledges his debt to the Roman empire:

Thou art welcome, Caius.
Thy Caesar knighted me; my youth I spent
Much under him; of him I gathered honour,
Which he to seek of me again perforce
Behoves me keep at utterance. I am perfect
That the Pannonians and Dalmatians for
Their liberties are now in arms, a precedent
Which not to read would show the Britons cold;
So Caesar shall not find them.
(*Cymbeline* 3.1.67–75)

This display of hospitality and Cymbeline's memory of Roman honour alerts us to his error in following the Queen's demand to "remember" his British past rather than his uncle's debt to Julius Caesar and his own debt to Augustus. The break with Rome coincides with a familial rupture in the British royal household and its end coincides with the removal of the domestically disrupting Queen. In the final scene, featuring Cymbeline's reunion with his children, the Queen's malevolent influence is altogether purged when Cymbeline tells Innogen "O she was naught" (5.4.271), an expression of contempt which recalls Richard's consideration that being "unkinged" by Bolingbroke has made him "nothing" (5.5.38) and which suggests the same sense of feminized worthlessness (Williams 1994, 960–61). Loyalty to the biological family and Rome is restored and Cymbeline himself fulfils the role perverted by the Queen: "O what am I, / A mother to the birth of three? Ne'er mother / Rejoiced deliverance more"

(5.4.369–371). The decision to grant tribute coincides with familial reunion which reinforces the analogy between empire and family.

As Mikalachki pointed out, the Queen's speech in 3.1 is included by G. Wilson Knight with other Shakespearean examples of what he characterized as an Elizabethan post-Armada sentiment (Mikalachki 1995, 303n7). It is perhaps significant that the other Shakespearean examples of "island patriotism" noted by Wilson Knight come from Elizabethan, rather than Jacobean, plays: *Richard 2*, 2.1.31–68 (considered above); *3 Henry 6*, 4.1.39–46; and *King John*, 2.1.19–31 (Wilson Knight 1947, 136). In *King John* the duke of Austria promises to support Arthur's claim to the English throne and describes England as an island "hedged in with the main, / That water-walled bulwark" (26–27) in a speech which echoes Gaunt's fanciful and geographically erroneous description of England (2.1.46). For Austria, the water that surrounds the 'island' of England functions as a defence: "that white-faced shore, / Whose foot spurns back the ocean's roaring tides / And coops from other lands her islanders" (23–25). In *3 Henry 6* Hastings similarly describes the sea as a defence, a "fence impregnable" which has been given by God (43), though it is not clear whether the island he describes is England in particular or Britain as a whole. Presumably for a Jacobean audience the Queen's speech, with its emphasis on the defensive role of Britain's waters, would seem anachronistic since threat of invasion at the hands of Catholic powers had subsided: Ireland had been effectively subdued with the defeat of Hugh O'Neill, the Earl of Tyrone, in 1603 and James had made peace with Spain in 1604. Emphasis on the "natural bravery" of the isle would seem unnecessary during the reign of James, just as the strange vision of the island as a watery park undermines the Queen's desire to emphasize the efficacy of Britain's boundaries.

Cymbeline was first printed in the 1623 Folio, where the Queen refers to Britain "ribbed and paled in / With oaks unscalable" although most editors have emended this to "banks unscalable" or "rocks unscalable". Stanley Wells preferred the use of "banks" because it suggests the sea coast and a military embankment (Wells et al. 1987, 606). However, as Roger Warren has pointed out, "oaks" "makes good sense" since "Britain is imaged as a deer-park, where the protective pales ... are living trees" (Shakespeare 1998, 154n20). The Queen's reference in the Folio to Britain being "ribbed and paled in" with trees and water partly anthropomorphosizes the landscape of Britain, an inversion of people being figured as part of the landscape in

Jupiter's prophecy: Cymbeline is "a stately cedar" and his sons the branches which will be "jointed to the old stock, and freshly grow" so that Britain will be "fortunate and flourish in peace and plenty" (5.3.234–238). It is only after the Roman god's revelations that the symbol of the tree as protection against invasion and insularity is superseded by the tree as a symbol of renewal and of a new Britain which embraces internationalism. Why Cymbeline should be referred to as a cedar tree is not clear although, as J. M. Nosworthy pointed out, it is a symbol associated with the phoenix which represents Innogen and thus restoration (Shakespeare 1955, lxxxi–lxxxii). However, it might be that Cymbeline is figured as a cedar tree by way of answer to the Queen's vision of Britain. Her description in the Folio of the island as "ribbed and paled in / With oaks unscalable" associates the tree with defence and isolationism. As far as the Queen is concerned this natural feature, together with the sands "that will not bear your enemies' boats, / But suck them up to th'topmast" (3.1.21–22), is hostile to those outside Britain and Romans in particular; as Cloten puts it "Britain's a world / By itself" (3.1.12–13). Here, as in Gaunt's speech about England, the natural world is considered to be actively involved in protection against invasion and the landscape imagined as endorsing a particular political agenda, a recurring motif also of Spenser's *Faerie Queene*, as we saw in the previous chapter. Although the Queen does not go so far as to picture England as an island, her vision of a coastline densely packed with trees is similarly fanciful. Although 'Oaks' provides a metaphorical link with Jupiter's prophecy, unscalable 'banks' or 'rocks' fulfil just as well the notion of a landscape which aggressively defends itself against outsiders.

The Queen's speech and Cloten's comment that "Britain's a world By itself" (3.1.12–13) contrast with Innogen's reflection that "I' th' world's volume / Our Britain seems as of it but not in 't, / In a great pool a swan's nest" (3.4.138–40). As in *Richard 2*, internationalism is welcomed by those who challenge misguided rulers and insularity aligned with the weak or morally compromised. Alexander Leggatt noted that Innogen's speech, though apparently intended "to stress Britain's insignificance in comparison with the great world", has the effect of making Britain seem "special and precious" (Leggatt 1977, 204). Emrys Jones claimed that the play should be understood in the context of the Tudor-British myth: "at the time *Cymbeline* was written Milford Haven was chiefly associated with the landing there in 1485 of Henry Earl of Richmond; with, that is, the accession of

Henry VII to the throne" (Jones 1961, 93). For Innogen also Milford Haven is a special place and is appropriately named since it appears to offer her a refuge, a promise of happiness in the much longed-for reunion with Posthumus: "O for a horse with wings! Hear'st thou, Pisanio? / He is at Milford Haven" (3.2.48–49). Prompted by its name, she imagines it to be a place imbued with an almost spiritual significance: "Read and tell me ... how far it is / To this same blessed Milford. And by th' way/ Tell me how Wales was made so happy as / T' inherit such a haven" (3.2.49–61).

Ironically, Innogen will never reach Milford Haven and experiences only a monstrous parody of a reunion with Posthumus in her encounter with the headless corpse of Cloten (4.2.292–333). Yet before her horrific contact with Cloten she does experience a kind of spiritual connection with the Welsh landscape in the "burial" of her apparently dead body by Guiderius and Aviragus. Innogen-as-Fidele is figured in terms of the landscape itself when Aviragus compares her body to the flowers with which he intends to honour her:

> With fairest flowers
> Whilst summer lasts and I live here, Fidele,
> I'll sweeten thy sad grave. Thou shalt not lack
> The flower that's like thy face, pale primrose, nor
> The azured harebell, like thy veins; no, nor
> The leaf of eglantine, whom not to slander
> Outsweetened not thy breath. The ruddock would
> With charitable bill – O bill sore shaming
> Those rich-left heirs that let their fathers lie
> Without a monument! – bring thee all this,
> Yea, and furred moss besides, when flowers are none,
> To winter-ground thy corpse.
> (*Cymbeline* 4.2.219–229)

As Roger Warren noted, there is a sense of her body undergoing metamorphosis and of her becoming part of the natural world (Shakespeare 1998, 24). Yet, despite references to burying Innogen-as-Fidele, which implies that the body will be deposited either in the ground or in a tomb, it becomes apparent that she will remain above ground in a grave "upon the earth's face" (4.2.286). The moss will "winter-ground" the corpse, implying protection by the plant from harsh winter weather (Shakespeare 1998, 206n230), something only required if the body is exposed to the elements.

Innogen-as-Fidele is 'buried' in the same manner as Euriphile, whom the boys believed to be their mother, with her body left exposed to the open air. In *Cymbeline* the lack of interment and laying the "head to th'east" (4.2.256) function as reminders that this is a pagan ritual (Shakespeare 1998, 207n256–7) since in Christian ritual, burial in the ground or in a tomb would ensure a return to the earth from which the body came and laying the head to the West would ensure that the body was facing Christ on the day of Judgement (Cressy 1997, 466). Usually, in texts aimed at a Christian audience, abandoning bodies in the open air without any burial rites is a contemptuous act which emphasizes a victim's foreignness, particularly their pagan status, and constitutes a punishment for their wrongdoing. As we saw in Chapter 2, abandoning the bodies of villains in the open air is a common feature of *The Faerie Queene* and in *Titus Andronicus* Lucius commands that Tamora's body be left in the open air for birds of prey to feed upon. But the lack of interment and the position of the body in *Cymbeline* are far from contemptuous and might connect with other aspects of the drama. Leaving Innogen-as-Fidele's body exposed to the air, with the suggestion that she becomes part of the air itself, prefigures the explication of Jupiter's oracle:

> The piece of tender air thy virtuous daughter,
> Which we call '*mollis aer*'; and '*mollis aer*'
> We term it '*mulier*', (to Posthumus) which '*mulier*' I divine
> Is this most constant wife, who even now
> Answering the letter of the oracle,
> Unknown to you, unsought, were clipped about
> With this most tender air.
> (*Cymbeline* 5.4.567–453)

The notion that Innogen-as-Fidele will form part of the Welsh landscape, part of its air rather than part of its earth, can only be understood in the context of the Roman explication, just as Cymbeline can only make sense of his responsibilities to others by not excluding Rome. Innogen's 'burial' and her adoption of a Latin name, Fidele, point to the Roman context of her sojourn in Wales. As Mikalachki put it, both Lucius and Milford Haven shape Innogen's identity and signal "how British national identity is formed from the interaction of the Roman invaders with the native land" (Mikalachki 1995, 317). As we saw in relation to *Richard 2*, Wales was a centre of Catholic dissent, which suggests that Rome carries a broader signification than its role in colonizing ancient Britain and indeed may signify early modern Rome as the centre of Catholic power. Cymbeline's reign coincided with the birth of Christ (Masten 2001, Ciii2v), as observed by Spenser in Book 2 of *The Faerie Queene*: "Next him *Tenantius* raignd, then *Kimbeline*, / What time th'eternall Lord in fleshly slime / Enwombed was ..." (2.10.50.1–3). Brian Gibbons argued that when writing his play Shakespeare was influenced by this reference to the reign of Cymbeline and Christ's birth and that Canto 10 of *The Faerie Queene* provided him with "a mythical but also a religious idea of providence in history" (Gibbons 1993, 30). In *Cymbeline* Wales as a place of refuge and renewal, the location where ancient Britain and Rome come together, may indicate Shakespeare's desire to emphasize the fact that British national identity was formed by its Catholic as well as its classical context. By recognizing the Christian context of the relationship between Rome and Wales Shakespeare may be questioning the view of those Protestant Reformers who believed the early church had degenerated: in *Cymbeline* Rome and Wales together are true to the spirit of the international Christian Church.

Belarius imagines that, like the herbs he scatters upon her body, Innogen-as-Fidele will be claimed by the earth:

> You were as flowers, now withered; even so
> These herblets shall, which we upon you strow.
> Come on, away; apart upon our knees
> The ground that gave them first has them again.
> Their pleasures here are past, so is their pain.
> (*Cymbeline* 4.2.287–291)

The expectation that Innogen will be absorbed into the earth is only conceptual, a fantasy, for she is not really dead. The burial scene carries political and ideological signification in prefiguring the transformation that will occur in the final scene of the play. When Jupiter's prophecy is fulfilled it is clear that Innogen will not become synonymous with Britain as its ruler just as earlier she did not become synonymous with Britain by becoming part of the landscape. This event of political significance must be understood as the obscure meaning of a botanical allegory when the cedar tree (Cymbeline) has its branches (his boys) restored. Here the governor of the land, like his daughter, is figured in terms of the landscape itself and the penetration by Rome co-exists with British grafting. The union of

Posthumus and Innogen is similarly constructed in terms of the natural world when Posthumus says to Innogen: "Hang there like fruit, my soul, / Till the tree die" (5.4.263–264). The botanical allegory of the cedar tree and its restored branches only comes about after the Queen and Cloten, the figures who have advocated Britain's insularity, have been removed from the play's action. More specifically, the rejoining of limbs to the body of the royal tree occurs as a consequence of the convergence of the previously isolated Wales (in the shape of Guiderius) with Britain (in the shape of Cloten) and the subsequent confrontation with Rome. The dismemberment of the "most incivil" prince (5.4.293), whose head is "lopped" from his shoulders, is reversed in the final scene when the "lopped branches", Cymbeline's two sons, are restored to the tree and the overwhelming theme is one of regrowth and renewal, particularly the renewal of familial bonds and the transformation of Britain's landscape which coincides with peace with Rome.

The History of King Lear

In *Richard 2* and *Cymbeline* the natural world is imagined by Gaunt and the Queen as an active participant in protection against invasion and thought by both to endorse a particular political agenda. In *The History of King Lear*, as in *Richard 2*, the landscape is subject to conceptual refiguring and, as in *Cymbeline*, familial politics dictate the politics of international relations. In the opening scene of the play Lear announces the plan he has devised and calls for his map: "Know we have divided / In three our kingdom" (1.37–38). At this point a division into three implies three 'equal' sections but Lear maintains that he will extend "the largest bounty ... Where merit doth most challenge it" (1.46–47). Curiously, this contradicts Gloucester's earlier comment that the divisions, pertaining to Goneril and Regan at least, are equal: "it appears not which of the dukes he values most; for qualities are so weighed that curiosity in neither can make choice of either's moiety" (1.4–6); although Lear encourages the inflation of proclamations of affection from each daughter he has apparently already made his decision about two-thirds of his kingdom. Presumably, even had she spoken as Lear had wished, Cordelia would only get the third that is left. As things turn out, he must quickly refigure the original boundaries and Cordelia's third is further divided into two: "Cornwall and Albany, / With my two daughters' dowers digest this third" (1.118–119). The territory awarded to Gonoril is described in vague terms by Lear: "Of all these bounds even from this line to this, / With shady forests and wide-skirted meads" (1.57–58) and the lands allotted to Regan are exactly the same, despite her more exaggerated proclamations of love. The non-specificity with which Lear describes the landscape has the effect of depoliticizing his actions since, with no mention of place names, he appears to be giving his daughters forests and meads rather than distinct territories. Like Gaunt, who endeavoured to influence royal behaviour in his mapping out of England, the "blessed plot" of his imagination, so too Lear draws Britain's boundaries in an effort to provoke proclamations of love from others.

Lear's division of his kingdom is a pivotal moment in the play and directorial decisions telling. Particularly relevant is whether the map is carried on to the stage and if so by whom, the size of the map, and whether or not the map is torn. In Jonathan Miller's film, with Michael Hordern as Lear, Kent enters holding the map while in Richard Eyre's film version of his production for the National Theatre, with Ian Holm as Lear, Gloucester holds the map (Miller 1982; Eyre 1997). Peter Holland described Nicolas Hytner's 1990 Royal Shakespeare Company production of the play with John Wood as Lear:

> When Wood's Lear put down the map which he had carried on to the stage
> in 1.1, seated himself in the throne and then realised that he could not
> reach the map, the line 'Give me the map *there*' (1.1.37, Wood's emphasis)
> became comic but it is not over-reading the moment to see his annoyance,
> as if it is someone else's fault that he cannot reach it rather than his own, as
> a small but indicative signpost to Lear's nature and the peremptory tone of
> the demand as the natural language for someone used to having every
> whim obeyed. (Holland 1997, 42)

Having Lear carry the map on stage suggests that he is in control, perhaps even dictatorial. It also suggests a degree of paranoia, as though no one else can be entrusted with the map. Holland also described Adrian Noble's 1993 Royal Shakespeare Company production of the play, with Robert Stephens as Lear:

> Noble's production was played out over a map of England which papered
> the stage floor and on which [the] Fool, gagged and with odd stockings like
> some bizarre footman, painted the red lines of the division of the kingdom,
> as the court – and Cornwall in particular – craned to see how the shares
> would be established. Gradually the paper map ripped and shredded from

the moment of Edgar's entry as Poor Tom in 3.6 until it was finally removed in the civil war of the last battle. (Holland 1997, 170)

Having a large map which gets ripped from the moment Poor Tom appears suggests the deterioration of Britain, particularly in the context of the dispossessed who roam its countryside. It also carries suggestions of a country literally being pulled apart. Yet Holland noted that Noble did not fully make use of the set's potential:

> ... the production did not seek to explore the politics of the play's view of nation. Only the careful nature of the apportionment of the three shares, with Cordelia's third a wedge that prevented the lands given to Goneril and Regan from touching at any point along their borders, suggested a politics of rule here. Instead the line from individual through family led without interruption to the pitiless universe beneath which their characters crawled. (Holland 1997, 170)

In Peter Brook's film, with Paul Scofield as Lear, there is no sign of the map until, when giving Goneril her portion of land, a rug-like material on the ground is pulled back to reveal a three-dimensional representation consisting of stone and earth and divided with strings and pins (1971). This seems to support the notion, referred to above, that Lear speaks about the division of the map as though the land itself, rather than a visual representation of it, had been carved up. Grigori Kozintsev's film, with Yuri Jarvet as Lear, has Lear grab at the map in anger when Cordelia speaks, he tears at the map, throws it to the ground and kicks it when saying "Cornwall and Albany, / With my two daughters' dowers digest this third" (1.119–120). When speaking the words "Be Kent unmannerly / When Lear is mad" (1.137–138) Kent kneels down and pulls two torn pieces of map together. This suggests that Lear is unbalanced, violent and perhaps even dangerous but that Kent is a cohesive influence, one who can mend the harm done by Lear if given half a chance (Kozintsev 1969). Barry Kyle's 2001 production of the play at Shakespeare's Globe in London, with Julian Glover as Lear, used a three-dimensional "earth map" that became a sand-pit of sodden earth (Bessell 2002, 64) for the mad Lear to romp in and which appeared to emphasize not only Lear's childishness but also the fragility of the kingdom which is easily destroyed.

The non-specificity with which Lear describes the territories allotted to Gonoril and Regan is in direct contrast to the specificity put on place names throughout the play beginning with a conversation between Kent and Gloucester, and Kent stating: "I thought the King had more affected the duke of Albany than Cornwall" (1.1–2). Opening with a discussion about these two characters, and by implication the territories they govern, indicates the drama's preoccupation with British history and British nationhood. 'Albany' or 'Albania' is an ambiguous term and might signify either Scotland or Britain: the Latin word 'Albania' meaning Scotland (OED *Albania sb* 1) and the Latin adjective 'Albus', meaning white (OED *Albion*), suggests the whole island of Britain via the white cliffs of Dover which feature so conspicuously in the play. Thomas Cooper in *Thesaurus Linguae Romanae et Britannicae* (1565) noted that Britain "was named *Albion, ab albis rupibus*, of white rockes, because that that unto them, that come by sea, from the east or southe, the bankes and rockes of this Ile doe appeare whyte" (Cooper 1565, A6v). Allusion to Scotland would suggest Celtic cultural alterity while allusion to the white cliffs of Dover would prepare an audience for Albany being a character more sympathetic to the dilemma facing Lear. As Andrew Gurr indicated, there was a dangerous topicality to the play's opening reference to Albany and Cornwall when the play was performed at Court in 1606:

> For the two play-earls to specify rivalry between the two named play-dukes Albany and Cornwall in the presence of the two real dukes, Prince Henry, who had just been made Duke of Cornwall, and his young brother, who had been the Duke of Albany since 1601, and to do so explicitly in the context of a disunited kingdom, was an audacious and extremely risky attempt to make the courtiers sit up and take note of how the old play had been rewritten in order to emphasize its application to the current debate over the union of the two kingdoms of England and Scotland. (Gurr 2002, 44)

That Lear's champion, Cordelia, comes to England with a French army adds further controversy and complicates straightforward nationalistic identities since Lear's enemies fight on the British side and his supporters on the French.

Place names chosen by Shakespeare prove particularly significant when we compare his version of the story with the source material used by him: the anonymous play *King Leir* which, according to Richard Knowles, Shakespeare would have known from the first edition printed in 1605 (2002, 35). Critics have long recognized the influence of *King Leir* on several Shakespeare plays but, as Jacqueline Pearson pointed out, the influence is most obvious "in plays dealing with the abdication or defeat of kings" (Pearson 1982, 115). In *King Leir* Gonorill is married to the King of Cornwall and Ragan to the king of Cambria, or Wales, another marginal territory. In *The History of King Lear* Cordelia, having been rejected by the duke of Burgundy, marries the King of France. In the source play however, Leir tells his counsellors that he intends by "policy" to "match her to some King within this ile" (1.66) and later to "match her with a King of Brittany" (1.91). It seems clear that 'Brittany' refers to Britain, not a part of France, since the Gallian (or French) King states his intention to "sayle for Brittany" in order to see "these three Nymphes, the daughters of King *Leir*" (4.347) and later refers to his sailing to "the Brittish shore" (4.380).

Leir's decision to trick Cordella into marriage follows the advice of his nobles that he marry his daughters "with some of your neighbour Kings, / Bordring within the bounds of Albion, / By whose united friendship, this our state / May be protected 'gainst all forrayne hate" (1.52–55). Although the phrase "Bordring within the bounds of Albion" could refer to land which lies next to Albion, Leir, having listened to his counsellors advice, explicitly states his desire to marry Cordella to a king "within this ile", that is Albion or Brittany. Curiously, in scene two, and without explanation, Skalliger, one of Leir's counsellors, tells Gonorill and Ragan of their father's plan to marry Cordella to "the rich king of Hibernia" (2.139), that is, Ireland, which might suggest that the anonymous author of *King Leir* imagined Ireland as part of the island of Britain in rather the same way that John of Gaunt imagines England to be an island in *Richard 2*. Despite the pronouncements made by Leir in the first scene, Geoffrey Bullough, Stanley Wells and Tiffany Stern have stated, without question, that Leir intends to marry Cordella to the King of Ireland, when our only source for this information is Skalliger (Bullough 1973a, 278; Shakespeare 2000b, 21; Anon 2002, 99n89). In Shakespeare's play and the source play the youngest daughter marries the king of France and any mention of Ireland, along with the ambiguous location of Brittany, is omitted from *The History of King Lear*. As in *Richard 2*, Shakespeare chose to omit his source's material on Ireland. In *King Leir* Cordella's marriage is bound up with her refusal to flatter Leir since she marries France independently of her father's choice, unlike Shakespeare's Cordelia who marries a suitor chosen by her father when his other choice rejects her.

The author of *King Leir* was apparently familiar with the Leir story from

Book 2 of Spenser's *Faerie Queene* but, like Shakespeare, made important changes to the narrative. In Spenser's poem no mention is made of Cornwall, Gonorill is married to the king of Scotland, Regan to the king of Cambria, and Cordelia "sent to *Aganip* of *Celtica*" (2.10.29.5). A. C. Hamilton pointed out that 'Celtica' means France (Spenser 1977, 263) and the OED concurs that "by Cæsar the name *Celtæ* was restricted to the people of middle Gaul (*Gallia Celtica*), but most other Roman writers used it of all the Galli or Gauls ..." (Celt *sb*1). In the source play, Leir praises the Gallian, or French, party as "Genovestan Gauls, Surnamed Red-shanks, for your chivalry" (5.6.29–30). Sidney Lee noted that the use of the word 'Genovestan' is puzzling since "the French prince who was Lear's son-in-law has no obvious relation with a region so far to the south" (Anon 1909, 117). More importantly, Lee claimed that the author of *King Leir* may have been misled by Spenser into confusing France with Ireland: "Nor does there seem any other example of giving the Gauls the surname of Redshanks, a designation commonly applied by Elizabethan writers only to Irish Celts or Gaelic Scots, from their habit of going bare-legged. Spenser calls the Gaulish home of Cordelia's husband Celtica, and hence the old dramatist may have been led to bestow on its inhabitants a descriptive appellation usually reserved for the Celts of Ireland or Scotland" (Anon 1909, 117).

Spenser's use of the term 'Celtica' and the misunderstanding this appears to have provoked on the part of the author of *King Leir* may constitute a wider process of allusion to Ireland in the context of other rebellions. Andrew Hadfield pointed out that although Ireland is not directly referred to in Shakespeare's plays written after *Henry 5* (apart from fleeting references in *Macbeth* and *Henry 8*), some of them "are concerned with the problems of civil war and international conflict" and so it would be surprising "were none of these to cast at least a glance over the Irish sea" (Hadfield 1997a, 52–53). One of the reasons given by Hadfield for Shakespeare's avoidance of direct reference to Irish issues is political sensitivity concerning the Nine Years War, a period of protracted resistance against the English in Ireland led by Hugh O'Neill, the Earl of Tyrone. If we accept Hadfield's suggestion that "the ghostly presence of Ireland haunts many of Shakespeare's works", some of which can be read as "displaced allegories of Irish events" (Hadfield 1997a, 52) it is likely that the French invaders in *The History of King Lear* would remind English audiences of the threat posed to English nationhood by Irish rebellion. Whether or not Shakespeare makes direct reference to Ireland in particular English history plays, Ireland functions as a subtext in both tetralogies, as Hadfield and Highley independently have found. In *1 Henry 4* the rebellion in Ireland by Hugh O'Neill, Earl of Tyrone, (contemporaneous with the play's production, not the history it shows) is obliquely figured in the mainland rebellions that threaten Henry's rule; in *Henry 5*, Essex's Irish campaign is directly referred to by the Chorus and in *2 Henry 6* there are Irish dimensions to the traitors York and Cade (Highley 1997, 86–109; 134–163; 40–66). Highley detected an Irish subtext in writing which is apparently concerned with Wales (for example David Powel's chronicle *The Historie of Cambria now called Wales* and George Peele's play *Edward I*) and has explored what he refers to as:

> the representational strategies developed by writers both in and out of the theater for handling the 'problem' of Ireland in ways that preserved the fictional distance required by the spoken and unspoken rules of censorship surrounding the performance and publication of texts. (Highley 1997, 67)

Similarly, Lisa Hopkins identified an Irish subtext to *Henry 5* and concluded that "beneath the fields of France loom the Irish bogs" (Hopkins 1997, 14), an observation which is particularly relevant to the possible confusion of France with Ireland, as identified by Lee, in Shakespeare's source play *King Leir*.

In *King Leir* the King of France leads the French army against Lear's English enemies, with Lear second in command. In Shakespeare's *The History of King Lear*, just as all mention of Ireland is omitted so the invasion by France becomes less straightforward when the king of France returns home (an action which is not explained) and Cordelia alone leads the French army. The Gentleman who tells Kent this news claims that France has left in his place "The Maréchal of France, Monsieur la Far" (17.9) but, as R. A. Foakes put it "the 'Marshall of France' is never heard of again; and Cordelia alone appears with the French army ..." (Shakespeare 1997, 317). Monsieur la Far is indeed "far" from England, far from the action of the play, but French military might possibly is evoked at the sight of a young woman leading the French army against the English. Even though it is clear that Cordelia is not a Frenchwoman, she is a French queen and may call to mind that other martial maid, Joan of Arc, denounced as a French whore or 'quean' (OED *sb* 1) in *1 Henry 6*, a play which provides the Protestant propagandist view that Joan was a witch as well as a whore (Fitzpatrick 2000, 72–75).

Stanley Wells and T. W. Craik have pointed out the resemblance between the name for the Marshal in *The History of King Lear*, 'La Far', and the French soldier, Le Fer, in *Henry 5* (Shakespeare 2000b, 223n9; Shakespeare 1995, 299n26). The scene in which the latter solider appears is worth considering for what it tells us about Shakespeare's interest in nomenclature and nationhood:

> PISTOL Come hither boy.
> Ask me this slave in French
> What is his name.
> BOY Écoutez: comment êtes-vous appelé?
> FRENCH SOLDIER Monsieur le Fer.
> BOY He says his name is Master Fer.
> PISTOL Master Fer? I'll fer him, and firk him, and ferret him. Discuss the same in French unto him.
> BOY I do not know the French for fer and ferret and firk.
> PISTOL Bid him prepare, for I will cut his throat.
> (*Henry 5* 4.4.27.23–32)

The French soldier's name is aggressively punned upon by Pistol. Craik claimed that "I'll fer him" is a meaningless repetition but it seems clear that Pistol wants to convey the idea that he'll go for, that is attack, the Frenchman: "I'll for him". As Craik noted, citing the OED, "firk" could mean "beat" but was also used with overtones of "fuck", and "ferret", meaning to "worry" "as a ferret worries a rabbit" or to "search thoroughly" (Shakespeare 1995, 300). Earlier in this encounter Pistol misunderstands the French word 'Qualité' (FRENCH SOLDIER "Je pense que vous êtes le gentilhomme de bon qualité". PISTOL "Qualité? 'Calin o custure me!'" 4.4.2–4) which, as Malone pointed out, reminds Pistol of the Irish refrain of a popular song: "Caleno custore me" (4.4.7.4) which "represents the Irish words 'calin og a' stor' (young maiden, my treasure)" (Shakespeare 1995, 297). Here the French soldier is feminized not only by his nervousness but by Pistol's threats to penetrate him, possibly suggested by the fact that the soldier's words trigger thoughts of a young maiden. The aggressive and incompetent English soldier interrogates the weak Frenchman who provokes the memory of Irish words and presumably Ireland itself. While in *The History of King Lear* the French, led by the female Cordelia, penetrate

England (an unsettling depiction of the Francized English as heroic), here the ignoble English soldier Pistol threatens to penetrate the Frenchman who reminds him of Ireland. Arguably France functions at least partially as a code for Ireland in this scene from *Henry 5* and in *The History of King Lear* where reference to other marginal places, Scotland and Cornwall, would remind English audiences of nearby alterity and rebellion. As we saw in the Introduction, a provincial touring company of recusant players performed numerous plays including 'king Lere' in 1610 at Gowthwaite Hall in Yorkshire and although it is not known whether this was Shakespeare's play or the anonymous source play *King Leir,* either play would have presented the audience with the prospect of invasion by Catholic France. The lines on Lear's map invite the playhouse audience to consider the parcelling of their country in a way which might separate their present home (London, for most playgoers) from their place of birth (not London, for most Londoners) and invasion by a Catholic country in Shakespeare's play, albeit welcome, would presumably have caused unease even allowing for Catholic sympathies amongst the playgoers: being a Catholic in early modern England did not necessarily mean being unpatriotic.

France may function partially as a code for Ireland in *The History of King Lear* because overt reference to England's closest neighbour, coupled with the foreign invasion depicted in the drama, might have provoked the text's suppression and even prosecution. In the scene featuring Pistol and Le Fer from *Henry 5,* the Irish context is oblique and the humour of the scene masks Pistol's aggression toward the foreign enemy. English nationalism is undermined in this scene since Pistol is hardly the epitome of English courage, but it functions clearly elsewhere in the play, in the Chorus's celebration of Henry's triumphant return from France to England:

> Were now the General of our gracious Empress
> As in good time he may – from Ireland coming,
> Bringing rebellion broachèd on his sword,
> How many would the peaceful city quit
> To welcome him! Much more, and much more cause,
> Did they this Harry.
> (*Henry 5* 5.Chorus.30–35)

English success against the French, considered via reference to the suppression of Irish rebellion, reminds the audience that porous borders cannot easily contain the enemy. The allusion to Essex's potential success in

Ireland and what Gary Taylor has referred to as "the sting in its tale" (Shakespeare 1982, 7) brings us rather neatly back to *Richard 2* and internal insurrection, reminding us that in *The History of King Lear* it is an English woman who leads the French army against her fellow English nationals and Lear's own subjects who take up arms against their king.

Edgar's conceptual manipulation of the landscape in the Dover-cliff scene echoes Lear's carving of the map in the first scene of the play and the location of the fictitious cliff is significant in relation to the play's wider concerns about nationhood and borderlands. As Jonathan Goldberg noted, Dover is initially invoked as a counterforce to the annihilative forces of the storm, but the only vision of Dover ultimately offered is Edgar's description of the cliff: "Dover Cliff exists only in Edgar's lines and nowhere else in the play" (Goldberg 1988, 247). Dover thus emerges as "the place of illusion – the illusion of the desire voiced by Kent or Gloucester, the illusion of recovery and the illusion of respite and end" (Goldberg 1988, 247). Since Edgar is responsible for, and entirely in control of, the illusion offered to Gloucester and the playhouse audience, he emerges as a slippery figure who cannot be fully trusted, something recognized by David Scott Kastan who commented on Edgar's peculiarly theatrical double duplicity: he is an actor, or vagabond, playing an aristocrat playing a vagabond (Kastan 1999, 163). As Kastan put it, Edgar's role-playing is "fraudulent" and his "spectacular counterfeiting" takes in Lear, who wrongly believes him to be "the thing itself", "unaccommodated man" (Kastan 1999, 163), and his own father, who believes his description of the landscape to be truthful. Edgar's capacity to deceive might also take in the playhouse audience since they would not necessarily know that the fictive location in which he leads the blind Gloucester is not a cliff. As Philip Maguire pointed out, the play's first audiences expected guidance from the players "to determine the locale of the action being played", but the exchange between Gloucester ("Methinks the ground is even", 20.3) and Edgar ("Horrible steep", 20.4) "would have left Globe audiences without any certain way of deciding which character's account of where they are is accurate" (McGuire 1994, 89). During what McGuire called the "theatrical disorientation" experienced by the Globe audience watching *The History of King Lear* a reference by Edgar to his "deficient sight" (20.23) is especially suggestive:

The 'deficient sight' of which Edgar speaks is a reference to what he says is his own vertiginous disorientation, but it also refers to the eyeless Gloucester, who will soon throw himself off what he thinks is the cliff on which he stands. In addition, 'deficient sight' glances at how, during performances at the Globe, audiences were called upon to accept that in matters of locale what their eyes see is 'deficient'. (McGuire 1994, 90)

The preoccupation with seeing and watching in the Dover-cliff scene might also suggest broader political issues to do with borders and national security, particularly the watching or surveillance between Dover and mainland Europe, something which, as we shall see, figures in one of Shakespeare's sources and a play which might have been influenced by, or indeed influenced, *The History of King Lear*.

John J. M. Tobin traced Shakespeare's many borrowings from Thomas Nashe and noted that in *Pierce Penilesse*, published in 1592, "there is much ado about bastards, compulsive planetary influence, adultery, corrupt justice, hell, blindness, Fortune's wheel and Dover cliff" and of particular interest are the items "absorbed into the fabric of *The History of King Lear*" which appear on three consecutive pages of Nashe's text: "where in the midst of a discussion of *'Hell'* as '...a place of horror, *stench*, and *darknesse*,' where 'Lust' and 'fornication' are particularly punished, we find its location as distant from heaven as Calais from Dover: 'for, as a man standing on Callis sands may see men walking on Dover Clyffes, so easily may you discerne heaven from the farthest part of Hell'" (Tobin 2003, 227). It is not surprising that the old enemy France, in particular Calais, which fell in 1558, should be compared to hell but the notion that "a man standing on Callis sands may see men walking on Dover Clyffes" is palpably untrue: although the distance between Dover and Calais is the shortest route between Britain and France it is not possible to see people 30 miles (48 kilometres) away. In addition to the parallels between *Pierce Penilesse* and *The History of King Lear* noted by Tobin, it is possible that Shakespeare used the Calais-Dover reference to inform Edgar's elaborate fictional description of where they are during the Dover-cliff scene, particularly the lie that he can see men walking on the beach below: "The fishermen that walk upon the beach / Appear like mice" (20.18). The reference to Calais in *Pierce Penilesse* is particularly significant for Shakespeare's play, which dramatizes an invasion by France. Nashe's work was published just four years after the Spanish Armada, which suggests an allusion to English anxiety about foreign surveillance and the reality that the island of Britain needed to defend itself from foreign invaders who, because Catholic, are characterized as hellish.

According to the Chadwyck Healey Literature Online database, the only other mention of the Dover cliffs in a literary work published before 1605 is in another prose text, John Lyly's *Euphues and his England* (1580) where Euphues, a young Athenian accompanied by his friend Philautus, journeys to "the noble Isle of *England*" and spends time "viewing the Castel of *Douer*, the Pyre, the Cliffes, the Road, and Towne" (Chadwyck-Healey 2003; Lyly 1902, 35) but unlike *Pierce Penilesse,* Lyly's text does not appear to have particularly influenced Shakespeare in his writing of *The History of King Lear*. The Dover cliffs also feature in Thomas Heywood's play *If You Know Not Me You Know Nobody, Part 2*. Madeleine Doran and Alfred Harbage concurred that Heywood's play, which was first published in 1606, was likely to have been first performed in 1604–5 (Heywood 1935, xiv; Harbage 1964, 92). As with Heywood's play, it is difficult to know for sure when *The History of King Lear*, first printed in the 1608 Quarto, was first performed. Harbage considered 1605–1606 most likely (Harbage 1964, 92) and Stanley Wells claimed that evidence points to Shakespeare having written "all or most of *The History of King Lear* in the later part of 1605" and although it was apparently not ready for a performance at court that Christmas, it may already have played at the Globe (Shakespeare 2000b, 14). Although we cannot tell for sure which of the two plays were performed first, and therefore in which direction influence may have occurred, it is clear that they share concerns about foreign invasion, nationhood, national boundaries and in particular Dover as a liminal place where seeing is highly significant.

Of particular interest are the last two scenes of Heywood's play, dramatizing the threat to Britain from the Spanish Armada. As O. Rauchbauer pointed out, these demonstrate "God's providence in regard to the Queen, which finally culminates in the miraculous defeat of the Armada" and were influenced by J. Aske's poem *Elizabetha Triumphans*, 1588 (Rauchbauer 1997, 144). At the beginning of scene 17 Queen Elizabeth, informed by a Post of the battle between the English and Spanish, enquires "Where did the royall Nauies first incounter?" to which the Post replies "From Douer Cliffes we might discerne them ioyne, / But such a cloud of smoke inuiron'd them, / We could discouer nought of their proceedings" (17.2560–2563). The English at Dover literally cannot see the enemy because they are surrounded by smoke, but there is also a suggestion that the Spanish cannot be seen because they are duplicitous. The OED shows that 'smoke' indicating "fumes of incense" was current in this period (OED smoke *sb* 1. b.) and in Heywood's play it emphasizes the religious dimensions of the English struggle against the foreign invader. The Catholic enemy concealing themselves behind smoke also suggests the obscurity with which Catholicism was associated in Protestant propaganda. As Douglas D. Waters pointed out, "It was commonplace to call the blinding result of Roman false teaching, including the Mass, a 'mist'," and he gives examples from the writings of John Jewel and Richard Hooker to support his claim that a mist conjured by the witch Duessa in Spenser's *Faerie Queene* "may symbolize, in the theological or anagogical allegory, the confusing and blinding influence 'the falsehood of the pope's mass' was thought to have upon the Protestant mind" (Waters 1970, 46). The problem of not being able to see the foreign enemy is repeated in the description given by the Post of the capture of Sir Martin Furbisher:

> The Spanish Fleet cast in a warlike Ranke
> Like a halfe Moone, or to a full bent bow,
> Wait for aduantage: when amongst the rest
> Sir *Martin Furbisher* blinded with smoke,
> And fir'd in heart with emulating honour,
> Gaue the proud Spaniard a broad side of shot:
> But being within the compasse of their danger,
> The distant corners of the gripled Fleet
> Circled him round: this valiant *Furbisher*,
> With all his braue and gallant followers,
> Are foulded in deaths armes.
> (*If You Know Not Me You Know Nobody, Part 2* 17.2574–2584)

Like Gloucester in *The History of King Lear,* Furbisher, despite being blinded, remains loyal to his monarch and his honourable actions are compared with the pride that consumes the Spanish invader. Although Furbisher is captured, his Admiral, Sir Francis Drake, bravely fights on, leading a second Post to conclude that "England nere bred / Men that at sea fight better managed" (17.2591–92). Drake, described by a Captain as "standing bare-head, brauely on the decke" (17.2615), fights with vehemence and English bravado saves the day:

> he waued his war-like sword,
> And with a bold defiance to the foe.
> The watch-word giuen, his Ordinance let flie
> With such a furie, that it broke their rankes,
> Shotter'd their sides and made their war-like shippes
> Like drunkards reele, and tumble side to side:
> (*If You Know Not Me You Know Nobody, Part 2* 17.2617–2622)

Noble English victory against the Spanish – associated here with gluttonous degeneracy when their warlike ships are likened to drunkards – is divinely sanctioned: the Captain claims their victory is "the will of heauen" (17.2623) and the "true spirit" of Drake compared to "the Spaniards scoffe" (17.2624–26). After praising Drake, Elizabeth claims that she, "A mayden Queene will be your Generall" (17.2639), a parallel with Cordelia who is a leader of men loyal to the British crown in Shakespeare's play. Elizabeth's statement toward the end of the play, "those that for vs would bleed, / Shall find vs kinde to them and to their feed" (18.2691–2692) matches *The History of King Lear* when Edgar, son of the loyal Gloucester who has bled for Lear, is asked by Albany at the play's end to "Rule in this kingdom and the gored state sustain" (24.315).

The notion that there was divine validation of English victory is reinforced when Elizabeth, having been informed about Spanish prisoners, announces "England's God be prais'd" (18.2645) and this religious dimension is underlined when she orders "commandement to the Deane of Powles, / He not forget in his next learned Sermon, / To celebrate this conquest at Powles Crosse" (18.2679–2681). More references to God follow with "thankes to heauen in vniuersall Prayer: / For tho our enemies by ouerthrowne, / Tis by the hand of heauen, and not our owne" (18.2682–85). In *The History of King Lear* Queen Cordelia's return to Britain is similarly figured as evidence of divine intervention in British political affairs: Kent refers to the letter he receives from Cordelia as a miracle (7.157–167) and at various other junctures in the play she is depicted as a Christ-like figure, as noted by Geoffrey L. Bickersteth (1946, 26), Nasheeb Shaheen (1987, 145–46) and Alexander Leggatt (1988b, 28). Helen Hackett recorded various examples of Queen Elizabeth as a Christ-like figure, for example E. K.'s gloss on the April Eclogue of Spenser's *Shepheardes Calender* where the conception of Elizabeth resembles that of Christ himself (Hackett 1995, 109). As in the battle with the Armada dramatized by Heywood, the image of Elizabeth as Christ reinforces the notion that English political affairs are directed by God. Yet although Heywood's play is a straightforward celebration of English triumph against the Catholic invader, Shakespeare's play is problematized by the divinely sanctioned queen being on the side of the foreign invaders. As with the Dover-cliff scene where the audience is disoriented by not knowing whose account of reality they should believe, so here the audience might well be discomfited by a saintly figure leading French forces against the villainous English, even if she has announced that "No blown ambition doth our arms incite, / But love, dear love, and our aged father's right" (18.28–29). If some members of the original audience for *The History of King Lear* were familiar with the story of this ancient king they would have expected a happy ending. Other expectations are similarly subverted: it might be supposed that a play about British history would depict French defeat as cause for celebration but in *The History of King Lear* the French defeat is tragic.

It is striking that two plays performed shortly after the death of Elizabeth and James' accession to the throne should mention the Dover cliffs when there had hitherto been little dramatic interest in the geographical feature. At the close of Heywood's play Elizabeth is given the last word: "Towards London march we to a peacefull throne, / We wish no warres, yet we must guard our owne" (18.2698–99). At the close of *The History of King Lear* Albany is the last to speak: "The oldest have borne most. We that are young / Shall never see so much, nor live so long" (24.320–321). In both endings there is a sense of new beginnings after momentous events. Heywood's play in particular may allude to James' conciliatory stance toward foreign enemies, which allowed him a preoccupation with national issues. Just as Heywood's title *If You Know Not Me You Know Nobody* plays with the notion of recognition – the title page of the first part of the play, published in 1605, containing the unmistakable image of Elizabeth and the subtitle of parts 1 and 2 referring to her "troubles" and her "victorie" respectively – so *The History of King Lear* ends with a reference to seeing. In both plays there is a sense that the new monarch, James, deems watching at Dover unnecessary and that domestic issues will take precedence.

In *Richard 2, Cymbeline* and *The History of King Lear* those who are overly reliant on fantastical manipulations of Britain's landscape are shown to be weak, incompetent rulers and/or morally suspect. In these plays conceptual refigurings of the landscape prove ineffectual when juxtaposed with military action, and internationalism, rather than insularity, is rewarded. Gaunt's fantasy, which imagines England as a country "bound in with the triumphant sea" (2.1.61), a celebration of isolationism echoed by the Queen's encomium in *Cymbeline*, is implicitly challenged by Innogen's recognition that "I' th' world's volume / Our Britain seems as of it but not in 't, / In a great pool a swan's nest" (3.4.138–140) and by Cymbeline's final embracement of Rome, a coming together of British and foreign powers echoed in Cordelia's leadership of the French army which invades Britain in order to defend Lear. In these plays topographical manipulation is undermined by geographical reality and political pragmatism which indicate the shortcomings of those who would reshape the land for their own purposes. The next chapter will consider *Henry 4* and *Macbeth* where prophecy and rumour dominate and the concept of topographical manipulation is used to explore England's relations with its troublesome borderlands.

CHAPTER 4

↬

Celtic alterity and the force of prophesy: 1 Henry 4, 2 Henry 4 *and* Macbeth

W E SAW IN THE previous chapter that Richard's banishment of Bolingbroke and Mowbray provokes very different responses from each man: whilst Mowbray considers absence from England and his beloved language nothing less than torture, Bolingbroke, in the notion that the sun shines in other places besides England, shows himself to be an internationalist. In *Richard 2* Bolingbroke does not embrace banishment, he calls it "an enforced pilgrimage" (1.3.264), but he does not fight it either since he makes no effort to persuade Richard against it and he rejects Gaunt's suggestions that he imagine it a pleasurable journey (1.3.262). In the closing scene of *Richard 2* Bolingbroke announces his intention to make reparation for Richard's death and speaks once again of travel abroad with a religious objective, another kind of "enforced pilgrimage" because of Richard: "I'll make a voyage to the Holy Land / To wash this blood off from my guilty hand" (5.6.49–50). Bolingbroke, the pragmatist, has become king but has also become prone to imaginings and superstition after Richard's death – he is more like Richard than critics have been willing to admit.

1 Henry 4 and 2 Henry 4

It is not clear in the closing scene of *Richard 2* whether the excursion intended by Henry will be contemplative or bloody, but in the opening scene of *1 Henry 4* it is evident that Henry's aim is to shift future violence outward, away from English soil and no longer between English men, to "be no more

[120]

opposed / Against acquaintance, kindred, and allies" (1.1.15–16), and to focus rather on the common enemy, "To chase these pagans in those holy fields" (1.1.24). The plan is for foreign blood to be spilt in order to avoid further English bloodshed and to make up for the bloodshed of one very significant Englishman, Richard. That Henry's plans are halted by internal strife is ironic as is the sense that, despite his history as a man who takes control and makes things happen, Henry, having achieved kingship, has little control over the course of future events. Discussion moves quickly and, within the space of several lines, focus shifts from plans to visit the Holy Land to the resolution of internal matters; travel to distant locations must remain part of the imagination for the time being since Henry is forced to deal with the more mundane reality of England's troublesome borderlands.

At the beginning of *2 Henry 4* Rumour enters to present the induction and proclaims that "Upon my tongues continual slanders ride, / The which in every language I pronounce, / Stuffing the ears of men with false reports" (1.1.6–8). Although she does not appear literally in *1 Henry 4*, rumour – diverse reports and their impact upon reputation – plays a pivotal role in the play and nowhere is this more evident than in the representation of the Welsh, part of the coalition of rebels that must be destroyed by Henry before he can undertake his journey to the Holy Land. According to Westmorland, the Welsh are not unlike the pagans against whom Henry wishes to fight:

> the noble Mortimer,
> Leading the men of Herefordshire to fight
> Against the irregular and wild Glyndŵr,
> Was by the rude hands of that Welshman taken,
> A thousand of his people butcherèd,
> Upon whose dead corpse' there was such misuse,
> Such beastly shameless transformation,
> By those Welshwomen done as may not be
> Without much shame retold or spoken of.
> (*1 Henry 4* 1.1.38–46)

This incident is referred to in Holinshed's Chronicles as one that "honest eares would be ashamed to heare, and continent toongs to speake thereof" (Holinshed 1587, Ddd6v) but is in fact related in detail a few pages later: "the women of Wales cut off their priuities and put one part thereof into the mouths of euerie dead man ... and not so contented, they did cut off their noses and thrust them into their tails as they laie on the ground mangled and defaced" (Holinshed 1587, Eee4v). The author of this report, Abraham Fleming, justified his decision to describe the incident: "This was a verie ignominious deed, and a worsse not committed among the barbarous: which though it make the reader to read it, and the hearer to heare it, ashamed: yet because it was a thing doone in open fight, and left testified in historie; I see little reason whie it should not be imparted in our mother toong ..." (Holinshed 1587, Eee4v). Westmorland informs Henry, and the audience, that barbarous foes live within the island of Britain and these threatening, if less exotic, domestic issues must be dealt with before glorious foreign wars can be undertaken. Henry's big plan in the name of international Christianity is thus undercut by reports of savage behaviour close to home and his lengthy opening speech, assessing past action and planning a glorious foreign campaign, made null and void. Westmorland's description of "the noble Mortimer" pitched against "the irregular and wild Glyndŵr" (1.1.38; 40) pitches English civility against Welsh savagery, but his report of a wild and brutish rebel contrasts with that offered to Henry by Hotspur. Although Hotspur's immediate intention is to defend Mortimer against charges of rebellion, he also praises Glyndŵr:

> Revolted Mortimer?
> He never did fall off, my sovereign liege,
> But by the chance of war. To prove that true
> Needs no more but one tongue for all those wounds,
> Those mouthed wounds, which valiantly he took
> When on the gentle Severn's sedgy bank,
> In single opposition, hand to hand,
> He did confound the best part of an hour
> In changing hardiment with great Glyndŵr.
> (1 Henry 4 1.3.93–101)

Henry rejects Hotspur's report of Mortimer's heroism as fantasy: "He never did encounter with Glyndŵr ... . / He durst as well have met the devil alone / As Owain Glyndŵr for an enemy" (1.3.114–117). In Westmorland's report of the encounter between Mortimer and Glyndŵr the latter is granted a prodigious aspect with the suggestion that Mortimer and his men were defeated by Glyndŵr alone. Similarly Henry characterizes Glyndŵr as demonic, he is "that great magician" (1.3.83) and later Falstaff will refer to "that devil Glyndŵr" (2.4.357) and "he of Wales that gave Amamon the bastinado and made Lucifer cuckold and swore the devil his true liegeman upon the cross of a Welsh hook" (2.5.325–328). The repeated coupling of Glyndŵr with malevolent supernatural forces serves to enhance his reputation as a formidable enemy. The characterisation may also serve Henry as a useful metaphor for rebellion with the notion that Glyndŵr wields demonic powers serving to undermine his political objectives. Yet Henry's opinion of Glyndŵr as demonic does not contradict Hotspur's characterisation of Glyndŵr as a great warrior, indicating that, contrary to Christopher Highley's assertion, Henry does not altogether withhold his admiration for the Welshman (Highley 1997, 94). That Glyndŵr is reported to be brutish, in league with demonic forces, and a great warrior serves to enforce his reputation as a daunting foe and thus perhaps alleviates Henry's failure to push through his plan to attack the pagans in the holy land: defeating the demonic within the bounds of Britain will be a suitable, if necessary, substitute before larger projects can be undertaken.

Glyndŵr's reputation as a potent warrior with magical powers was available to Shakespeare primarily from Holinshed who also noted Glyndŵr's early education in England:

> He was first set to studie the lawes of the realme, and became an vtter barrester, or an apprentise of the law (as they terme him) and serued king Richard at Flint castell, when he was taken by Henrie duke of Lancaster, though other haue written that he serued this king Henrie the fourth, before he came to atteine the crowne, in roome of an esquier (Holinshed 1587, Ddd5v).

Glyndŵr's early years, being "trained up in the English court" resemble those of the Irish rebel Hugh O'Neill, the Earl of Tyrone, although, as Hiram Morgan pointed out, there is no evidence for the popular assumption that O'Neill was raised in the Sidney household in England (Morgan 1993, 92); O'Neill himself referred to his education amongst the English rather than in England itself and Morgan claimed that "Hugh O'Neill was a ward of Giles Hovenden, an English settler in Laois" (Morgan 1993, 93). As we saw in the previous chapter, Tyrone was considered by some Welsh to be a descendant of Glyndŵr, and Christopher Highley argued that Shakespeare expected his audience to make connections between them, "weaving into the fabric of the play a displaced representation of Tyrone's resistance to English authority in Ireland" (Highley 1997, 87). According to Morgan, their experiences were similar and so was the way in which they were regarded by English commentators. David J. Baker referred to English anxieties about those in Ireland who did not conform to the categories created by the colonist: "The hybrid – either the degenerate Englishman or the incompletely assimilated Irishman – could become, for the colonial power, a figure of threatening ambiguity ..." (Baker 1992, 40) and Hadfield and McVeagh noted that "O'Neill troubled and enraged English writers not just because of the danger and disruption he caused, nor simply for the audacity of his nearly successful war, but because he was a transgressive and hybrid figure who in many ways resembled them (Hadfield & McVeagh 1994, 89). In Sir John Harington's famous account of his meeting with O'Neill he noted that "the Earl used far greater respect to me than I expected, and began debasing his own manner of hard life, comparing himself to wolves, that fill thier bellies sometime, and fast as long for it" (Maxwell 1923, 338). This modesty (or affectation) from O'Neill is contradicted by Harington's observations about O'Neill's sons – "in English clothes like a nobleman's sons ... both of them learning the English tongue" – and O'Neill's interest in poetry: "I gave them, not without the advice of Sir William Warren, my English translation of Ariosto, which I got at Dublin; which their teachers took very thankfully, and soon after shewed it to the Earl, who called to see it openly, and would needs hear some part of it read" (Maxwell 1923, 338). O'Neill's pleasure in the English translation of Italian poetry makes it difficult to present him as a mere savage and in Shakespeare's *1 Henry 4* Glyndŵr's reputation is shown to be similarly heterogeneous. Glyndŵr, like O'Neill, did not fit colonial categories and in *1 Henry 4* the co-existence of Glyndŵr's alterity and his civilized nature – his concern for his daughter and his command of music in the scene set in Wales – proves unsettling.

When we first meet Glyndŵr in 3.1 he bears little resemblance to the play's earlier descriptions of him and details are altered from Holinshed. An importance change is the venue for the alliance between the rebels and the personalities involved: in Holinshed the alliance is confirmed in the house of the Archdeacon of Bangor by the rebels' deputies while Shakespeare depicts the meeting in Glyndŵr's home, making it a more personal and familial compact. Although Shakespeare's Glyndŵr is both civilized and gracious, Highley contended that the domestication of Glyndŵr, the revision of his "fearful reputation", presents him as "an object of ridicule" and that Falstaff's "satirical vignette of Glyndŵr mastering the forces of Hell" prepares us for Hotspur's "thorough demystification of the Welshman's

prodigious self-image and magical pretensions", a process further reinforced through Hotspur's criticisms which associate Glyndŵr with "traits
stereotyped as feminine" (Highley 1997, 95). Highley's theory is that
Shakespeare is undermining the Welsh Glyndŵr as part of a contemporary
propaganda war against the Irish Tyrone.

Highley's argument for parallels between Glyndŵr and Tyrone is convincing, but less plausible is the notion that Shakespeare is attacking
Glyndŵr. The magical powers that Glyndŵr boasts of appear to be genuine
at least once in the play, when he summons music for his daughter to sing:

> those musicians that shall play to you
> Hang in the air a thousand leagues from hence,
> And straight they shall be here. Sit and attend.
> (*1 Henry 4* 3.1.219–221)

David Bevington noted that "Whether Glendower is to be perceived as a
powerful magician in thus summoning music is a complex question" but
that "In general his claims to magical powers are undercut by Hotspur's sar-
donic witticisms" (Shakespeare 1987, 219n2244.1). Similarly David Scott
Kastan pointed out that Hotspur "jokingly admits that Glendower seemingly has successfully called musicians" and "gibes that he is not surprised to
discover that Welsh can be used to call satanic spirits, though he is presumably aware, as is the audience of the play, that the musicians in the theatre
company are most likely sitting behind a curtain in the music gallery and so
might indeed be said to 'Hang in the air'" (Kastan 2002, 254n226) –
although Kastan is wrong to assume that the musicians would be in the
gallery because, as Richard Hosley pointed out, they were usually situated
inside the tiring house (Hosley 1960, 116–18). Whether or not Shakespeare
wished us to think that Glyndŵr summoned the music supernaturally or
played a trick upon his audience, having previously secreted musicians
about the place, is less important than the fact that magic appears to occur.
Although Hotspur's response to the apparent magic is typically mocking,
he does not deny that Glyndŵr has done what he said he would and on this
occasion Hotspur's mocking is challenged not by Glyndŵr, as it has been
throughout the scene, but by someone who should be partial to Hotspur,
his wife, Lady Percy:

> Then should you be nothing but musical,
> For you are altogether governed by humours.

Lie still, ye thief, and hear the lady sing in Welsh.
(*1 Henry 4* 3.1.228–230)

Hotspur has been admonished twice before, by Mortimer and Worcester, for his behaviour toward Glyndŵr. Mortimer presents a positive account of Glyndŵr, thus undermining Hotspur's characterisation of him, and undermining Highley's conclusion that Hotspur's words necessarily represent the view of Glyndŵr that Shakespeare wanted his audience to adopt:

> In faith, he is a worthy gentleman,
> Exceedingly well read, and profited
> In strange concealments, valiant as a lion,
> And wondrous affable, and as bountiful
> As mines of India. Shall I tell you, cousin?
> He holds your temper in a high respect,
> And curbs himself even of his natural scope
> When you come 'cross his humour; faith, he does.
> (*1 Henry 4* 3.1.160–167)

Hotspur's attempts to undermine Glyndŵr ultimately fail because his characterisations are not to be trusted. When admonishing Hotspur, Worcester is unequivocal in his criticism:

> In faith, my lord, you are too wilful-blame,
> And since your coming hither have done enough
> To put him quite besides his patience.
> You must needs learn, lord, to amend this fault.
> Though sometimes it show greatness, courage, blood –
> And that's the dearest grace it renders you –
> Yet oftentimes it doth present harsh rage,
> Defect of manners, want of government,
> Pride, haughtiness, opinion, and disdain,
> The least of which haunting a nobleman
> Loseth men's hearts, and leaves behind a stain
> Upon the beauty of all parts besides,
> Beguiling them of commendation.
> (*1 Henry 4* 3.1.172–184)

Hotspur's response is typically blunt: "Well, I am schooled. Good manners be your speed!" (3.1.185–86) which John Dover Wilson noted was a reference to the uselessness of manners on the battlefield (Shakespeare 1946,

[126]

161n188). Hotspur has previously criticized Glyndŵr for his courtly accomplishments and Worcester's comments, though a useful corrective to Hotspur's jibing, are in turn undercut by Hotspur's pragmatic view of manners in battle. Hotspur speaks sense but Shakespeare presents alternate points of view on Glyndŵr.

Far from undermining Glyndŵr in particular, the overall effect of the scene set in Wales is to undermine the rebels in general, presenting them as a squabbling and distracted group, full of "unprofitable chat" (3.1.60). Hotspur cannot even remember one of the essentials of any well-run rebellion: "A plague upon it, I have forgot the map!" (3.1.5). In a scene which pre-echoes Lear's carving up of his kingdom, the rebels decide to "divide our right, / According to our threefold order ta'en" (3.1.66–67). Here geographical reality proves inconvenient to the division of land and Hotspur, unhappy with his share, wants to force a new route for the river Trent: "It shall not wind with such a deep indent, / To rob me of so rich a bottom here" (3.1.101–102). His desire to reshape the landscape and force the river to divert its natural direction is initially refused by Glyndŵr but political expediency succeeds over topographical reality and Glyndŵr gives in: "Come, you shall have Trent turn'd" (3.1.132). Hotspur's response, that he does not care about the land itself since he will "give thrice so much land / To any well-deserving friend" but will split hairs "in the way of bargain" (3.1.133–35), shows him not only to be argumentative but boastful, a characteristic usually attributed to Glyndŵr. For Hotspur arguing is its own reward and he is less interested in real gains. Ultimately, however, the argument over topographical division is pointless because the rebels will not enjoy power. Retrospective irony makes it clear that the division is a fantasy and indeed a waste of time. What appears to be at work here is a comment on the nature of the rebellion: a disorganized, competitive, and petty affair. In particular Hotspur's arrogance in wishing to force human intervention upon the natural world and the pointlessness of his arguing contrasts strikingly with Glyndŵr who behaves in a conciliatory and pragmatic manner when negotiation is called for and, as we shall see, is more in tune with the natural world, much to the frustration of Bolingbroke.

The rebels' grand designs come to nothing when things do not go according to plan, their failure to achieve their ambition in direct contrast to Henry's successful rebellion against Richard. Yet Henry also experiences failure when his planned excursion to the Holy Land does not take place. In both cases, Henry's intention to travel abroad and the rebels' plan to divide Britain between them, prophecy plays a key role in the events that unfold. In *2 Henry 4* Henry announces: "It hath been prophesied to me many years / I should not die but in Jerusalem, / Which vainly I supposed the Holy Land" (4.3.365–367). Earlier in the play Henry, anxious about his past and how it relates to current disloyalties, speaks to Warwick about Richard:

> You, cousin Neville, as I may remember –
> When Richard, with his eye brimful of tears,
> Then checked and rated by Northumberland,
> Did speak these words, now proved a prophecy? –
> "Northumberland, thou ladder by the which
> My cousin Bolingbroke ascends my throne" –
> Though then, God knows, I had no such intent,
> But that necessity so bowed the state
> That I and greatness were compelled to kiss –
> "The time shall come" – thus did he follow it –
> "The time will come that foul sin, gathering head,
> Shall break into corruption"; so went on,
> Foretelling this same time's condition,
> And the division of our amity.
> (*2 Henry 4* 3.1.62–74)

As mentioned in chapter 4, the theories of Elizabethan culture developed by "old" historicists such as E. M. W. Tillyard and Lily B. Campbell read the second tetralogy as an orthodox condemnation of regicide. Henry's belief in the fulfilment of Richard's prophecy articulates the Tudor myth, the notion that, as Nicolas Grene put it, "England was cursed for the primal crime of the disposition and murder of Richard II, and for that crime the house of Lancaster was visited with the whole vicious circle of civil war, only finally exorcised with the union of York and Lancaster in the accession of Richmond as Henry VII" (Grene 2002, 45). Tillyard read the history plays as "the grandly consistent embodiment of the orthodox political and social morality of the Elizabethan period, preaching order and hierarchy, con-demning factious power-seeking and the anarchy of civil war to which it led, commending the divinely sanctioned centralised monarchy of the Tudors" (Grene 2002, 45). Although Henry's recollection of Richard's words apparently substantiates Tillyard's reading of the plays (and his read-ing of Shakespeare's attitude to power and order) the matter is more com-plex than Tillyard acknowledged. Tillyard's theory has been challenged by numerous critics, among them H. A. Kelly, who showed that the *Chronicles*, from which Tillyard claimed Shakespeare absorbed the Tudor myth, reflected different and contending historiographical myths: there was also a "Lancaster myth" and a "York myth". Kelly's analysis of the annals and contemporary accounts on which the *Chronicles* were based showed that successive histories of divine providential intervention had in fact been altered to suit a particular political regime (Kelly 1970, 297–306). Subsequent critics have suggested that the history plays are not univocal. As Graham Holderness put it, "Several post-Tillyard critics discussing the English history plays have observed that historiography in this period was not a passive reflector of medieval providential theology nor a loyal transmitter of Tudor political commonplace, but a varied and changing activity producing different and competing methods and forms" (Holderness 1985, 23). That Henry anxiously contemplates the impact of his "foul sin" against Richard does not suggest that Shakespeare believed the Tudor myth to be true nor that the play is a straightforward condemnation of Henry's accession to the throne. However, it is equally true that Shakespeare does not present a straightforward condemnation of Welsh rebellion: the meeting between the rebels is disorganized and they engage in petty squabbling but Glyndŵr in particular is a striking and attractive adversary.

Richard speaks prophecies in *Richard 2* and Henry announces his belief in prophecies in *1* and *2 Henry 4* but, surprisingly, the man most associated with prophecy, Glyndŵr, says nothing on the subject himself. Although Glyndŵr speaks about natural portents at the time of his birth and apparently has the supernatural ability to conjure music in the scene set in Wales, he is mainly linked with prophecy by what others say about him. In this sense, prophecy is intimately bound up with rumour and reputation, concepts which are central to all three plays. Remarkably, critics are responsible for repeating the kind of rumours which surround Glyndŵr in the plays, for example David Bevington noted that "Glendower's superstitious belief in prophecies prevents him from becoming an effective military force at Shrewsbury" (Shakespeare 1987, 219–220 n224.1), an assertion based not on what Glyndŵr himself says but on what is said about him. Vernon reports that Glyndŵr "cannot draw his power this fourteen days" (4.1.128) but does not say why and in a later scene it is the Archbishop of York who claims that Glyndŵr "comes not in, o'erruled by prophecies" (4.4.18). Shakespeare's source material, Daniel's *Ciuil Warres* and Holinshed's

Chronicles, differs on whether there was a Welsh presence at the battle of Shrewsbury. Although Daniel reported that Glyndŵr "The ioyning with the *Welsh* they had decreed / Was hereby stopt ... " (Daniel 1595, R1v), Holinshed claimed that the Welshmen "came to the aid of the Persies, and refreshed the wearied people with new succours" (Holinshed 1587, Ddd6v), although he does not mention whether or not Glyndŵr was present. Highley noted that it is Shakespeare's invention that Glyndŵr stays away because of prophecies but, like Bevington, made no reference to this reason being reported second-hand, notable omissions given that throughout the play Glyndŵr is associated with rumour, conjecture and reputation (Highley 1997, 97).

We might wonder why Shakespeare's play links Glyndŵr's absence from the battle of Shrewsbury with rumours of prophecies but allows no statement from Glyndŵr himself. We might also wonder why Shakespeare alters the location of the rebels' meeting, staging it in Glyndŵr's house and with women present. Highley claimed that this was part of Shakespeare's agenda to undermine Glyndŵr, who is "surprisingly at ease in the company of women" and represented as "a fussing, over-protective parent", suggesting that the women, and particularly Glyndŵr's daughter, have a feminizing influence upon Glyndŵr (Highley 1997, 95). But this is simply not the case. As Matthew Greenfield pointed out, "Glendower presides over a seduction ... His daughter's weeping, her music, and her sexuality, all represented as a kind of overflowing or incontinence, work to feminize her husband and rob him of an Englishness that is gendered male" (Greenfield 2002, 74). Glyndŵr "presides over", that is he directs and controls the feminizing of the English Mortimer. The interest shown in his daughter's welfare, which Highley puts down to fussiness, is not so different from that shown by Henry for Hal, although there is no evidence with Glyndŵr of Henry's peevish desire to switch his offspring for another (1.1.77–94). Terence Hawkes noted that Mortimer's situation, whereby he is seduced and captivated by a Circe-like Welsh woman, "undoubtedly echoes that of his hapless English comrades at Bryn Glas" (Hawkes 2002, 34), where happened the "beastly shameless transformation" reported by Westmorland in 1.1. That the figurative emasculation of the English Mortimer is anticipated by the literal emasculation of other Englishmen suggests that the effeminizing process in Wales – both during the violation of English soldiers at Bryn Glas and the seduction of Mortimer in Glyndŵr's home – is primarily a nationalistic one.

For Hawkes, the subversive abilities of Glyndŵr's daughter are located specifically in "the strongly suasive powers" of the Welsh language; its feminine, seductive, and narcotic nature has the capacity to create a "bower of bliss" whose modes dissolve and transcend the male, order-giving boundaries of an English-speaking world" (Hawkes 2002, 31).

Hawkes used the term "bower of bliss" to describe the scene set in Wales without specifically saying that it comes from Spenser's *Faerie Queene*. Stephen Greenblatt famously connected the Bower of Bliss episode from Book 2 of Spenser's poem to colonialism, Ireland and religious iconoclasm. According to Greenblatt, the Bower of Bliss represents a threat to civility and the threat of absorption by that which is characterized as alien (Greenblatt 1980, 172–73). Acrasia, the Circe figure who leads military men astray, is undoubtedly similar to Glyndŵr's daughter, but whereas Spenser's episode ends with Guyon's aggressive destruction of the Bower, Mortimer is effectively subdued. In this he is more like Verdant, the young knight who has abandoned his arms and lies in a post-coital embrace with Acrasia (*Faerie Queene* 2.12.78–80), than Guyon who violently over-reacts in order to avoid the seduction he may secretly desire. It is likely that Shakespeare was influenced by this episode from Spenser's *Faerie Queene* when composing *1 Henry 4*: Books 1–3 of Spenser's poem were published in 1590 and Books 1–6 and the Mutabilitie Cantos in 1596. *1 Henry 4* was entered in the Stationers' Register on 25 February 1598 and quarto editions first appeared in the same year (Shakespeare 1987, 2). As Hawkes pointed out, the seductive power of Welsh alerts the audience to the subversive "and in a complex sense 'effeminate' role" of Welsh culture in early modern Britain and when Hotspur rejects these charms – "I had rather hear Lady my brach howl in Irish" (3.1.230) – the audience is reminded of "the larger Celtic world that its own commitment to English and Englishness had long been trying to suppress" (Hawkes 2002, 31). It is the Welsh language and Welsh culture in general which work to undermine English masculinity rather than Welsh women specifically.

Jean Howard and Phyllis Rackin claimed that Glyndŵr's daughter is a symbol of alterity who is excluded from "the linguistic community" of men since "she speaks a language that announces her otherness" (Howard & Rackin 1997, 170). Yet Mortimer and Hotspur are also excluded from the linguistic community of the Welsh since they cannot understand the conversations between Glyndŵr and his daughter. Important military business is conducted in English but in the scene set in Wales Mortimer and Hotspur's inability to speak Welsh makes them outsiders. While Howard and Rackin saw the speaking of Welsh as disempowering, Greenfield thought it possible that, in metadramatic terms, it creates a boundary which excludes the theatre audience and, rather than signifying alterity, allows Glyndŵr's daughter "some degree of autonomy or privacy" (Bullough 1973b, 75). Greenfield's reading allows for the possibility that Glyndŵr's daughter, and Welshness in general, is represented by Shakespeare in a more positive light than is usually acknowledged. This is supported by Hawkes' claim that Shakespeare's playing company had Welsh speakers and "It may well be that an acquaintance with Welsh people in London accounts for Shakespeare's portrayal of Glyndŵr as more sympathetic than his sources would encourage" (Hawkes 2002, 33). Yet Hawkes also emphasized the utter strangeness of the Welsh language to English ears, both modern and Tudor:

> To most of those familiar with the major European tongues, Welsh would have seemed – as it still does – entirely exotic. In its written form, the apparent senseless conjunction of consonants generates blankness, if not bewilderment. In its spoken form, its requirement of unachievable phonemes, such as /ll/, mark it as impossibly alien, utterly estranging (Hawkes 2002, 33).

The co-existence of the familiar (Welsh members of the company, the Welsh in London) and the exotic (the Welsh language) is embodied in the figure of Glyndŵr himself. Glyndŵr is very much in control, especially in the scene set in Wales, where, aside from being the powerful paterfamilias on his home ground, he is the only person present who understands everything that is said. Glyndŵr's bilingualism is a source of power since it affords him access to the English-speaking court while those English in his court do not have the same advantage. If Hawkes is right, and part of the scene set in Wales was written or influenced by Welsh speakers, then Welshness is given a voice and allowed the freedom to create in a specifically English space; the writing of English history provides a subtle and complex picture of the infamous Welsh rebel, Glyndŵr. Highley's suggestion that Glyndŵr's rebellion is "a displaced representation of Tyrone's resistance to English authority in Ireland" (Highley 1997, 87) is a plausible one, but if we accept that the depiction of Glyndŵr is more nuanced and sympathetic than Highley allows, then important questions are raised about the possibility of the theatre's sympathy for Welsh and Irish nationalism.

Hawkes emphasized the suasive powers of the Welsh language and the complex effeminate role of Welsh culture in relation to the figurative emasculation of Mortimer and the dissolution of his Englishness. But the Welsh landscape also has a central role to play in the transformation effected upon Mortimer. Hotspur's description of the battle between Mortimer and Glyndŵr, which praises both men, also connects them very intimately with the Welsh landscape via the river Severn:

> Three times they breathed and three times did they drink,
> Upon agreement, of swift Severn's flood,
> Who, then affrighted with their bloody looks,
> Ran fearfully among the trembling reeds,
> And hid his crisp head in the hollow bank,
> Bloodstainèd with these valiant combatants.
> (*1 Henry 4* 1.3.101–106)

There is little distinction between Welshman and Englishman in Hotspur's description of the fight where each man breathes, and drinks "three times" and "upon agreement". That the combatants drink from the river Severn as it runs through Wales – the historical location of the combat being Bryn Glas, where the Welsh women defiled the bodies of English soldiers – suggests that the water itself might prove partial, providing a kind of magical sustenance to "that great magician, damned Glyndŵr" (1.3.83). Yet Hotspur's report that the river is fearful of their "bloody looks", hiding itself in the hollow bank, implies that the landscape itself refuses to take sides, either because each man is so great or because the river, which runs through England and Wales, is caught between the two, thus prefiguring Mortimer's switch in loyalty. The water has been stained with the blood of "these valiant combatants", which suggests that, united by their valour, they share their blood with the river and thus each other. As in Spenser's river-marriage canto, discussed in Chapter 2, this blood-mingling is linked to miscegenation. Philip Schwyzer noted that Mortimer "unites his blood with Owain Glyndŵr's not once but twice – first literally, and with potent symbolism, in the waters of the Severn as they do battle on its banks (1.3.102–7), and then in marriage with Glyndŵr's daughter" (Schwyzer 1997, 36). The dissolution of boundaries between Englishman and Welshman, effected by the blood which mingles in the Welsh river and in each other's veins, is certainly solemnized by marriage, but the overwhelming effect of Mortimer's blood seeping into the Welsh landscape is to suggest that his loyalty to Wales will run deep and that the landscape itself, as much as his bewitching Welsh wife and fellow rebels, now expects and will receive that loyalty.

Mortimer's battle with Glyndŵr, which sees him drink from and bleed into the Welsh river, marks his transition from loyal Englishman to loyal Welsh husband and rebel while Glyndŵr is intimately linked with the Welsh landscape throughout the play and believes that he receives sustenance from it. Although the Welsh landscape favours neither man in Shakespeare's description of the battle between Mortimer and Glyndŵr, Glyndŵr is convinced that, unlike the English landscape which has "daub[ed] her lips with her own children's blood" (1.1.6), the Welsh landscape has supported him in past encounters with the English king:

> Three times hath Henry Bolingbroke made head
> Against my power; thrice from the banks of Wye
> And sandy-bottomed Severn have I sent him
> Bootless home, and weather-beaten back.
> (1 Henry 4 3.1.61–64)

Both Mortimer and Bolingbroke have confronted Glyndŵr in Wales and Glyndŵr's lyrical description of events suggests that the landscape from which his power emanates imbues him with the strength to resist Henry, thus casting the very landscape itself as a supporter of his rebellion. As in Hotspur's report of Glyndŵr's battle with Mortimer, it is Welsh water which is the source of powerful Welsh resistance but, unlike the battle between Glyndŵr and Mortimer, where the Welsh landscape was impartial, there is little indication that Henry receives sustenance from the rivers Wye and Severn. Glyndŵr's manipulation of the natural world, to the detriment of Bolingbroke, is recorded by Holinshed:

> About mid of August, the king to chastise the presumptuous attempts of the Welshmen, went with a great power of men into Wales, to pursue the capteine of the Welsh rebell Owen Glendouer, but in effect he lost his labor; for Owen conueied himselfe out of the waie, into his knowen lurking places, and (as was thought) through art magike, he caused such foule weather of winds, tempest, raine, snow, and haile to be raised, for the annoiance of the kings armie, that the like had not been heard of; in such sort, that the king was constreined to return home, hauing caused his people yet to spoile and burne first a great part of the countrie (Holinshed 1587, Ddd6v).

As well as the belief in Glyndŵr's ability to raise storms is the notion that he is capable of merging into the very landscape itself by moving "into his knowen lurking places". Like Malengin in Spenser's *Faerie Queene*, who resembles the figure of the Irish rebel, Glyndŵr flees into the landscape from which he gains strength. As we saw in Chapter 2, Malengin's resistance is short-lived: Talus destroys him, breaking his bones into pieces "as small as sandy grayle" (5.9.19.4) and the landscape, which previously afforded Malengin support, effectively switches allegiance, colluding with Talus and absorbing the dust of Malengin's malevolent body in order to leave little trace of him behind. However, in Holinshed's report, quoted above, there is an overwhelming sense that Wales supports Glyndŵr's resistance and, instead of inflicting violence upon the body of the rebellious Glyndŵr, Henry spoils and burns his country, an act which suggests that aggression toward the landscape which has proved partial to Welsh rebellion is the next best thing to exacting revenge upon the body of the rebel himself.

Just as Glyndŵr disappears into the landscape in Holinshed's account of his rebellion so he disappears from *1 Henry 4* after 3.1. In Holinshed's description of Glyndŵr's death, rumour and the Welsh landscape converge in what constitutes a striking inversion of earlier reports, in both Holinshed and *1 Henry 4*, of Glyndŵr's victories:

> The Welsh rebell Owen Glendouer made an end of his wretched life in this tenth yeare of King Henrie his reigne, being driven now in his latter time (as we find recorded) to such miserie, that in manner despairing of all comfort, he fled into desert places and solitarie caves, where being destitute of all releefe and succour, dreeading to shew his face to anie creature, and finallie lacking meat to susteine nature, for mere hunger and lack of food, miserablie pined awaie and died. (Holinshed 1587, Fff2v)

R. R. Davies agreed with Adam of Usk, the English medieval chronicler, who claimed that Glendower spent his last days "hiding in the open country and in caves and in the thickets of the mountains" (Davies 1997, 326) but no mention is made of Glendower starving to death. As Elissa R. Henken outlined in her study of Glyndŵr, there is disagreement among historians as to how Glyndŵr spent his last years with some, like Holinshed, believing him to have starved to death, alone and miserable in the desolate Welsh landscape, and others believing him to have died in relative comfort at the house of one of his daughters (Henken 1996, 64–66). As the *Dictionary of*

National Biography pointed out, it was English writers of the early modern period who "believed that he died of sheer starvation among the mountains" (Stephen & Lee 1921–1922, 1313). Given the lack of evidence, Holinshed's account is a fantasy of Glyndŵr's demise where he retreats into the landscape with which he has always been associated but, crucially, the landscape is indifferent toward him, providing no relief to his condition. Most importantly, the fantasy presents a Glyndŵr who is afraid ("dreeading to shew his face") and thus bears little resemblance to Holinshed's earlier descriptions of him. Glyndŵr, like Tyrone, took advantage of his country's difficult terrain when resisting English authority and it is no surprise that Holinshed should wish to connect his fantastical demise with a particular tactic of guerrilla warfare: the starvation of the indigenous population advocated by Irenius in the *View*. The Welsh leader, whose men "had laine lurking in the woods, mounteines and marishes" (Holinshed 1587, Eee2r) in order to hide from and attack the English, now lurks in the same environment but is powerless to save himself.

Glyndŵr is mentioned only briefly at the conclusion of *1 Henry 4* when Henry announces his intention to go to Wales "To fight with Glyndŵr and the Earl of March" (5.5.40–43) and although he is referred to by name twice in *2 Henry 4* he does not make an appearance. In *2 Henry 4* Warwick encourages Henry to ignore stories about the strength of their enemy since "Rumour doth double, like the voice and echo, / The numbers of the feared" (3.1.97–99) and announces that he has "receiv'd / A certain instance that Glyndŵr is dead" (3.1.102–103), an instance that is never verified by evidence or impartial observation. Crucially, Shakespeare ignores Holinshed's account of Glyndŵr's ignoble demise and, unlike his Irish counterpart Tyrone, who fled to Rome after the failure of his rebellion, Glyndŵr remains at large in the Welsh landscape. Rumour abounds in both plays and that there is no confirmation of Glyndŵr's demise is unsettling for the English forces. It is also rather disappointing, since we might expect between Henry and Glyndŵr the kind of show-down we get between Prince Harry and Hotspur. Most importantly, however, no evidence of Glyndŵr's demise, ignoble or otherwise, underpins his reputation as a prodigious and enigmatic enemy who remains a potent, because unseen, threat to Henry's reign. In both plays grand schemes are undermined and anticlimax is a dominant feature: Henry's expectations of a glorious Holy War at the beginning of *1 Henry 4* are frustrated, as are the rebels' plans to divide Britain amongst themselves. Ironically, Henry will go to Jerusalem only via the Jerusalem Chamber, in which he will die. The ultimate meaning of the prophecy that he "should not die but in Jerusalem" (4.3.366) is really rather mundane: a room in England replaces an exotic and challenging journey and the result is rather tawdry; it is not glorious for a warrior king to die at home. At the conclusion of *2 Henry 4* it becomes clear that Henry has fallen short of John of Gaunt's definition of English kings in his encomium of England: "Renowned for their deeds as far from home / For Christian service and true chivalry /As is the sepulchre, in stubborn Jewry" (*Richard 2* 2.1.53–55). A splendid reputation based on military conquest is not to be had by Henry and though the Welsh rebellion fails, the ghost of Glyndŵr lingers. Henry, who had desired to "read the book of fate" (*2 Henry 4* 3.1.44), is resigned to prophetic misinterpretation and faith in rumour; unable to control the future in the way he hoped possible at the outset of *1 Henry 4*, he dies off-stage, aware that his son is keen to inherit the crown he took from Richard.

Macbeth

In the plays discussed above, grand designs come to nothing and prophecy proves to be misleading. For Henry, Wales not the Holy Land proves to be the centre of alterity and although rebellion is quashed Glyndŵr remains a haunting presence. As in *1* and *2 Henry 4* prophecy plays a key role in the events that unfold in *Macbeth*: the misunderstanding of prophecy as a trigger for usurpation is central as is rebellion and the desire of a monarch to control his future. Like Henry, Macbeth is preoccupied by his involvement in the act of regicide and as king must defeat the civil rebellion which ensues. The first prophecy is fairly straightforward but those which follow, and on which his safety depends, prove more difficult to direct. Macbeth's erroneous interpretation of the prophecies shows that, like King Henry 4, he has interpreted literally when a more subtle understanding of what would come to pass was required.

The first apparition, "an armed head", warns Macbeth to "beware Macduff" but is apparently contradicted by the second apparition, "a bloody child", which assures him that he may "laugh to scorn / The power of man, for none of woman born / Shall harm Macbeth." (4.1.79–81). Macbeth's efforts to negotiate these two prophecies results in him covering all bases: he believes both but will take no chances:

> Then live, Macduff – what need I fear of thee?
> But yet I'll make assurance double sure,
> And take a bond of fate thou shalt not live,
> That I may tell pale-hearted fear it lies,
> And sleep in spite of thunder.
> (*Macbeth* 4.1.82–86)

Given the initial warning to "beware Macduff" Macbeth is rightly cautious; it is the third apparition, "a child crowned, with a tree in his hand", in which he places most faith. The apparition announces that "Macbeth shall never vanquished be until / Great Birnam Wood to high Dunsinane Hill / Shall come against him" (4.1.90–94) and, understandably, Macbeth thinks himself safe because trees cannot move:

> That will never be.
> Who can impress the forest, bid the tree
> Unfix his earth-bound root? Sweet bodements, good!
> Rebellious dead, rise never till the wood
> Of Birnam rise, and on 's high place Macbeth
> Shall live the lease of nature, pay his breath
> To time and mortal custom.
> (*Macbeth* 4.1.95–100)

Macbeth thinks that Birnam Wood coming to Dunsinane, something seemingly impossible, can only be achieved by supernatural means and the playgoer might expect to see this accomplished on stage. The outcome, an old military stratagem, rules out supernatural intervention and the playgoer, though not Macbeth, knows what to expect, having heard Malcolm command that "every soldier hew him down a bough / And bear 't before him" (5.4.2–3). Although we might feel disappointed that supernatural intervention will not be staged there is an undeniably pleasurable moment of realization for the playgoer when it becomes clear that Malcolm's plan will seemingly fulfil the prophecy. In the tense atmosphere of Dunsinane castle a messenger tells Macbeth "anon me thought / The wood began to move" (5.5.35–36) but we know this to be an illusion; supernatural involvement can be excluded by the playgoer who realizes that "Birnam Wood comes to Dunsinane" via trickery.

The trickery and illusion which replace the implied supernatural event may frustrate audience expectations but the outcome is, nevertheless, a curious one. Instead of supernatural forces manipulating the landscape, having "the tree / Unfix his earth-bound root" and walk towards Dunsinane, human ingenuity manipulates the natural world; what Macduff calls "Industrious soldiership" (5.4.17) triumphs over Macbeth's passive acceptance of prophecy. Malcolm is certainly unaware that his military stratagem fulfils the prophecy but that it does so suggests either a spiritual dimension to human resourcefulness or coincidence. The former would seem to endorse Tillyard's view of what most Elizabethans believed about social order and providence, that God or his agents would punish those who violated God's order (Tillyard 1943, 17–25), but the fulfilment of the prophecy, and the resultant punishment of the violator, Macbeth, is problematized by the source of the prophecy: the witches cannot be considered agents of God. Yet the difficulty surrounding the source of the prophecy is partially offset by the fact that Malcolm's efforts have a blessed dimension via the mandate of a saintly English king, "the most pious Edward" (3.6.27). The belief that Edward was capable of curing scrofula, also called the king's illness, by touching a victim is dramatized in the play. The English doctor tells Malcolm that the king is attended by "a crew of wretched souls / That stay his cure" (4.3.141–142). Edward is both pastor and physician and the doctor's presence unnecessary since Edward's touch can cure the physical ailment. Moreover, as Malcolm tells Macduff, Edward's gift will pass through the royal line:

> To the succeeding royalty he leaves
> The healing benediction. With this strange virtue
> He hath a heavenly gift of prophecy,
> And sundry blessings hang about his throne
> That speak him full of grace.
> (*Macbeth* 4.3.156–160)

The hereditary nature of Edward's gift glances at the prophecy which leaves Macbeth childless; Edward's ability to prophesy and the blessings that attend his throne contrast sharply with Macbeth's slavish adherence to the prophecies of others, his inability to see how they could be fulfilled without supernatural means, and the lack of security which attends his kingship from the outset.

The English doctor is redundant because Edward inhabits his role, whereas in the Scottish court the doctor who attends Lady Macbeth is powerless to assist her psychological disorder: "This disease is beyond my practice" (5.1.56). The doctor announces that "More needs she the divine than the physician" (5.1.72), but benign spiritual power is absent from Scotland under the reign of Macbeth who, unlike Edward, cannot control the prophetic power to which he has access. Whereas Malcolm has the support of a healer who possesses "a heavenly gift of prophecy" Macbeth has only "th'equivocation of the fiend" (5.6.43) on which to rely, a topical allusion to the Jesuitical doctrine of equivocation and the trial of the Jesuit priest Henry Garnett, accused of complicity in the Gunpowder Plot (Shakespeare 1951, xvi–xix). While Scotland is at the mercy of the equivocating fiend, the English court is apparently a location to which benevolent forces gravitate: Lennox wishes that "Some holy angel / Fly to the court of England" so Macduff's message may accelerate "a swift blessing" to Scotland which stands "Under a hand accursed" (3.6.46–50). Yet England is also a source of violence, albeit violence against a tyrant. As far as Lady Macduff is concerned, England is also a place which harbours traitors: "What had he done to make him fly the land? ... His flight was madness. When our actions do not, / Our fears do make us traitors" (4.2.1–5).

As David Scott Kastan has pointed out, the binaries apparently at work in the play are not entirely stable: the same violence which characterizes Macbeth's rule was necessary to keep Duncan king in the first place, something clearly outlined from the outset of the play when the "unexplained revolt" against Duncan's rule "is put down by Macbeth's brutal defense of Duncan's authority" (Kastan 1999, 167). That Duncan is complicit in the violence of the play has also been noted by Derek Cohen: Duncan's delight in the Captain's report of Macbeth's slaughter of Macdonald implicates him in the violence of the play, he is "attracted to and made part of it, and in death he becomes its central image, from voyeur of violence to its most crucial and evidentiary martyr" (Cohen 1993, 127). Thinking along the same lines, John Turner noted the sense in which Macbeth, although admittedly tyrannical, becomes "a scapegoat, bearing all the violence in his society, unifying it by his death and thereby preventing the thanes from understanding those political contradictions and psychological ambivalences that have caused the violence in which they are even now implicated" (Holderness, Potter & Turner 1988, 143). Macbeth is a violent warrior but so too is his nemesis Macduff and the apparition which foretells Macduff's success, a bloody child, seems to underline the violence surrounding the play's politics of kingship identified by Kastan, Cohen and Turner. Macbeth's reign is violent but, as Kastan observed, so too is his defeat:

"Though the play would see Macbeth's violence as aberrative and blasphemous, as that which assails sovereign authority and must be repudiated, it offers no obvious alternative to that violence as that which is necessary to construct and defend sovereignty" (Kastan 1999, 178). That both Duncan and Macbeth are referred to as "gracious" reinforces Kastan's argument that moral contrast in the play "is unnervingly unsettled by the text's compelling strategies of repetition and resemblance" (Kastan 1999, 166), though the similarity of both men is undermined by those speaking about them: Duncan is referred to as "gracious" twice by the noble Lennox (3.6.2; 3.6.10) and once by Macbeth himself (3.1.67) whereas Macbeth is called "gracious" only by Seyton and a servant (5.3.31; 5.5.28) and in both cases the word is used more as a courteous reference to his stature rather than as an estimation of character. While it is true to say that Duncan and others are implicated in the play's violence, the natural world, as we shall see, is imbued with a particular moral agenda.

Macbeth cannot understand why the physician who attends his wife cannot cure her. When told by the doctor that "she is troubled with thick-coming fancies / That keep her from her rest" (5.3.39–40) he responds "Cure her of that: / Canst thou not minister to a mind diseased ... / Cleanse the fraught bosom of that perilous stuff / Which weighs upon the heart? (5.3.39–47). Macbeth's inability to read the spiritual dimension to his wife's condition is echoed in his attitude to the realm of Scotland:

> If thou couldst, doctor, cast
> The water of my land, find her disease,
> And purge it to a sound and pristine health,
> I would applaud thee to the very echo,
> That should applaud again.
> (*Macbeth* 5.4.49–53)

Macbeth implies that he knows no reason why the land is sick but if the disease could be identified it would again be healthy. Rather than introspection he projects blame onto external forces: "What rhubarb, cyme, or what purgative drug / Would scour these English hence? Hear'st thou of them?" (5.4.54–55). Just as Henry endeavoured to direct civil disorder outward and toward the pagans in the Holy Land at the beginning of *1 Henry 4* so Macbeth considers that Scotland would be healthy if only the English were absent, ignoring the antagonism toward his own rule inside Scotland and those Scottish rebels who accompany the English in their invasion. That

Scotland itself is sick and injured under the rule of Macbeth is reinforced by the noble men who oppose him. Macduff and Malcolm describe Scotland as a country which bleeds (4.3.32–34; 4.3.40) and Caithness figures Malcolm as the antidote to Scotland's sickness: "Meet we the medicine of the sickly weal, / And with him pour we in our country's purge, / Each drop of us" (5.2.24–28), a metaphor built upon by Lennox who figures their self-sacrifice as a purge which will "dew the sovereign flower and drown the weeds" (5.2.30). Lennox claims that Scotland is a "suffering country, / Under a hand accursed" (3.6.49–50) and Macduff believes that heaven itself empathizes with Scotland's pain:

> Each new morn
> New widows howl, new orphans cry, new sorrows
> Strike heaven on the face that it resounds
> As if it felt with Scotland and yelled out
> Like syllable of dolour.
> (*Macbeth* 4.3.5–9)

Malcolm and his fellow rebels use the notion of a sick Scotland, a land suffering under Macbeth's tyranny, to underpin the moral purpose of their actions: intervention from a healthy England, which is governed by a sacred monarch, will cauterize the wound inflicted by Macbeth and heal the country's illness. While Scotland is repeatedly represented as a sick country under Macbeth's governance, England is twice referred to by Malcolm as "gracious" (4.3.44; 4.3.190) and depicted as a place of refuge where Malcolm "is received / Of the most pious Edward with such grace / That the malevolence of fortune nothing / Takes from his high respect" (3.6.26–29). Although Duncan is a weak king in Holinshed, Macbeth claims that Shakespeare's Duncan is a good king – "So clear in his great office, that his virtues / Will plead like angels, trumpet-tongued against / The deep damnation of his taking off" (1.7.18–20) – and under Duncan's reign Scotland is not sick. A sick Scotland under Macbeth's rule is apparently Shakespeare's invention since no mention of the land suffering sickness appears in Holinshed, Shakespeare's main source, which tends rather to focus on the misery of the Scots under Macbeth. Moreover, disturbances in the natural world coincide with the killing of Duncan:

> LENNOX: The night has been unruly. Where we lay
> Our chimneys were blown down, and, as they say,
> Lamentings heard i' th' air, strange screams of death,

And prophesying with accents terrible
Of dire combustion and confused events
New-hatched to th' woeful time. The obscure bird
Clamoured the livelong night. Some say the earth
Was feverous and did shake.
(*Macbeth* 2.3.55–62)

Similarly, after Duncan's death has been reported, Ross and the Old Man discuss strangely dark days and the unnatural behaviour of animals (2.4.1–19). The pathetic fallacy reported in the play appears to suggest that the moral depravity of Macbeth's violence against Duncan has provoked the very landscape itself to react violently against the murder of God's anointed representative on earth but is in fact typical of the characters' tendency to equate the human and natural worlds. In *Richard 2* the Welsh Captain reported similar natural occurrences and took them as signs that "the King is dead" (2.4.7) when in fact his reading them so made them so: it is the disbandment of the Welsh which caused, or at least contributed to, Richard's defeat. Commenting on Elizabethan attitudes toward social order and providence, Tillyard claimed that "Commonest of all correspondences in poetry is that between the storms and earthquakes of the great world and the stormy passions of man" (Tillyard 1943, 100) but just as *1 Henry 4* and *2 Henry 4* do not present a straightforward condemnation of Bolingbroke's accession to the throne (as Tillyard claimed they did) so too there is no simplistic moral centre in *Macbeth*. Although Macbeth's enemies might appear justified in ousting Macbeth, a justification apparently underlined by the natural world's endorsement of their actions (something we also saw in Spenser's *Faerie Queene* and explored in Chapter 3) his enemies are morally compromised by their participation in violence and, as David Scott Kastan pointed out, the play ends with a distinct lack of moral closure (Kastan 1999, 178).

As in *Richard 2*, *1 Henry 4*, and *2 Henry 4* violence is intimately connected with kingship in *Macbeth* and that violence also characterizes the Scottish landscape. As mentioned above, disturbances in the natural world coincide with the killing of Duncan, but the landscape corresponds with the play's action from the very outset. In the Folio the witches are located in a troubled natural environment, first appearing in thunder and lightning (1.1) and later specifically upon a heath which Macbeth describes as "blasted" (1.3.77). For Michael Goldman the opening scene of the play, "the sudden thunder and menace at the beginning" (Goldman 1985, 98), may have been influenced by the Gunpowder Plot:

> The image of that catastrophe – an explosive manifestation of evil, absolute and as if out of nowhere, the sense that value and order could be wiped out in an instant – contributed, I think to the investigation of evil that Shakespeare felt compelled to make in *Macbeth*. And so he began his play with a terrible noise, followed instantly by a loathsome and, for the moment, incomprehensible apparition:

> *Thunder and lightning. Enter three* WITCHES.

> This effect, so clear and definite in the text, is strangely muted in most modern productions. But it is plain that Shakespeare wanted to begin with a bang; he wanted to shock his audience. (Goldman 1985, 98)

We cannot know for sure whether or not Shakespeare "wanted to begin with a bang" since the play was first printed in 1623 and with added material by Thomas Middleton for a posthumous revival. Goldman is careful to assert that he does not think that the play's beginning "is anything like a deliberate allusion to the Gunpowder plot" merely that "an English audience recently familiar with the Plot would have been especially sensitive to the moral and metaphysical overtones of the opening scenes (Goldman 1985, 98–99). Although it is feasible that an audience would have recognized allusions to such a recent and momentous event, theatre audiences would have been familiar with the convention of thunder and lightning to introduce the supernatural (Thomson 1999, 11), much as audiences of horror films are today, and of course the Gunpowder Plot did not actually produce a bang. Nevertheless Goldman is right to emphasize the noise of this first scene and the fact that "Macbeth is meant as a noisy and frightening play" (Goldman 1985, 98). This first scene is very short and, as Goldman noted, it "should rush past us before we can recover. We do not need time to get accustomed to the witches. They are not supposed to be intelligible but frightening, uncanny, obscure" (Goldman 1985, 98).

In Holinshed the witches are located not on a heath but "in the middest of a laund", a "laund" being "an open space among woods, a glade (= Latin *saltus*); untilled ground, pasture" (OED Laund *sb*). Again, Shakespeare's manipulation of his source is telling: Holinshed's location is arguably less sinister than Shakespeare's "blasted heath" (1.3.77), the word "blasted" meaning "Balefully or perniciously blown or breathed upon; stricken by meteoric or supernatural agency, as parching wind, lightning, an alleged malignant planet, the wrath and curse of heaven; blighted" (OED blasted *a* 1). John Turner noted the significance of this location: "It is on the heath, by the battlefield, that the sisters tempt Macbeth, seeking (it seems) to exploit the dependence of the gentle weal upon war; for it is there and now, in this most marginal place and time, that Macbeth and his country are most vulnerable" (Holderness, Potter & Turner 1988, 137). For Terry Eagleton the witches are "heroines", exiles from an oppressive and violent hierarchical social order who inhabit "their own sisterly community on its shadowy borderlands, refusing all truck with its tribal bickerings and military honours" (Eagleton 1986, 2). In *Macbeth* the heath is indeed a "shadowy borderland", a transitional place, somewhere that is experienced on the way to or from someplace else and with a life-altering potential. Macbeth and Banquo are returning from the wars and on their way to Forres, they are in neither one place nor the other when they encounter the figures who will encourage Macbeth to shape his future. Unlike Glyndŵr, Macbeth does not manipulate the landscape, on the contrary it is manipulated by those who will effectively control him and he tracks his rise by the names of places that, as it were, fall on him.

The witches do not merely inhabit the malignant landscape of the "blasted heath" but actually appear to be part of it. Having announced that Macbeth "shalt be King hereafter" (1.3.50) and Banquo "shalt get kings, though thou be none" (1.3.67), the witches vanish and Banquo comments "The earth hath bubbles, as the water has, / And these are of them; wither are they vanished?" to which Macbeth replies "Into the air; and what seemed corporal melted / As breath into the wind" (1.3.79–82). Like Glyndŵr, thought by Holinshed to be capable of merging into the very landscape by moving "into his knowen lurking places" (Holinshed 1587, Ddd6v), the witches disappear into their environment at will. It is their status as witches which enables the weird sisters to manipulate the natural world, evident in their earlier plan to torture a sailor by raising a storm at sea: "Sleep shall neither night nor day / Hang upon his penthouse lid; / He shall live a man forbid" (1.3.20–22). Yet Shakespeare's witches have limited powers – "Though his bark cannot be lost, / Yet it shall be tempest-tossed" (1.3.24–25) – something they readily acknowledge even if Macbeth does not. As Alan McFarlane pointed out, those who believed in sorcery thought a witch's power "was limited to a few miles" (MacFarlane 1970, 168) and so perhaps it is the distance of the sailor's boat from the shore which means that it "cannot be lost".

As we have seen, the witches in *Macbeth* are capable of manipulating the landscape and of making themselves seem part of it and, before the murder of Duncan, Macbeth makes an effort to extract complicity from the very earth itself:

> Thou sure and firm-set earth,
> Hear not my steps which way they walk, for fear
> Thy very stones prate of my whereabout,
> And take the present horror from the time,
> Which now suits with it.
> (*Macbeth* 2.1.56–60)

By the time Banquo's ghost appears at the banquet Macbeth is convinced that he cannot escape retribution and that the natural world will tell what he has done:

> It will have blood, they say: blood will have blood.
> Stones have been known to move, and trees to speak;
> Augures, and understood relations, have
> By maggot-pies and choughs, and rooks brought forth
> The secret'st man of blood.
> (*Macbeth* 3.4.123–126)

Like Henry 4, Macbeth is less able to direct future events than he had hoped and his belief that he can expect the support of the natural and supernatural world, shown to be ill-founded. It seems that if a sin is unnatural enough then the natural and supernatural world will not conspire against its concealment:

> The time has been
> That, when the brains were out, the man would die,
> And there an end. But now they rise again
> With twenty mortal murders on their crowns,
> And push us from our stools.
> (*Macbeth* 3.4.77–81)

Later Macbeth will curse the witches: "Infected be the air whereon they ride, / And damned all those that trust them." (4.1.155–156). Ironically the air of Scotland has already been described as sick, or infected, by Macbeth and by the noblemen who oppose him and Macbeth's curses will rebound on himself when his "cursed head" is displayed by Macduff (5.7.86).

Macbeth is a violent play and blood is of central significance with the words "blood" and "bloody" appearing 11 and 16 times respectively. Of course "blood" also connotes lineage, a primary concern in the play and crucial to the ambitions of Macbeth. The play's first act of violence, Macbeth's killing of Macdonald, reported by the Captain in 1.2, is similar to Westmorland's description of "the noble Mortimer" pitched against "the irregular and wild Glyndŵr" at the beginning of *1 Henry 4*. We are told how "brave Macbeth ... with his brandished steel / Which smoked with bloody execution / Like Valour's minion, carv'd out his passage / Till he fac'd the slave ... [and]... unseamed him from the nave to th'chops" (1.2.16–22). As Derek Cohen pointed out, the reference to Macbeth carving out his passage "is no neutral description of the warrior's progress, but a terrible image of bloody slaughter as Macbeth makes a corridor of bodies between himself and Macdonald. The smoking sword speaks not only of the hidden demonism of the hero, but also the wrath with which he wreaks his right-eous havoc" (Cohen 1993, 130). The brutality of Macbeth's slaughter of a traitor will of course be surpassed by the stabbing of Duncan, urged on by Lady Macbeth, who is more bloodthirsty, though more ignorant of killing, than her soldier-husband ("who would have thought the old man to have had so much blood in him", 5.1.37–38), and the slaughter of Macduff's wife, children and servants, all victims of the bloody violence initiated by the witches and the provocation for promises of retribution by Macduff (4.3.232–237).

In the plays considered in this chapter, blood is both literal and imag-ined, and when imagined is invariably associated with guilt. Before com-mitting the murder of Duncan, Macbeth imagines that he sees a bloody dagger in front of him but realizes it is not real. It is only after the murder of Duncan that there is a particular focus on the symbolic potency of hands stained with blood. Macbeth's believes his bloody hand to denote a crime of such magnitude that it will alter the natural colour of the entire sea, "Making the greene one red" (2.2.61), which echoes Henry's desire toward the end of *Richard 2* to "wash this blood off from my guilty hand" (5.6.50). The OED records frequent use in the sixteenth century of the adjective "red hand", meaning "red-handed" ("In the very act of crime, having the evi-dences of guilt still upon the person" OED red-handed *a.* 1). The image of the bloody hands may also suggest what Art J. Hughes referred to as the "internal Gaelic controversy as to which clan could most strongly lay claim to the heraldic emblem of the Red Hand" (Hughes 1988, 85), suggesting Shakespeare's interest in Gaelic symbols when writing plays about Scottish and Welsh history. Lady Macbeth thinks that washing the blood from their hands is a practical matter – "A little water clears us of this deed" (2.2.65) – only to discover that physical cleanliness is no index of absolution. Macbeth's anxiety that the blood on his hands will entirely pollute, and thus alter, the water – "Making the greene one red" (2.2.61) – imagines symbolic guilt as transferable and indelible. Washing with water carries connotations of Christian purification and here Shakespeare takes the notion of blood that will not wash off and uses it for psychological metaphor. The connection between washing and Christian ritual in the context of kingship was also made by Richard 2 who commented that "Not all the water in the rough rude sea / Can wash the balm off from an anointed king" (3.2.50–51). Initially, but only temporarily, the Macbeths succeeded in transferring suspicion of guilt by besmirching Duncan's innocent attendants with blood and similarly Henry cannot rid himself of the belief that, having never reached the Holy Land to wash Richard's blood from his hands, Richard's curse has indeed come to pass.

Ultimately neither Henry nor Macbeth can control his environment in the way each was led to believe was possible. Indeed, the issue of controlling the environment functions as a crucial determinant in the works of Shakespeare and Spenser and the distinctions we can draw between them as writers. As we saw in previous chapters, Spenser's *View* and much of his poetry is characterized by the fantasy that topographical manipulation will bring about the dreamed-of pastoral idyll and a landscape that currently impedes the establishment of English rule will become an active participant in the colonial poet's agenda. Unlike Spenser, who remained distinctly optimistic about the possibility of topographical manipulation, which he saw as a prerequisite for colonial rule, Shakespeare appears to be suggesting that the ideological transformation of land which rulers routinely employ in the rhetoric of self-justification can be turned against them. The key to understanding the role of landscape in writings by Shakespeare and Spenser might well be their status: Spenser the frustrated colonist demonstrating an almost neurotic desire to re-shape the landscape which currently inhibits the control of his enemies and Shakespeare, possibly a secret Catholic, alert to the difficulties surrounding the relationship between topographical manipulation, power, rebellion and the marginalized.

Conclusion

W E SAW IN THE introduction to this book that the most commonly held belief about Shakespeare today is that his plays are universal and timeless, a belief partly due to the apparent indeterminacy of his writings. Where Spenser has been seen as a poet of firm opinions, a major force in the propagation of Elizabethan Protestant nationalism, it is not clear where Shakespeare's political and religious loyalties lie. Spenser is traditionally thought of as being specific to his time, an Elizabethan poet involved in the colonizing of sixteenth-century Ireland, but Shakespeare has been conceived of in broader terms and his multivalency has been used to suggest that he was Catholic. Genre also determines the traditional view of each writer: Spenser the poet is considered a univocal and solitary figure where Shakespeare is seen as a man of the theatre, collaborating with other agencies, a reality which is believed to have impacted upon the creative process. In this conclusion I'd like to revisit some of the common assumptions about each writer in the context of their attitudes to topographical manipulation. The notion of Spenser as Elizabeth's poet exiled in Ireland requires modification, as does that of Shakespeare the unknowable man of the theatre. Just as Spenser's reputation as Elizabeth's poet of Empire does not tell the whole truth about his ambivalent feelings toward Elizabeth and Ireland, so too Shakespeare's reputation as the mysterious and multivalent dramatist does not take into account certain aspects of his biography and writings.

Spenser

Although Spenser is remembered primarily as a poet, we saw in the Introduction that he worked as a civil servant in colonial Ireland, participated in the violence used to suppress the colonized people and wrote a dialogue advocating severe treatment of the indigenous population. His letters and prose writing allow us to know something of his intentions and meanings and, given his connections with the Sidney/Leicester faction, we can also infer something of his political and religious affiliations. Spenser's reputation is that of the Protestant poet in exile whose admiration for Elizabeth is matched only by his hatred of the rebellious Irish, but this is not quite the full story. In order to fully understand Spenser's attitude toward Elizabeth and Ireland it is necessary to re-visit Book 5 of *The Faerie Queene*, the *Mutabilitie Cantos* and the *View*.

Spenser is regarded as something of a monarch-pleaser but, besides being officially censured over Book 5 of *The Faerie Queene* by James 1 who rightly perceived the villainous Duessa to represent his mother Mary Stuart, as noted by Richard McCabe (McCabe 1987, 224), he also risked the disapproval of Elizabeth. Although, as we saw in the Introduction, she is praised throughout *The Faerie Queene* – Elizabeth is his muse, a divine figure whose brightness is an indication of English Protestant virtue, a chaste, beautiful and sacred monarch – criticism of her rule is also apparent. Despite encomiums of Elizabeth in the proems to Books 1–4 and in Book 6 there is no mention of her in the proem to Book 5. This omission signals the subversive nature of Book 5 which is particularly evident in the depictions of its female rulers Radigund and Mercilla. The Amazon Radigund is a sexually aggressive ruler whose metaphorical emasculation of the male knight Artegall destabilizes sexual hierarchies. She thus functions as a foil to Britomart, the ideal female Christian knight who relinquishes power to Artegall, her husband. Although we might conclude that at this point in his allegory Spenser is denouncing female rule in general, just as John Knox had done in his *First Blast of the Trumpet Against the Monstrous Regiment of Women* published in 1558, there is evidence that Spenser is ridiculing a particular aspect of Elizabeth's governance, her policies on Ireland.

As noted in the Introduction, there are clear parallels between Artegall and Lord Grey which indicate an Irish dimension to the Radigund episode: Radigund's humiliating treatment of Artegall echoes Elizabeth's recall of her deputy from Ireland in 1582 which, in Spenser's view, had the effect of furthering rebellion in Ireland. In the *View* Spenser proclaims that justice must not be undermined by pity, and the negative consequences of showing pity are demonstrated in Book 5 of *The Faerie Queene*: Artegall makes the mistake of showing pity to Radigund, to whom he is sexually attracted, and is at once vanquished (5.5.13–17) and Britomart's pity toward the people of Radegone (5.7.36.4–9) threatens to frustrate the imposition of order. But it is Mercilla's pity toward Duessa that is especially telling. The eventual beheading of Duessa, an act prefigured by the beheading of Radigund earlier in Book 5, takes place only after prevarication on the part of Mercilla. Although Mercilla has been described as "a mayden Queene of high renowne" (5.8.17.2) who "doth support, and strongly beateth downe /The malice of her foes, which her enuy" (5.8.17.5–6), her compassion towards Duessa is a grave error of judgement:

> But she, whose Princely breast was touched nere
> With piteous ruth of her so wretched plight,
> Though plaine she saw by all, that she did heare,
> That she of death was guiltie found by right,
> Yet would not let iust vengeance on her light;
> But rather let in stead thereof to fall
> Few perling drops from her faire lampes of light;
> The which she couering with her purple pall
> Would haue the passion hid, and vp arose withall.
> (*The Faerie Queene* 5.9.50.1–9)

As A. C. Hamilton noted, Elizabeth's three-month delay in allowing justice to proceed against Mary Stuart is marked by three stanzas (Spenser 1977, 597) and the reader must wait until the next canto to learn of Duessa's execution. As John D. Staines put it, "Although portraying Elizabeth as Mercilla appears to idealize her virtues, evoking her 'myld' mercy at this point also reminds the reader of those less flattering depictions of the queen's mercy, the complaints of the Council, Parliament, and Protestant propagandists that her mercy was reckless" (Staines 2001, 301). One of those who would have thought Elizabeth's mercy reckless had a distinct Irish connection. As Richard McCabe observed, Lord Grey was a commissioner involved in the trial of Mary and the one most keen to see her executed (McCabe 1987, 239). For Andrew Hadfield "Mercilla is shown to understand far too little about the territories she rules, a pointed contrast to the likes of Lord Grey or Spenser himself" (Hadfield 1997b, 167). Spenser believed Elizabeth's capacity for compassion constituted a serious hindrance to the suppression of rebellion in Ireland. For Spenser, Elizabeth's recalling of Grey from Ireland was a dangerous precedent and he feared her abandonment of the New English colonists in Ireland. The imaginative presence of Elizabeth 1 pervades *The Faerie Queene* in its title and in the characters of Gloriana and Belphoebe, as we saw in the Introduction, as well as via Radigund and Mercilla. Elizabeth is also present in the figures of Cynthia and Diana in the *Mutabilitie Cantos* where Spenser presents a fantasy that implicates Elizabeth in the utter waste of her colony.

Cynthia was a name used for Elizabeth (Raleigh called his poem about her "Ocean to Cynthia") and she was often referred to as Diana. Likening Elizabeth to Diana, the beautiful and chaste goddess of the moon and of hunting, could suggest flattery but also criticism of the queen. Andrew Hadfield detected an attack on the queen's policies and her ageing, virginal state in the figure of Cynthia who "is described as never standing still, a double-edged reference to Elizabeth's inconstant policies and the mutability of her own body, which had been beyond childbearing age since the 1580s, leaving the succession uncertain" (Hadfield 1997b, 189). This "double-edged reference" to Elizabeth might also be found in the figure of Mutabilitie. The story of Mutabilitie's attempted displacement of Cynthia and the inset story of Molanna's betrayal of Diana position rebellious and disloyal figures against Elizabeth. These figures might represent the colonized people of Ireland who rebel against the English crown but they might just as easily represent something more subtle, as might Mutabilitie herself.

There is some evidence that Mutabilitie's attempt to oust Cynthia from her throne carries allusions to rebellion in Ireland: Mutabilitie threatens violence against Cynthia "And there-with lifting vp her golden wand, / Threatned to strike her if she did with-stand" (7.6.13.4–5). Additionally, she wears an "vncouth" habit (7.6.13.9), a word also used to describe the arrested development of the Old English – the first wave of colonizers who failed to subdue the Irish in the twelfth century – in the *View* (Spenser 1949, 118) and of the villainous Archimago and Maleger in Book 2 of *The Faerie Queene* (2.1.8.2; 2.11.27.5). Mutabilitie is beautiful but she has an alien nature, she is "of strange and forraine race", a description which echoes the emphasis on the Irish as strange and savage by early modern English writers. Yet although there are indications that Mutabilitie's rebellion signifies an Irish one against the crown there are also signs that the story of a powerful, beautiful and changeable woman "fraught with pride and impudence" (7.6.25.2) describes the queen herself who will not take advice from men such as Grey and Spenser. In Mutabilitie's rebellion we can perhaps detect Elizabeth's unnatural and wilful rejection of the proper course for reform in Ireland and, in the threat to the representatives of Elizabeth (Cynthia and Diana), a warning to the queen of the consequences of her policy on Ireland.

The degeneration of the world, lamented by the narrator in the Proem to Book 5 of *The Faerie Queene*, is expanded upon in the story of Mutabilitie's rebellion and cosmic change signals Spenser's anxiety about local change and degeneration in Ireland, something fully expressed in the *View*. Mutabilitie has inverted the positive aspects of existence that were in place before her intervention, bringing about degeneration, loss and moral corruption. She has demolished not only the laws of nature "But eke of Iustice, and of Policie" (7.6.6.2) and it is the responsibility of Artegall and Talus in Book 5 to put those laws back into place, an echo of Grey's task in Ireland before his reform was interrupted by Elizabeth's recall. Mutabilitie's rebellion against the empire of the gods perhaps suggests Irish rebellion against the governance of Elizabeth but the rebellion against empire by one "bold woman" might also suggest that it is the actions of the English queen rather than her Irish subjects which will "thrust faire *Phoebe* from her siluer bed, / And eke our selues from heauens high Empire" (7.6.21.1–4).

Another example of rebellion and disloyalty against a moon goddess in the *Mutabilitie Cantos* (and briefly mentioned in Chapter 2) is the story of Molanna's betrayal of Diana. Here Spenser imagines Ireland as a favourite holiday resort for the gods until the disloyalty of one of Diana's nymphs, who takes a bribe from Faunus so he can see Diana bathing. As in the story of Mutabilitie's rebellion, a woman (Diana's nymph) is the source of treachery but here the woman against whom she rebels (Diana) is primarily at fault. When Ireland was blessed by the presence of Diana it prospered:

> Whylome, when *IRELAND* florished in fame
> Of wealths and goodnesse, far aboue the rest
> Of all that beare the *British* Islands name,
> The Gods then vs'd (for pleasure and for rest)
> Oft to resort there-to, when seem'd them best:
> But none of all there-in more pleasure found,
> Then *Cynthia*; that is soueraine Queene profest

Of woods and forrests, which therein abound,
Sprinkled with wholsom waters, more then most on ground.
(*The Faerie Queene* 7.6.38.1–9)

Spenser's fantasy is that Ireland was once wealthy, fertile and inhabited by gods but rebellion and, most importantly, Diana's reaction to that rebellion has altered the place:

Arlo through *Dianaes* spights
Beeing of old the best and fairest Hill
(That was in all this holy-Islands hights)
Was made the most vnpleasant, and most ill.
The Faerie Queene 7.6.37.5–9)

The story suggests treachery by the indigenous people since the nymph who is made "corrupt" and betrays Diana is native to the land: as William Keach points out, 'Molanna' is Spenser's name for the Irish river Behanna (Keach 1990, 60). Yet the story also depicts Diana's (Elizabeth's) treachery by stressing her departure from Arlo hill as desertion: she has "abandond" the brook, and "quite forsooke" the forests and countryside:

Them all, and all that she so deare did way,
Thence-forth she left; and parting from the place,
There-on an heauy haplesse curse did lay,
To weet, that Wolues, where she was wont to space,
Should harbour'd be, and all those Woods deface,
And Thieues should rob and spoile that Coast around.
Since which, those Woods, and all that goodly Chase,
Doth to this day with Wolues and Thieues abound:
Which too-too true that lands in-dwellers since haue found.
(*The Faerie Queene* 7.6.55.1–9)

Spenser's fantasy of what Ireland once was and what it might be again is undermined by Elizabeth's political and military disengagement. In the *View* Eudoxus tells Irenius that Ireland's problems "proceede rather of the vnsoundnes of the Counsells and Plottes, which youe saie haue bynne often tymes laied for her reformacions or of faintnes in followinge and effectinge the same, then of anye suche fatall Course or appointment of god as youe misdeeme ..." (Spenser 1949, 44). By not listening to men such as Spenser, Elizabeth has doomed Ireland to rebellion and degeneration.

Another story involving Diana, Faunus and an unfortunate nymph is

detailed in Book 2 of *The Faerie Queene*. Guyon, who has tried without success to clean the bloody hands of Ruddymane in a well, is told the story of
the well by the Palmer. A virgin, one of Flora's nymphs, being chased by the
lustful Faunus, asked Diana to allow her to die a maid, whereby Diana
transformed her into stone pouring out tears as water. Ruddymane's hands
cannot be cleansed because the well will not allow its pure water (which suggests the chastity of the nymph and Diana) to be stained (2.2.1–9). Here
Spenser indulges in the kind of fantasy we've seen in previous chapters, incorporating the notion that the landscape itself actively participates in the author's
political agenda by not allowing the blood which is a sign of sin to make its
mark on the landscape. His later story in the *Mutabilitie Cantos* is an inversion
of this one in Book 2: in the story featuring Guyon the water in the well remains
pure because of the intervention of Diana whilst in the *Mutabilitie Cantos* the
water of Ireland and the land itself have been made impure because of Diana's
abandonment. The fantasy that the landscape is benevolent is overturned in
the later story when the water in which Diana used to bathe has become tainted
and the landscape made degenerate by her curse:

> Thence-forth abandond her delicious brooke;
> In whose sweet streame, before that bad occasion,
> So much delight to bathe her limbes she tooke:
> Ne onely her, but also quite forsooke
> All those faire forrests about *Arlo* hid,
> And all that Mountaine, which doth over-looke
> The richest champian that may else be rid,
> And the faire *Shure*, in which are thousand Salmons bred.
> (*The Faerie Queene* 7.6.54.2–9)

It is likely that Spenser's enthusiasm for imagining topographical participation in the colonial project began to wane as the support of Elizabeth was
less forthcoming and Irish resistance in the colony grew stronger. For
Spenser, mutability, degeneration and waste occur in Ireland not only as a
direct result of native rebellion but because of Diana's actions. There is a
solid foundation to Helen Hackett's claim that Spenser uses lunar imagery
in the *Mutabilitie Cantos* to question rather than endorse the elevation of
Elizabeth as a sacred icon, and that his criticism of the queen "is partly gen-
erated by dissent from Elizabeth's Irish policy" (Hackett 1995, 191). In
Spenser's fantasy of Ireland's history Diana has, by her absence and by
actively making decisions which cause harm, damned it to be a desolate

wasteland, something that Elizabeth might alter if she had the political will. The *Mutabilitie Cantos* thus constitute not only a criticism of the rebellious Irish and degenerate Old English in Ireland but an extended criticism of Elizabeth's policy on Ireland.

Nicholas Canny wondered why Spenser abandoned his epic poem when it was only half-written and suggested that he became disillusioned by the failure of his poetical efforts to promote moral improvement and political reform. Since poetry had exposed Spenser to criticism, Canny concluded that Spenser made the decision to try a less oblique form of writing and thus composed the *View*, using a format which allowed a greater directness than was possible with allegory (Canny 2001, 27–31). This was not the first time Spenser had worked outside the genre for which he is best known because his correspondence with Harvey makes reference to nine plays written by Spenser, now lost (Spenser 1949, 471). As Naseeb Shaheen pointed out, "Spenser's interest in drama could have been aroused as early as his grammar school days when the boys performed plays under Mulcaster" and noted that the October eclogue of the *Calender* "suggests that he yearned for the inspiration needed to write tragedy and dignify the stage" (Shaheen 1976, 47–48).

Although Philip Sidney stressed that poetry need not take the form of verse, Spenser's interest in writing for the stage and his later shift into publishing prose have often been overlooked in order to consolidate his reputation as one of England's foremost Renaissance poets. Moreover, his criticism of Elizabeth's Irish policy in *The Faerie Queene* and the *View* undermines his reputation as "Elizabeths Arschkissende [arse-kissing] Poet" (Marx 1974, 305). As we saw in the Introduction, Spenserians have long been embarrassed by the *View* and efforts have been made to minimize its significance, primarily because it advocates violence against the recalcitrant Irish. Yet although Spenser undoubtedly thought Ireland a dangerous place inhabited by barbaric and inferior inhabitants, a more positive view of the land and its people emerges.

As Colin Burrow pointed out, the status of exiled poet has long been conferred on Spenser, who was compared to the banished Ovid and thus associated with a tradition of poets who had offended the authorities (Burrow 2000, 37). Julia Reinhard Lupton noted that, as with the poetics of Ovid, exile and metamorphosis are central to Spenser's writing and the *View* constitutes "the exile's complaint from a barbarous land at the edges of empire" (Lupton 1993, 102). Yet, as Christopher Highley pointed out, feelings of displacement and exile co-existed with opportunity. While Barnabe Googe felt compelled to take a position in Ireland, regarded it as a form of exile, and returned to England as soon as possible, Spenser chose to stay in the colony. Unlike Googe, Spenser was not a gentleman by birth and Ireland, with its less rigid social and legal codes, afforded opportunities for such men (Highley 1997, 13–15). Highley claimed that Spenser created a court for himself in his poetry but, as Willy Maley noted, Ireland itself functioned as an alternative court. The viceregal system in Ireland, unique in early modern Europe, complicated the relationship of court and colony, and undermines the common idea that Spenser had to choose between them. The viceroy ruled as an absolute monarch and therefore Ireland was not an inferior location. This surrogate monarchical authority was a locus of power in its own right from which the English court could be criticized (Maley 1997, 99). Similarly Andrew Hadfield noted "the development of an alternative Englishness in Ireland" where "the Englishness of 'the shepheardes nation' is more English than the English, being a return to first principles lost at court ... " (Hadfield 1997b, 17). The notion of Spenser as a poet of exile is also undermined by Maley's proposition that Rosalinde, Colin Clout's object of desire, might represent Ireland and thus "Spenser's acquisition of an Irish estate represents the fulfilment of his youthful passion, not its displacement" (Maley 1997, 29). Nicholas Canny concurred that far from being alienated from the queen and court, his only reward being exile and a small irregularly paid pension, Spenser had been given an estate in the Munster plantation for which there was substantial competition and so his being in Ireland could be regarded as something of an achievement (Canny 2001, 35–36).

It is ironic that the weaker social and legal codes that existed in Ireland, and which benefited Spenser and his fellow colonists, are condemned throughout the *View* and such contradictions occur throughout Spenser's writing. As we have seen in previous chapters, Spenser's poetry and prose writings are alert to the dangers inherent in the landscape, a landscape that largely resembles the Irish interior, but there is a distinct sense of optimism that the natural world, if properly managed, can be supportive. The English court is attractive but it lacks grace and, despite its dangers, Ireland provides the society of shepherds with the possibility of refuge, its potential order represented by the vision of the dance of the Graces on

Mount Acidale depicted in Book 6 of *The Faerie Queene*. Denunciation of Irish customs dominates the *View* but there are moments when we can discern a grudging admiration for that which Spenser desires to alter. Although Spenser comments on the dangers lurking within Irish woods he is alert to their beauty and this tendency toward ambivalence exists throughout the tract. As we saw in chapter 2, Spenser desires a refiguring of the landscape in order to achieve a tactical advantage against the Irish rebels and criminals he deplores but he also advocates using their tactics, leaving the reader with the impression that he admires their military ingenuity: the English can learn from the Irish practice of using the landscape for shelter and the element of surprise to attack the enemy.

A particularly striking example of Spenser's ambivalence is his denigration of the Celtic poets, or the bards, which co-exists with envy that they are "had in so high regard and estimation amongst them that none dare displease them for fear to run into reproach through their offence" (Spenser 1970, 72). There is a palpable tension between Spenser's outrage that these bards should be above the law and his admiration that they should command respect from others. Spenser's announcement in his *Letter to Raleigh* that he must guard against "gealous opinions and misconstructions" (Spenser 1977, 737) shows that English poets did not enjoy the same high status as that achieved by the Irish bards. Spenser's interest in Irish poetry was noted by Roland M. Smith who challenged A. C. Judson's assertion that Spenser 'invented' stories about the rivers around Kilcolman castle. Spenser himself states that the stories told in *Colin Clout Comes Home Againe* are old and they closely resemble "local folk-traditions as well as legends in the Irish place-name collections preserved in both prose and verse" which Spenser would have learnt either from his Irish tutor or from the natives about Kilcolman (Smith 1935, 1047–48). Christopher Highley drew attention to the bardic overtones of Spenser's sonnet to the Earl of Ormond and Ossory in the 1590 edition of *The Faerie Queene* and *Colin Clout Comes Home Againe* (Highley 1997, 23–33) and argued that

> the appropriation of a bardic persona ... represents part of a larger effort by Spenser to reconceive his cultural identity. That reconceptualization involves shifting his emotional center from England to Ireland, thinking of himself as more fully grounded in his adopted homeland, and of reconciling himself and his fellow settlers to a life away from their ancestral home (Highley 1997, 33).

Spenser's reputation as a poet of firm opinions, a characterisation which largely depends on his reputation as a dominant force in the propagation of Elizabethan Protestant nationalism, requires qualification since Ireland remained his home for nearly twenty years and admiration for certain aspects of Irish culture ameliorates his denunciation of them.

Spenser's claim that the Old English have "degenerated and growen all-moste meare Irishe yea and more malitious to the Englishe than the verye Irishe themselves" (Spenser 1949, 96) betrays anxiety about the process of alteration that occurs as a result of colonization and so it is perhaps ironic that a desire to alter the world around him should feature so heavily in his writings. It is perhaps Spenser's awareness of the potency of Irish influence upon English colonizers which triggers the passionate pleas for topographical manipulation in the *View*, which are mirrored in his desire to create a pastoral idyll in his poetry. Irish success at alteration has impacted upon Spenser and conditioned his approach to power and control and it is this, coupled with his admiration for particular aspects of Irish culture and criticism of Elizabeth, which serves to problematize simplistic notions about identity, exile and influence. The various characterizations of Spenser – fervent supporter of Elizabeth, romantic poet, exile, hater of all things Irish – fail to capture the complexity of his views. So too with Shakespeare neat categories prove to be inadequate.

Shakespeare

As we saw in the introduction, the rise of 'bardolatry' was determined by the belief that Shakespeare depicted the human condition, a view popular amongst the Romantics. Hazlitt's praise of Shakespeare's mind, which he believed "contained a universe of thought and feeling within itself" (Hazlitt 1908, 71–72) helped propagate the idea that Shakespeare must necessarily be equipped with a remarkable and unusual sensitivity to his fellow man and woman. Unlike the reputation accorded to Spenser as a poet of firm opinions and a major force in the propagation of Elizabethan Protestant nationalism, Shakespeare is traditionally thought of as a more opaque and indeterminate writer, a reputation enhanced by the rising speculation surrounding his religious loyalties; if Shakespeare was Catholic then that might explain his tendency to remain hidden. The multivalency of Shakespeare's work apparently signals his ability to empathize with all, but this does not sit easily with Katherine Duncan Jones' recent portrait of Shakespeare as a particularly uncharitable man.

As Duncan Jones pointed out, Shakespeare by the early 1600s "had become spectacularly wealthy", a wealth in no small part due to his "lease of tithes [which] brought him major profit from the humble toil of the yeomen and labourers of Stratford", people who were particularly vulnerable having recently experienced starvation due to bad harvests. Yet as Duncan-Jones noted, "Despite his evident prosperity, there continues to be no evidence that Shakespeare was engaged in any charitable activity, either on behalf of the poor of Stratford, or those of St Giles, Cripplegate, the parish where he now lodged in London" (Duncan-Jones 2001, 183–84). When compared with his contemporary, the actor-manager Edward Alleyn, who established many charitable foundations and "was active in collecting the parish dues that provided alms for the poor", Shakespeare, who "repeatedly avoided paying parish dues", comes off rather badly (Pearson 1982, 150). Although, as Duncan-Jones put it, "the purchase of monopolies and taxes had become a perfectly normal way of raising income during the Elizabethan period" and "Shakespeare was only procuring for himself the kind of benefit that more socially elevated individuals were awarded by the crown" (Duncan-Jones 2001, 184–85), the source of his considerable income raises troubling questions about a writer celebrated for his humanity.

Just as Shakespeare's reputation as a sensitive observer of the human condition is compromised by his apparent lack of charity, so too his reputation as a man of the theatre, unconcerned about publication, is open to question. We saw in the Introduction that the Romantic notion of dramatic writing as poetry writ large and Shakespeare as a poet unsullied by the theatre, which dominated Shakespeare studies for many years, was replaced by the consensus that Shakespeare was primarily a man of the theatre, writing his plays for actors and audiences and indifferent to any potential readership and therefore to publication. The rise in stage-centred critical thinking emphasized Shakespeare's role within the theatre industry and the role of multiple agencies in the composition of his plays. As well as the impact of the censor and the market, alterations to his scripts, most likely suggested in rehearsal by himself and colleagues, interfere with the subsequent Romantic notion of Shakespeare as a solitary genius as did his participation in co- and multiple-authorship. The rise in the stage-centred study of Shakespeare has emphasized the generic distinction between dramatists and poets. We might easily think that poets, traditionally considered univocal and solitary figures, have more control over their material than dramatists and, although poets might fall foul of the censor, drama is to a greater degree dependent on external factors which impact upon the creative process.

But there is evidence that Shakespeare was concerned about his reputation, eager to establish himself as a poet as well as a playwright and keen for his work to be published. In an important new study Lukas Erne argued that the traditional view of Shakespeare, largely propagated by his biographer Sidney Lee in the nineteenth century, as a writer who "had little interest in his writings as personal property and even less interest in posterity" (Erne 2003, 2), is flawed. Erne cited the printer William Jaggard's misattribution to Shakespeare of poems by Thomas Heywood in a collection called *The Passionate Pilgrim* (1599), which angered both writers. In a letter appended to his *Apology for Actors* (1612) Heywood stated:

> I must necessarily insert a manifest iniury done me in that worke, by taking the two Epistles of *Paris to Helen* and *Helen to Paris*, and printing them in a less volume, vnder the name of another, which may put the world in opinion I might steale them from him; and hee to doe himselfe right, hath since published them in his owne name: but as I must acknowledge my lines not worthy his [Shakespeare's] patronage, vnder whom he [Jaggard] hath published them, so the Author [Shakespeare] I know much offended with M. *Iaggard* (that altogether vnknowne to him) presumed to make so bold with his name. (quoted in Erne 2003, 1)

As Erne pointed out "This incident presents us with a picture of an unfamiliar Shakespeare: keenly aware of what is and what is not his literary property, concerned about his reputation, proud of his name and unwilling to have it associated with lines that did not flow from his pen" (Erne 2003, 2). The notion that Shakespeare was not interested in how future generations would regard him and his writing is challenged by Erne, who pointed to the sonnets: "No reader can ignore how prominently the theme of poetry as immortalization figures in them" (Erne 2003, 5). As Erne indicated, this was noted by J. B. Leishman, who in 1961 could claim that no critic of the sonnets had hitherto commented on the discrepancy between Shakespeare's alleged lack of interest in literary fame and his repeated references to the immortalizing power of poetry.

A number of Shakespeare's plays had already been performed when an outbreak of plague closed London's theatres between 1592 and 1594 and it is commonly believed that Shakespeare took advantage of this lull to write his two narrative poems *Venus and Adonis*, published in 1593, and *The Rape of Lucrece*, published the following year. It is ironic, given the argument that Shakespeare should be considered a literary writer, that his poetry, so successful in his own lifetime, should have been broadly neglected by the critics after his death. Colin Burrow neatly summed up their publication history:

> An earlier string of institutional accidents effectively divided the poems (often unthinkingly stigmatized by the dire privative prefix of 'the *non*-dramatic works') from the plays. The poems were not included in the First Folio of Shakespeare's *Comedies, Histories and Tragedies* of 1623. This was partly because many of those responsible for putting the volume together were men of the theatre. But it was also because *Venus and Adonis* and *Lucrece* were extremely popular, and remained marketable commodities in their own right throughout the seventeenth century.... In the eighteenth-century collected editions of Shakespeare ... the poems and sonnets were usually either left out altogether, or shuffled off in final volumes or appendices to the dramatic works.... (Burrow 2002, 2)

Burrow lamented that "despite some splendid reappraisals over the last fifty years" Shakespeare's poetry is still consigned "to the edges of the canon" and rightly pointed out: "If collected editions wished to reflect how Shakespeare wished to be thought of in the 1590s, or how he was generally regarded before the folio of 1623, then *Venus and Adonis* should be at the front of those editions: this was the first work to which he attached his name, and it was the work which made his name" (Burrow 2002, 3). Francis Meres' praise of Shakespeare in his *Palladis Tamia* (1598) compared Shakespeare to Plautus in comedy and Seneca in tragedy but, significantly, began by praising his poetry, suggesting its precedence in the minds of his admirers: "As the soule of *Euphorbus* was thought to liue in *Pythagoras*: so the sweete wittie soule of *Ouid* liues in mellifluous & hony-tongued *Shakespeare*, witnes his *Venus* and *Adonis*, his *Lucrece*, his sugred Sonnets among his priuate friends, &C" (Meres 1598, Oo1v–Oo2r). Yet, as Erne pointed out, we should not assume that Shakespeare supervised the printing of his narrative poems, something often taken for granted since the texts "are remarkably clean by comparison with those of the quarto playtexts" which Erne explained as being due to "Richard Field's printing rather than William Shakespeare's proofreading" (Erne 2003, 96). The argument that Shakespeare cared more about his poems than his plays because he provided dedications only for the former is also dismissed by Erne as an action which "simply reflects the conventions of the time" (Erne 2003, 98). Shakespeare was unlikely to have supervised the printing of his plays, not because he cared nothing for them but because, on the one hand, supervising the printing of a play was a time-consuming business, and on the other, plays "were considered unimportant publications and comparatively little effort went into their printing" (Erne 2003, 96). So it seems that the realities of the industry itself as well as Shakespeare's numerous commitments rather than his lack of interest explains why he did not oversee the printing of his plays.

We have seen that the notion of Shakespeare as a man of the theatre came to dominate Shakespeare Studies in the latter part of the twentieth century and was perhaps most fully expressed by the editors of the Oxford Complete Works who were influenced by Jerome McGann's notion of the socialized text. They emphasized the plays as performance rather than literature by moving away from a focus on Shakespeare's authorial manuscripts, something previous editors tended to do, and considering the theatre as the completion of Shakespeare's work. Responding to Andrew Gurr's call for attention to "the inherent difference between the original company's own written playbook and the text the players performed" (Gurr 1999, 70), Erne challenged the practice of privileging the play-as-performed, and thus Shakespeare as primarily a man of the theatre, over the authorial manuscript:

> ... many of Shakespeare's plays existed in two significantly different forms in the late sixteenth and in the seventeenth centuries. On the one hand, Shakespeare produced 'authorial manuscripts,' instances of what John Webster called the 'poem' and what some title pages refer to as 'the true original copy.' On the other hand, there were manuscripts that had undergone the company's preparation for actual performance, what Webster calls 'the play,' or, in other words, the text 'as it has been sundry times performed.' Whereas texts in the former group were of a length which actors found impossible to reconcile with the requirements of performance, the latter had been reduced to what was compatible with the 'two hours traffic of our stage.' Contrary to the theatrical scripts, the raison d'être of the long 'poems', I have argued, was basically literary (Erne 2003, 192)

The notion that Shakespeare distinguished between the product that got performed and that which he intended for publication undermines the idea that Shakespeare was primarily a dramatist. It also makes Shakespeare less collaborative a writer than was hitherto accepted since those texts which were not handed over to the company, his "long 'poems'", were not subject to the demands which performance placed upon a text. More significantly, if Shakespeare really conceived of himself as a poet then perhaps the Romantics, long ridiculed for their belief that Shakespeare should be read, have a point and the generic distinction between published play-texts (although not the plays as performed) and poetry is a false one. The rise in the stage-centred study of Shakespeare has perhaps enhanced his reputation as a multivalent author: the theatre industry, by its very nature collaborative, stands apart from the traditional conception of poets as univocal and solitary figures. But if Shakespeare privileged his poetry over those texts which got performed (and his emphasis on immortality in the sonnets would seem to suggest this) then perhaps he asserted a greater degree of control over his intellectual materi-al intended for publication and his opinions on particular matters are less opaque than hitherto acknowledged.

We saw that Spenser's poetry and prose betray a desire to manipulate the world around him, a preoccupation with fantasies of metamorphosing the landscape (by unification, dissection and even elimination) and of the landscape endorsing a particular political agenda. We also saw that these efforts to control and contain subversive elements in the landscape of Fairyland and Ireland are not always successful. Genre again comes into the frame: drama necessarily voices differences of opinions and, unlike Spenser's *Faerie Queene*, Shakespeare's plays contain no narratorial voice over the top of characters' conversations. Although this might suggest that Shakespeare's views are unknowable, certain patterns begin to emerge. While Shakespeare's writing is to some extent multivalent, his characters presenting a range of views not matched by any of Spenser's imaginative material, we can discern in the plays a similar preoccupation with fantasies of metamorphosis and topographical endorsement of a political agenda. As with Spenser there is also an acknowledgement that human efforts to control and contain the landscape cannot always be privileged over geo-graphical reality or moral imperative.

Shakespeare, like Spenser, demonstrates a preoccupation with fantasies of metamorphosing the landscape but seems to be suggesting that fantasies centred on the landscape are invoked by the powerless and are ultimately ineffectual; the imagination is no substitute for political pragmatism and successful governance. Internationalism is welcomed by those who challenge misguided rulers and insularity aligned with the weak or morally compromised, a pattern which suggests Shakespeare's approval of the internationalist and conciliatory policies toward traditional foreign enemies adopted by James 1. Decisions made by Shakespeare in shaping his sources suggest specific loyalties, and a distinct sympathy for Welsh and Irish nationalism emerges which, given the strength of Catholicism in both countries, may indicate Shakespeare's religious loyalties. All fantasies involving the manipulation of the landscape by its elimination or dissection are shown to be highly presumptuous and, moreover, remain unfulfilled: there are limits to human power over the natural world.

Claims for Shakespeare's Catholic sympathies appear more convincing when we consider that, unlike many of his contemporaries, he did not tend towards anti-Catholic propaganda in his plays. In the Introduction it was noted that Ernst Honigmann believed the theory of Shakespeare's Catholicism difficult to reconcile with the anti-Catholic tone of some of his early plays, for example the anti-Catholic bias toward Humphry in 1 Henry 6 and 2 Henry 6 and in the rhetoric of King John. We might also note the extraordinarily anti-Catholic scenes featuring Joan La Pucelle (Joan of Arc) in 1 Henry 6 as evidence of Shakespeare's Protestant loyalties, but only if we think Shakespeare was responsible for those scenes. Gary Taylor, who noted that Shakespeare removed most of the anti-Catholic polemic of his source when writing King John (Taylor 1985, 99), argued that Shakespeare wrote 1 Henry 6 in collaboration with at least two authors, one of whom was Thomas Nashe. The other authors Taylor labelled as X and Y, noting "The identities of X and Y are unknown, though Y has particular links with Locrine ... and both have strong similarities to the dramatic writings of Robert Greene and George Peele" (Wells et al. 1987, 217). It is not clear how collaboration occurred in the early modern theatre, whether plays were divided amongst authors according to scenes, speeches, characters, or whether some other method was used, for example revision by one author of another's work. How the process might have worked is outlined by Brian Vickers (2002, 18–43) but Gordon McMullan is more circumspect about our ability to pin down who was responsible for what (2000a, 180–99). According to one model of authorship (that particular authors were responsible for particular scenes) Gary Taylor assigns those scenes featuring Joan

La Pucelle to authors other than Shakespeare, the one exception being 4.7. which he considered might have had mixed authorship, possibly Shakespeare and Y (Wells et al. 1987, 217). Throughout the play, French comments on Joan's goodness are undercut by English insults denouncing her as a witch and a strumpet but it is act 5, which Taylor believed was written by Y, where anti-Catholic propaganda is most clearly operating since the English are shown to be right.

1 Henry 6 is one of Shakespeare's earliest plays and he seems not to have co-authored another for many years. Critics usually assume that Shakespeare was learning his trade and stopped collaborating when he had gained sufficient expertise as a playwright, but it is also possible that he felt uncomfortable about the lack of control co-authoring offered, an idea which reinforces Erne's point that he was "concerned about his reputation, proud of his name and unwilling to have it associated with lines that did not flow from his pen" (Erne 2003, 2); perhaps as a secret Catholic Shakespeare wanted to limit any further association with the kind of vulgar anti-Catholic propaganda represented in the scenes featuring Joan La Pucelle. Shakespeare would not have been able to protest against his co-author's anti-Catholic scenes, since this would have meant announcing Catholic sympathies, but his other plays provide subtle indications of where his religious sympathies lay.

In addition to those plays mentioned in the Introduction, *Sir Thomas More* suggests particular loyalties, especially in its depiction of More himself. This is an inherently interesting text since part of it probably represents the only creative writing by Shakespeare that has survived in his own handwriting. The play exists solely as British Library manuscript Harley 7368, in several hands, and comprising 22 sheets. Most of the writing is in the hand of Anthony Munday, although 'additional' sheets in different hands have been inserted. John Jowett used stylistic analysis to argue that Henry Chettle (not Munday as is usually claimed) composed the first scene of the play and that several others composed "over one-third of the original text" (Jowett 1989, 147–48). The front of the first sheet contains a provisional licence from Edmund Tilney, the state censor, requiring alterations before public performance. The 'additions' might represent changes to the play made after Tilney's objections were known but this explanation is difficult to sustain because in some ways the changes (such as the rewriting of the scene in which More quells the rioters) make matters worse. This problem is treated in the Revels edition of the play by its editors Vittorio Gabrieli and Giorgio Melchiori (Munday 1990) and more fully in Scott McMillin's book *The Elizabethan theatre and 'The Book of Sir Thomas More'* (McMillin 1987). McMillin and the Revels editors concur, as do most scholars, that Shakespeare is probably the composer and writer of Hand D and hence of the scene which depicts events leading up to the riots of Londoners against resident foreigners on May Day 1517. The riot's leaders – John Lincoln, Williamson and his wife Doll, George and Ralph Betts, and Sherwin – are angry at the behaviour of foreigners in London and have planned a violent uprising against them. Shakespeare's contribution comes before the entry of Sheriff More of London, sent by the authorities to calm the situation. In response to Betts' comment that they want "the removing of the strangers, which cannot choose but much advantage the poor handicrafts of the city" (2.3.76–77) More pleads for compassion and tolerance:

> Grant them removed, and grant that this your noise
> Hath chid down all the majesty of England.
> Imagine that you see the wretched strangers,
> Their babies at their backs, with their poor luggage
> Plodding to th' ports and coasts for transportation,
> And that you sit as kings in your desires,
> Authority quite silenced by your brawl
> And you in ruff of your opinions clothed:
> What had you got? I'll tell you. You had taught
> How insolence and strong hand should prevail,
> How order should be quelled
> (*Sir Thomas More* 2.3.78–88)

More's appeasement of the rioters is a powerful piece of rhetoric, the pathetic image of miserable people appealing to the humanity of his listeners. Although it might be argued that the behaviour of the foreigners in 1.1 undermines More's speech, it is clear that More's reference to "babies" is a focus on the innocent, suggesting that they and their parents must not suffer for the sins of the few. More also appeals to the Londoners' sense of reason and self-preservation, arguing that if they use violence to rid themselves of foreigners then some day violence might be used by others to get rid of them: "other ruffians ... Would shark on you and men like ravenous fishes / Would feed on one another" (2.3.90–93).

More urges obedience to the King since he is God's anointed representative on earth (an echo of Gaunt's speech to the Duchess of Gloucester in *Richard 2*, 1.2) and warns that the xenophobic Londoners face becoming like the people they despise:

> Say now the King,
> As he is clement if th' offender mourn,
> Should so much come too short of your great trespass
> As but to banish you: whither would you go?
> What country, by the nature of your error,
> Should give you harbour? Go you to France or Flanders,
> To any German province, Spain or Portugal,
> Nay, anywhere that not adheres to England,
> Why, you must needs be strangers.
> (*Sir Thomas More* 2.3.133–141)

Having become strangers, they too would face local contempt:

> Would you be pleased
> To find a nation of such barbarous temper
> That breaking out in hideous violence
> Would not afford you an abode on earth,
> Whet their detested knives against your throats,
> Spurn you like dogs, and like as if that God
> Owed not nor made not you, nor that the elements
> Were not all appropriate to your comforts
> But chartered unto them, what would you think
> To be thus used? This is the strangers' case,
> And this your mountainish inhumanity.
> (*Sir Thomas More* 2.3.141–151)

While not wishing to draw any simplistic parallels, it seems likely that these scenes hit upon concerns current around the time of composition: the plea from More, a Catholic martyr, for tolerance on behalf of strangers is a Christian response to the suffering of humanity but it might also echo the feelings of English Catholics who, during the early years of James' rule, hoped for greater toleration of their religious beliefs than was granted during the reign of Elizabeth. As Philip Caraman pointed out, the Jesuit priests John Gerard and Henry Garnet both "cherished hopes of toleration" and Garnet, in a letter written three weeks after Elizabeth's death, stated "there has happened a great alteration ... Great fears were: but all are turned into greatest security: and a golden time we have of unexpected freedom abroad" (Caraman 1964, 305). More warns against rebellion, just as any loyal English Catholic would have recoiled from insurrection against their monarch and the description of strangers wandering the earth trying to find succour conjures images of recusant priests and their Catholic supporters who suffered "mountainish inhumanity" at the hands of their captors and is remarkably similar to Edgar's plight in *King Lear*, the Catholic dimensions of which have been discussed in the Introduction. In More's soliloquy, also thought to have been written by Shakespeare (3.1.1–21), he announces himself as a man of God who is suspicious toward the "gay skins" of secular advancement "Either of honour, office, wealth and calling" (3.1.18; 3.1.15), a scene which reinforces the view of More as an honest, morally upright and principled man. That most of the manuscript is in the hand of Anthony Munday does not mean that Munday necessarily composed the play as it existed before the additions. Indeed, as Thomas Merriam pointed out, given the play's positive depiction of More, it is unlikely that Munday, an anti-Catholic recusant hunter, was involved in the creative process (Merriam 2000). The most likely scenario is that Munday transcribed a play that was penned by others, perhaps in order to bring Catholic sympathizers to the attention of the authorities.

From Shakespeare's apparent Catholic sympathies emerges the complex picture of an author who is perhaps more knowable than is usually acknowledged. Although he is commonly credited with the ability to speak from all corners, a substantial number of plays provide evidence of particular religious sympathies. The multivalency of his work, which apparently signals a remarkable sensitivity and ability to empathize with fellow human beings, sits uneasily with what seems to have been a distinct lack of charitableness. Genre has helped shape the notion that Shakespeare is unknowable (all opinions being voiced through dramatic characters) and although undoubtedly a man of the theatre it seems that, like Spenser, he was eager to establish himself as a poet and was concerned about his reputation, which may have led him to assert a substantial degree of control over his product. It is likely that Shakespeare is a rather more univocal author than the common image of him allows. Spenser's reputation as a univocal author is similarly problematic: although the opinions of Irenius dominate the *View*, it is nevertheless a prose dialogue (a form anticipated by the multivocal nature of *The Shepheardes Calender*), his desire to contain Ireland's violent reality is not always successful, and the narrator of *The Faerie Queene* lacks complete control of the narrative.

Although Spenser is concerned with topographical containment unhindered by reality, Shakespeare tends to have a more subtle approach to control and closure, an approach which is only partially dictated by genre. Spenser's poetry and prose reveal insecurity reflected in his efforts to manipulate the landscape according to his own political agenda, whilst Shakespeare's drama more objectively questions the relationship between topography and the individual. Spenser's political and religious conservatism contrasts with Shakespeare's political (and perhaps religious) radicalism, which emphasizes the vagaries of human desires and, ultimately, human inability to achieve complete control over the landscape. The current instability of the artificially (and violently) constructed United Kingdom is prefigured in writing by Shakespeare and Spenser, both writing at a time of renewed effort in extending and maintaining borders. For Shakespeare and Spenser place has a special function and both are preoccupied with the processes by which borders are manipulated and extended. Both writers produce work in which the consumer (reader or playhouse spectator) is fully encouraged to imagine fictive place 'x' while remaining aware of its likeness to real place 'y' (frequently, a part of the north-east Atlantic archipelago), but in exploiting this never-expressed freedom we can see two distinct responses to contemporary ideological pressures. One possible explanation for Shakespeare's artistic responses to ideology is his suppressed Catholicism which made him essentially a secret alien at the heart of London's cultural production. By contrast, Spenser's alterity was a product of his move to a place, Munster in Ireland, where English courtly ideology was distinctly abnormal. Spenser's desire to create a local courtly milieu, explored by Maley and Hadfield, can plausibly be explained as an attempt to neutralize this self-inflicted otherness. For many Shakespeareans, his possible Catholicism offers a materialist explanation for creative multivalency which has for several centuries been naively attributed to artistic sublimity and which sometimes only barely disguises a more opinionated stance. This avenue of historicism may yet fail to provide a way out of the idealist criticism which dominates most mainstream Shakespeare studies (in schools and in theatres), since he might still not have been a Catholic. Nonetheless, it seems clear that important light is thrown upon artistic works by the study of place as both a component of the artistic products (which inevitably have fictive locations) and a determinant in the artist's biography.

Works Cited

Anon. 1560. *The Bible and Holy Scriptures Conteyned in the Olde and Newe Testament. Translated According to the Ebrue and Greke. With Moste Profitable Annotations. [Geneva Version]*. Geneva. R. Hall.

Anon. 1909. *The Chronicle History of King Lear: The Original of Shakespeare's* King Lear. Ed. Sidney Lee. The Shakespeare Classics. 7. London. Chatto and Windus.

Anon. 2002. *King Leir*. Ed. Tiffany Stern. Globe Quartos. London. Nick Hern.

Aptekar, Jane. 1969. *Icons of Justice: Iconography and Thematic Imagery in Book V of* The Faerie Queene. New York. Columbia University Press.

Arnold, Matthew. 1965. *The Poems of Matthew Arnold*. Ed. Kenneth Allott. London. Longmans.

Baker, David J. 1992. ""Wildehirissheman": Colonialist Representation in Shakespeare's *Henry V*." *English Literary Renaissance*. 22.1. 37–61.

Baker, David J. 1993. "Off the Map: Charting Uncertainty in Renaissance Ireland." *Representing Ireland: Literature and the Origins of Conflict, 1534–1660*. Edited by Brendan Bradshaw, Andrew Hadfield and Willy Maley. Cambridge. Cambridge University Press. 76–92.

Bate, Jonathan. 2003. "'In the Script Factory: It is Time to Stop Worrying About Shakespeare's Collaborators, and to Start Appreciating Them': Review of Brian Vickers *Shakespeare, Co-Author: An Historical Study of Five Collaborative Plays* (Oxford: Oxford University Press, 2003)." *Times Literary Supplement*. 5520. 3–4.

Bearman, Robert. 2002. "Was William Shakespeare William Shakeshafte? Revisited." *Shakespeare Quarterly*. 53. 83–94.

Bennett, Josephine Waters. 1942. *The Evolution of* The Faerie Queene. New York. Burt Franklin.

Berger Junior, Harry. 1999. "*Ars Moriendi* in Progress, or John of Gaunt and the Practice of Strategic Dying." *Critical Essays on Shakespeare's* Richard II. Edited by Kirby Farrell. Critical Essays on British Literature. New York. G. K. Hall. 237–61.

Bessell, Jaq. 2002. "The 2001 Globe Season: The White Company: *King Lear.*" *Shakespeare's Globe: Research bulletin.* 21. 1–73.

Bickersteth, Geoffrey L. 1946. "The Golden World of *King Lear*: Annual Shakespeare Lecture of the British Academy." *Proceedings of the British Academy.* 32. 149–71.

Blenerhasset, Thomas. 1610. *A Direction for the Plantation in Ulster.* London. E. Allde for J. Budge.

Bradbrook, M. C. 1968. *Elizabethan Stage Conditions: A Study of Their Place in the Interpretation of Shakepeare's Plays.* Cambridge. Cambridge University Press.

Brink, Jean R. 1994. "Constructing the *View of the Present State of Ireland.*" *Spenser Studies.* 11. 203–28.

Brook, Peter. 1971. *King Lear.* Motion Picture. Athena Films.

Brooks-Davies, Douglas. 1990. "Una." *The Spenser Encyclopedia.* Edited by A. C. Hamilton. Toronto. University of Toronto Press. 704–05.

Brumbaugh, Barbara. 2000. "'Under the Pretty Tales of Wolves and Sheep': Sidney's Ambassadorial Table Talk and Protestant Hunting Dialogues." *Spenser Studies.* 14. 273–90.

Bullough, Geoffrey, ed. 1973a. *Narrative and Dramatic Sources of Shakespeare.* Vol. 7. 8 vols. London. Routledge and Kegan Paul.

Bullough, Geoffrey, ed. 1973b. *Narrative and Dramatic Sources of Shakespeare.* Vol. 4. 8 vols. London. Routledge and Kegan Paul.

Burrow, Colin, ed. 2002. *The Complete Sonnets and Poems.* The Oxford Shakespeare. Oxford. Oxford University Press.

Burrow, Colin. 2000. "'That Arch-poet of the Fairie Lond': A New Spenser Allusion." *Notes and Queries.* 47. 37.

Butlin, R. A. 1976. "Land and People, *c.* 1600." *A New History of Ireland.* 3. Edited by T. W. Moody, F. X. Martin and F. J. Byrne. Oxford. Oxford University Press. 142–67.

Calderwood, James L. 1971. *Shakespearean Metadrama: The Argument of the Play in* Titus Andronicus, Love's Labour's Lost, Romeo and Juliet, A Midsummer Night's Dream, *and* Richard II. Minneapolis. University of Minnesota Press.

Canny, Nicholas and Ciaran Brady. 1988. "Debate: Spenser's Irish Crisis: Humanism and Experience in the 1590s." *Past and Present.*120. 201–15.

Canny, Nicholas. 2001. *Making Ireland British: 1580–1650.* Oxford. Oxford University Press.

Caraman, Philip. 1964. *Henry Garnet 1555–1606 and the Gunpowder Plot.* London. Longmans.

Carroll, Clare. 1990. "The Construction of Gender and the Cultural and Political Other in *The Faerie Queene* 5 and *A View of the Present State of Ireland*: the Critics, the Context, and the Case of Radigund." *Criticism.* 32.2. 163–92.

Chadwyck-Healey. 2003. *Literature Online (LION) Database Internet Http//lion.chadwyck.co.uk.*

Chang, H. C. 1955. *Allegory and Courtesy in Spenser: A Chinese View*. Edinburgh. Edinburgh University Press.

Chettle, Henry. 1603. *Englandes Mourning Garment: Worne Here By Plaine Shepheardes; in Memorie of Their Mistresse, Elizabeth*. London. V. S. for Thomas Millington.

Cohen, Derek. 1993. *Shakespeare's Culture of Violence*. Basingstoke. Macmillan.

Coleridge, S. T. 1907. *Biographia Literaria*. Ed. J. Shawcross. Vol. 2. 2 vols. Oxford. Clarendon.

Coleridge, Samuel Taylor. 1918. *Coleridge's Literary Criticism*. Ed. J. W. Mackail. London. Humphrey Milford.

Coleridge, Samuel Taylor. 1960. *Shakespearean Criticism*. Ed. Thomas Middleton Raysor. Vol. 2. 2 vols. London. J. M. Dent.

Collinson, Patrick. 1985. "The Church: Religion and Its Manifestations." *William Shakespeare: His World, His Work, His Influence*. 1: His World. Edited by John F. Andrews. New York. Charles Scribner's Sons. 21–40.

Cooper, Helen. 1990. "Pastoral." *The Spenser Encyclopedia*. Edited by A. C. Hamilton. Toronto. University of Toronto Press. 529–32.

Cooper, Thomas. 1565. *Thesaurus Linguae Romanae and Britannicae. Accessit Dictionarium Historicum et Poeticum Propria Vocabula Virorum, Mulierum, . . . Complectens*. London. in aed. quondam Bertheleti, per H. Wykes.

Cressy, David. 1997. *Birth, Marriage, and Death: Ritual, Religion, and the Life-cycle in Tudor and Stuart England*. Oxford. Oxford University Press.

Daniel, Samuel. 1595. *The First Fowre Bookes of the Ciuile Warres Betweene the Two Houses of Lancaster and Yorke*. London. P. Short for S. Waterson.

Davies, R. R. 1997. *The Revolt of Owain Glyn Dŵr*. Oxford. Oxford University Press.

Davies, Sir John. 1612. *A Discoverie of the True Causes Why Ireland Was Never Entirely Subdued, Untill His Majesties Raigne*. London. W. Jaggard for J. Jaggard.

Dobson, Michael. 1992. *The Making of the National Poet: Shakespeare, Adaptation and Authorship, 1660–1769*. Oxford. Clarendon.

Duncan-Jones, Katherine. 2001. *Ungentle Shakespeare: Scenes From His Life*. Arden Shakespeare. London. Arden.

Eagleton, Terry. 1986. *William Shakespeare*. Rereading Literature. Oxford. Basil Blackwell.

Eliot, T. S. 1934. *Elizabethan Essays*. London. Faber and Faber.

Erne, Lukas. 2003. *Shakespeare as Literary Dramatist*. Cambridge. Cambridge University Press.

Eyre, Richard. 1997. *King Lear*. Motion Picture. British Broadcasting Corporation.

Falkiner, C. Litton. 1904. *Illustrations of Irish History and Topography, Mainly of the Seventeenth Century*. London. Longmans.

Falls, Mary Robert. 1953. "Spenser's Kirkrapine and the Elizabethans." *Studies in Philology*. 50. 457–75.

Fitzpatrick, Joan. 1998. "Spenser's Nationalistic Images of Beauty: The Ideal and the Other in Relation to Protestant England and Catholic Ireland in *The Faerie*

Queene Book 1." *Cahiers Elisabethains: Late Medieval and Renaissance English Studies*. 53. 13–26.

Fitzpatrick, Joan. 2000. *Irish Demons: English Writings on Ireland, the Irish and Gender By Spenser and His Contemporaries*. Lanham. University Press of America.

Fogarty, Anne. 1989. "The Colonization of Language: Narrative Structures in *A View of the Present State of Ireland* and *The Faerie Queene*, Book VI." *Spenser and Ireland: An Interdisciplinary Perspective*. Edited by Patricia Coughlan. Cork. Cork University Press. 75–108.

Fowler, Alastair. 1964. *Spenser and the Numbers of Time*. London. Routledge and Kegan Paul.

Gainsford, Thomas. 1618. *The Glory of England, or a True Description of Blessings, Whereby She Triumpheth Over All Nations*. London. E. Griffin for T. Norton.

Gibbons, Brian. 1993. *Shakespeare and Multiplicity*. Cambridge. Cambridge University Press.

Goddard, Harold C. 1951. *The Meaning of Shakespeare*. Chicago. University of Chicago Press.

Goldberg, Jonathan. 1988. "Perspectives: Dover Cliff and the Conditions of Representation." *Shakespeare and Deconstruction*. Edited by Douglas G. Atkins and David M. Bergeron. American University Studies. New York. Peter Lang. 245–65.

Goldman, Michael. 1985. *Acting and Action in Shakespearean Tragedy*. Princeton. Princeton University Press.

Gray, M. M. 1930. "The Influence of Spenser's Irish Experiences on *The Faerie Queene*." *Review of English Studies*. 6.21–24. 413–28.

Greenblatt, Stephen. 1980. *Renaissance Self-Fashioning: From More to Shakespeare*. Chicago and London. University of Chicago Press.

Greenfield, Matthew. 2002. "*I Henry IV*: Metatheatrical Britain." *British Identities and English Renaissance Literature*. Edited by David J. Baker and Willy Maley. Cambridge. Cambridge University Press. 71–80.

Greenlaw, Edwin A. 1912. "Spenser and British Imperialism." *Modern Philology*. 9.3. 347–70.

Grene, Nicholas. 2002. *Shakespeare's Serial History Plays*. Cambridge. Cambridge University Press.

Griffin, R. Morgan. 1999. "The Critical History of *Richard II*." *Critical Essays on Shakespeare's* Richard II. Edited by Kirby Farrell. Critical Essays on British Literature. New York. G. K. Hall. 23–40.

Gurr, Andrew. 1999. "Maximal and Minimal Texts: Shakespeare V. The Globe." *Shakespeare Survey*. 52. 68–87.

Gurr, Andrew. 2002. "Headgear as Signifier in *King Lear*." Ed. Peter Holland. *Shakespeare Survey*. 55: *King Lear* and Its Afterlife. 43–52.

Hackett, Helen. 1995. *Virgin Mother, Maiden Queen: Elizabeth I and the Cult of the Virgin Mary*. Basingstoke. Macmillan.

Hadfield, Andrew and John McVeagh, eds. 1994. *Strangers to That Land: British Perceptions of Ireland From the Reformation to the Famine*. Ulster Editions and Monographs. 5. Gerrards Cross, UK. Colin Smythe.

Hadfield, Andrew, ed. 2001. *The Cambridge Companion to Spenser*. Cambridge Companions to Literature. Cambridge. Cambridge University Press.

Hadfield, Andrew. 1994. "Was Spenser's *View of the Present State of Ireland* Censored? A Review of the Evidence." *Notes and Queries*. 239. 459–63.

Hadfield, Andrew. 1997a. "'Hitherto She Ne're Could Fancy Him': Shakespeare's 'British' Plays and the Exclusion of Ireland." *Shakespeare and Ireland: History, Politics, Culture*. Edited by Mark Thornton Burnett and Ramona Wray. Basingstoke. Macmillan. 47–67.

Hadfield, Andrew. 1997b. *Edmund Spenser's Irish Experience: Wilde Fruit and Salvage Soyl*. Oxford. Clarendon Press.

Hankins, John Erskine. 1971. *Source and Meaning in Spenser's Allegory: A Study of The Faerie Queene*. Oxford. Clarendon Press.

Harbage, Alfred. 1964. *Annals of English Drama 975–1700: An Analytical Record of All Plays, Extant or Lost, Chronologically Arranged and Indexed By Authors, Titles, Dramatic Companies*. Third edition. London. Routledge.

Hardin, Richard F. 1990. "Adicia, Souldan." *The Spenser Encyclopedia*. Edited by A. C. Hamilton. Toronto. University of Toronto Press. 7–8.

Hawkes, Terence. 1998. "Bryn Glas." *Post-Colonial Shakespeares*. Edited by Ania Loomba and Martin Orkin. New Accents. London. Routledge. 117–40.

Hawkes, Terence. 2002. *Shakespeare in the Present*. Accents on Shakespeare. London. Routledge.

Hazlitt, William. 1908. *Lectures on the English Poets*. The New Universal Library. London. Routledge.

Heaney, Seamus. 1975. *North*. London. Faber and Faber.

Henken, Elissa R. 1996. *National Redeemer: Owain Glyndŵr in Welsh Tradition*. Cardiff. University of Wales Press.

Henley, Pauline. 1928. *Spenser in Ireland*. Dublin. Cork University Press.

Heywood, Thomas. 1935. *If You Know Not Me You Know Nobody: Part II*. Prepared by Melanie Doran in consultation with W. W. Greg. Malone Society Reprints. Oxford. Oxford University Press.

Highley, Christopher. 1997. *Shakespeare, Spenser, and the Crisis in Ireland*. Cambridge Studies in Renaissance Literature and Culture. 23. Cambridge. Cambridge University Press.

Holderness, Graham, Nick Potter and John Turner. 1988. *Shakespeare: The Play of History*. Contemporary Interpretations of Shakespeare. Basingstoke. Macmillan.

Holderness, Graham. 1985. *Shakespeare's History*. Dublin. Gill and Macmillan.

Holinshed, Raphael. 1587. *Chronicles, Newlie Augmented and Continued By J. Hooker Alias Vowell Gent. and Others*. Vol. 3: All the Kings and Queenes of England in Their Orderlie Successions; Stow's Continuation of the Chronicles of England

From 1576 to 1586. 3 vols. London. [H. Denham,] at the expenses of J. Harison, G. Bishop, R. Newberie, H. Denham, and T. Woodcocke.

Holland, Peter. 1997. *English Shakespeare's: Shakespeare on the English Stage in the 1990s*. Cambridge. Cambridge University Press.

Honigmann, E. A. J. 1998. *Shakespeare: the 'Lost Years'.* 2nd edn. Manchester. Manchester University Press.

Hopkins, Lisa. 1997. "Neighbourhood in *Henry V." Shakespeare and Ireland: History, Politics, Culture*. Edited by Mark Thornton Burnett and Ramona Wray. Basingstoke. Macmillan. 9–26.

Hosley, Richard. 1960. "Was There a Music-room in Shakespeare's Globe?" *Shakespeare Survey*. 13. 113–23.

Hough, Graham. 1962. *A Preface to* The Faerie Queene. London. Gerald Duckworth.

Howard, Jean E. and Phyllis Rackin. 1997. *Engendering a Nation: A Feminist Account of Shakespeare's English Histories*. London. Routledge.

Hughes, Art J. 1988. "The Seventeenth-century Ulster/Scottish Contention of the Red Hand: Background and Significance." *Gaelic and Scots in Harmony: Proceedings of the Second International Conference on the Languages of Scotland*. Edited by Derick S. Thomson. Glasgow. University of Glasgow. 78–94.

Johnson, Samuel. 1765. *Mr Johnson's Preface to His Edition of Shakespear's Plays*. London. Printed for J. and R. Tonson, H. Woodfall, J. Rivington, R. Baldwin, L. Hawes, Clark and Collins, T. Longman, W. Johnston, T. Caslon, C. Corbet, T. Lownds, and the Executors of B. Dodd.

Jones, Emrys. 1961. "Stuart Cymbeline." *Essays in Criticism*. 11. 84–99.

Jones, H. S. V. 1919. *Spenser's Defense of Lord Grey*. University of Illinois Studies in Language and Literature. Urbana. University of Illinois Press.

Jones, H. S. V. 1930. *A Spenser Handbook*. New York. Appleton-Century-Crofts.

Jowett, John. 1989. "Henry Chettle and the Original Text of *Sir Thomas More." Shakespeare and* Sir Thomas More*: Essays on the Play and Its Shakespearian Interest*. Edited by T. H. Howard-Hill. Cambridge. Cambridge University Press. 131–49.

Judson, Alexander C. 1945. *The Life of Edmund Spenser*. The Works of Edmund Spenser: A Variorum Edition. 11. Baltimore. Johns Hopkins.

Kastan, David Scott. 1999. *Shakespeare After Theory*. London. Routledge.

Kastan, David Scott. 2002. *King Henry IV Part 1*. Arden Shakespeare. London. Arden Shakespeare.

Keach, William. 1990. "Arlo Hill." *The Spenser Encylopedia*. Edited by A. C. Hamilton. Toronto. University of Toronto Press. 60.

Kelly, Henry Ansgar. 1970. *Divine Providence in the England of Shakespeare's Histories*. Cambridge MA. Harvard University Press.

Kelsey, Lin and Richard S. Peterson. 2000. "Rereading Colin's Broken Pipe: Spenser and the Problem of Patronage." *Spenser Studies*. 14. 233–72.

Klein, Bernhard. 1998. "Partial Views: Shakespeare and the Map of Ireland."

online, internet, http://purl.oclc.org/emls/04-2/kleinpart.htm. *Early Modern Literary Studies*. 4.2. 5.1–20.

Knapp, Jeffrey. 1992. *An Empire Nowhere: England, America, and Literature From Utopia to* The Tempest. The New Historicism: Studies in Cultural Poetics. 16. Berkeley. University of California Press.

Knowles, Richard. 2002. "How Shakespeare Knew *King Leir*." Ed. Peter Holland. *Shakespeare Survey*. 55: *King Lear* and Its Afterlife. 12–35.

Kozintsev, Grigori. 1969. *Korol Lir*. Motion Picture. Lenfilm Studio.

Lamb, Charles. 1891. *The Dramatic Essays of Charles Lamb*. Ed. Brander Matthews. London. Chatto and Windus.

Leggatt, Alexander. 1977. "The Island of Miracles: An Approach to *Cymbeline*." *Shakespeare Studies*. 10. 191–209.

Leggatt, Alexander. 1988a. *Shakespeare's Political Drama: The History Plays and the Roman Plays*. London. Routledge.

Leggatt, Alexander. 1988b. King Lear. Harvester New Critical Introductions to Shakespeare. Hemel Hempstead. Harvester Wheatsheaf.

Lewis, C. S. 1936. *The Allegory of Love: A Study in Medieval Tradition*. London. Oxford University Press.

Lowell, James Russell. 1875. "Spenser." *North American Review*. 120. 334–94.

Lupton, Julia Reinhard. 1993. "Mapping Mutability: or, Spenser's Irish Plot." *Representing Ireland: Literature and the Origins of Conflict, 1534–1660*. Edited by Brendan Bradshaw, Andrew Hadfield and Willy Maley. Cambridge. Cambridge University Press. 93–115.

Lyly, John. 1902. *The Complete Works*. Ed. R. Warwick Bond. Vol. 2: Euphues and His England; The Plays. 3 vols. Oxford. Clarendon.

MacFarlane, Alan. 1970. *Witchcraft in Tudor and Stuart England: A Regional and Comparative Study*. London. Routledge & Kegan Paul.

Maley, Willy. 1994. *A Spenser Chronology*. Author Chronologies. Basingstoke. Macmillan.

Maley, Willy. 1997. *Salvaging Spenser*. Basingstoke. Macmillan.

Marx, Karl. 1974. *The Ethnological Notebooks: Studies of Morgan, Phear, Maine, Lubbock*. Ed. Lawrence Krader. Second edition. Assen. Van Gorcum.

Masten, Jeffrey. 2001. "More or Less: Editing the Collaborative." *Shakespeare Studies*. 29. 109–31.

Maxwell, Constantia. 1923. *Irish History From Contemporary Sources (1509–1610)*. London. Allen and Unwin.

McCabe, Richard A. 1987. "The Masks of Duessa: Spenser, Mary Queen of Scots, and James VI." *English Literary Renaissance*. 17. 224–42.

McCabe, Richard A. 1989. "The Fate of Irena: Spenser and Political Violence." *Spenser and Ireland: An Interdisciplinary Perspective*. Edited by Patricia Coughlan. Cork. Cork University Press. 109–25.

McCabe, Richard A. 1993. "Edmund Spenser, Poet of Exile." *Proceedings of the British Academy*. 80. 73–103.

McCracken, Eileen. 1959. "The Woodlands of Ireland Circa 1600." *Irish Historical Studies*. 11.44. 271–96.

McGann, Jerome J. 1983. *A Critique of Modern Textual Criticism*. Chicago. University of Chicago Press.

McGuire, Philip. 1994. *Shakespeare: The Jacobean Plays*. English Dramatists. Basingstoke. Macmillan.

McMillin, Scott. 1987. *The Elizabethan Theatre and* The Book of Sir Thomas More. Ithaca. Cornell University Press.

McNeir, Waldo F. 1969. "The Sacrifice of Serena: *The Faerie Queene* VI.viii.31–51." *Festschrift Fur Edgar Mertner*. Edited by Bernhard Fabian and Ulrich Suerbaum. Munich. Wilhelm Fink. 117–56.

Meres, Francis. 1598. *Palladis Tamia. Wits Treasury Being the Second Part of Wits Common Wealth*. London. P Short for C Burbie.

Merriam, Thomas. 2000. "An Unwarranted Assumption." *Notes and Queries*. 47. 438–41.

Mikalachki, Jodi. 1995. "The Masculine Romance of Roman Britain: *Cymbeline* and Early Modern English Nationalism." *Shakespeare Quarterly*. 46. 301–22.

Miller, Jonathan. 1982. *King Lear*. Motion Picture. British Broadcasting Corporation.

Milward, Peter. 1997. *The Catholicism of Shakespeare's Plays*. Southampton. The Saint Austin Press.

Milward, Peter. 1998. *Shakespeare and the Jesuits*. Letters to the Editor: Times Literary Supplement, January, p. 15.

Montrose, Louis Adrian. 1983. "Of Gentlemen and Shepherds: The Politics of Elizabethan Pastoral Form." *English Literary History*. 50.3. 415–59.

Montrose, Louis. 1993. "The Work of Gender in the Discourse of Discovery." *New World Encounters*. Edited by Stephen Greenblatt. Berkeley. University of California Press. 177–217.

Morgan, Hiram. 1993. *Tyrone's Rebellion: The Outbreak of the Nine Years War in Tudor Ireland*. Royal Historical Society Studies in history. 67. Woodbridge. Boydell.

Muir, Kenneth. 1951. "Samuel Harsnett and *King Lear*." *The Review of English Studies*. 2.5. 11–21.

Munday, Anthony. 1990. *Sir Thomas More*. (Revised by Henry Chettle, Thomas Dekker, Thomas Heywood and William Shakespeare) Ed Vittorio Gabrieli and Giorgio Melchiori. The Revels Plays. Manchester. Manchester University Press.

Niccols, Richard. 1610. "England's Eliza." *A Mirour for Magistrates. Newly Enlarged with a Last Part*. Edited by John Higgins and R. Niccols. London. F. Kyngston. Eee2r-Lll6r.

Nohrnberg, James. 1976. *The Analogy of* The Faerie Queene. Princeton. Princeton University Press.

Oruch, Jack B. 1967. "Spenser, Camden, and the Poetic Marriages of Rivers." *Studies in Philology*. 64.4. 606–24.

Osgood, Charles G. 1931. "Comments on the Moral Allegory of *The Faerie Queene*." *Modern Language Notes*. 46. 502–07.

Owens, Judith. 2000. "The Poetics of Accomodation in Spenser's 'Epithalamion'." *Studies in English Literature*. 40.1. 41–62.

Pearson, Jacqueline. 1982. "The Influence of *King Leir* on Shakespeare's *Richard II*." *Notes and Queries*. 227.29. 113–15.

Pocock, J. G. A. 1975. "British History: A Plea for a New Subject." *Journal of Modern History*. 47. 601–28.

Pollard, A. W. and G. R. Redgrave. 1976. *A Short-title Catalogue of Books Printed in England, Scotland, & Ireland and of English Books Printed Abroad 1475–1640*. Vol. 2: I–Z. 3 vols. London. The Bibliographical Society.

Quitslund, Jon A. 1990. "Beauty." *The Spenser Encyclopedia*. Edited by A. C. Hamilton. Toronto. University of Toronto Press. 81–82.

Rauchbauer, O. 1997. "The 'Armada Scene' in Thomas Heywood's 'If You Know Not Me You Know Nobody'." *Notes and Queries*. 222. 143–44.

Rich, Barnaby. 1610. *A New Description of Ireland: Wherein is Described the Disposition of the Irish*. London. [W. Jaggard] for T. Adams.

Roche, Thomas P. 1964. *The Kindly Flame: A Study of the Third and Fourth Books of Spenser's* Faerie Queene. Princeton, NJ. Princeton University Press.

Rollinson, Philip B. 1990. "Maleger." *The Spenser Encyclopedia*. Edited by A. C. Hamilton. Toronto. University of Toronto Press. 449–50.

Rosinger, Lawrence. 1968. "Spenser's Una and Queen Elizabeth." *English Language Notes*. 6. 12–17.

Sanford, Rhonda Lemke. 2002. *Maps and Memory in Early Modern England: A Sense of Place*. Early Modern Cultural Studies, 1500–1700. New York. Palgrave.

Schoenbaum, S. 1977. *William Shakespeare: A Compact Documentary Life*. Oxford. Clarendon.

Schwyzer, Philip. 1997. "Purity and Danger on the West Bank of the Severn: The Cultural Geography of *A Masque Presented at Ludlow Castle, 1634*." *Representations*. 60. 22–48.

Shaheen, Naseeb. 1976. *Biblical References in* The Faerie Queene. Memphis. Memphis State University Press.

Shaheen, Naseeb. 1987. *Biblical References in Shakespeare's Tragedies*. Newark, NJ. University of Delaware Press.

Shakespeare, William. 1946. *The First Part of the History of Henry IV*. Ed. John Dover Wilson. New Cambridge Shakespeare. Cambridge. Cambridge University Press.

Shakespeare, William. 1951. *Macbeth*. Ed. Kenneth Muir. The Arden Shakespeare. London. Methuen.

Shakespeare, William. 1955. *Cymbeline*. Ed. J. M. Nosworthy. The Arden Shakespeare. London. Methuen.

Shakespeare, William. 1961. *King Richard II*. Ed. Peter Ure. The Arden Shakespeare. London. Methuen.

Shakespeare, William. 1968. *The Norton Facsimile of the First Folio of Shakespeare*. Ed. Charlton Hinman. New York. W W Norton.

Shakespeare, William. 1982. *Henry V*. Ed. Gary Taylor. The Oxford Shakespeare. Oxford. Oxford University Press.

Shakespeare, William. 1987. *Henry IV, Part I*. Ed. David Bevington. The Oxford Shakespeare. Oxford. Oxford University Press.

Shakespeare, William. 1988. *The Complete Works: Compact Edition*. Ed. Stanley Wells, Gary Taylor, John Jowett, and William Montgomery. Oxford. Clarendon Press.

Shakespeare, William. 1995. *King Henry V*. The Arden Shakespeare. London. Routledge.

Shakespeare, William. 1997. *King Lear*. Ed. R. A. Foakes. The Arden Shakespeare. Walton-on-Thames. Thomas Nelson.

Shakespeare, William. 1998. *Cymbeline*. Ed. Roger Warren. The Oxford Shakespeare . Oxford. Oxford University Press.

Shakespeare, William. 2000a. *King Henry VIII*. Ed. Gordon McMullan. Arden Shakespeare. London. Arden.

Shakespeare, William. 2000b. *The History of King Lear*. Vol. Ed. Stanley Wells. The Oxford Shakespeare. Oxford. Oxford University Press.

Shakespeare, William. 2002. *King Richard II*. Ed. Charles R Forker. The Arden Shakespeare. London. Arden.

Shepherd, Simon. 1981. *Amazons and Warrior Women: Varieties of Feminism in Seventeenth-century Drama*. Brighton. Harvester.

Sidney, Sir Philip. 1965. *An Apology for Poetry: or the Defence of Poesy*. Ed. Geoffrey Shepperd. Nelson's Medieval and Renaissance Library. London. Nelson.

Sinfield, Alan. 1985. "'Give an Account of Shakespeare and Education, Showing Why You Think They Are Effective and What You Have Appreciated About Them. Support Your Comments with Precise References'." *Political Shakespeare: New Essays in Cultural Materialism*. Edited by Jonathan Dollimore and Alan Sinfield. Manchester. Manchester UP. 134–57.

Smith, Roland M. 1935. "Spenser's Irish River Stories." *Publications of the Modern Language Association of America*. 50. 1047–56.

Spenser, Edmund, ed. 1989. *The Shorter Poems*. Ed. William A Oram, Einar Bjorvand, Ronald Bond, Thomas H. Cain, Alexander Dunlop, Richard Schell. New Haven and London. Yale University Press.

Spenser, Edmund. 1898. *The Faerie Queene Book V*. Ed. Kate M. Warren. Vol. 5. 6 vols. London. Constable.

Spenser, Edmund. 1935. *The Faerie Queene: Book Four*. Ed. Ray Heffner. The Works of Edmund Spenser: A Variorum Edition. 4. Baltimore. Johns Hopkins.

Spenser, Edmund. 1943. *The Minor Poems Volume One*. Ed. Charles Grosvenor Osgood, Henry Gibbons Lotspeich, and Dorothy E. Mason. The Works of Edmund Spenser: A Variorum Edition. 7. Baltimore. Johns Hopkins.

Spenser, Edmund. 1949. *Prose Works*. Ed. Rudolf Gottfried. The Works of Edmund

Spenser: A Variorum Edition. 10. Baltimore. Johns Hopkins.

Spenser, Edmund. 1970. *A View of the Present State of Ireland*. Ed. W.L. Renwick. Oxford. Clarendon Press.

Spenser, Edmund. 1977. *The Faerie Queene*. Ed. A. C. Hamilton. Annotated English Poets. London. Longman.

Spenser, Edmund. 1982–1884. *The Complete Works in Verse and Prose*. Ed. Alexander B. Grosart. Vol. 1: Alexander B. Grosart 'Life of Spenser'; Aubrey de Vere 'Characteristics of Spenser's Poetry'; Edward Dowden 'Spenser the Poet and Teacher'; W. B. Philpot 'Certain Aspects of the Poetry of Spenser'; William Hubbard 'The Introspection and Outlook of Spenser'. 9 vols. London. Privately published.

Staines, John D. 2001. "Elizabeth, Mercilla, and the Rhetoric of Propaganda in Spenser's *Faerie Queene*." *Journal of medieval and early modern studies*. 31.2. 283–312.

Steadman, John M. 1990. "Error." *The Spenser Encyclopedia*. Edited by A. C. Hamilton. Toronto. University of Toronto Press. 252–53.

Stephen, Leslie and Sidney Lee. 1921–1922. *The Dictionary of National Biography: From the Earliest Times to 1900*. Vol. 7: Finch — Gloucester. 22 vols. London. Oxford University Press.

Taylor, Gary. 1985. "The Fortunes of Oldcastle." *Shakespeare Survey*. 38. 85–100.

Taylor, Gary. 1994. "Forms of Opposition: Shakespeare and Middleton." *English Literary Renaissance*. 24. 283–314.

Thomson, Leslie. 1999. "The Meaning of *Thunder and Lightning*: Stage Directions and Audience Expectations." *Early Theatre*. 2. 11–24.

Tillyard, E. M. W. 1943. *The Elizabethan World Picture*. London. Chatto and Windus.

Tobin, John J. M. 2003. "Sources and Cruces." *In Arden: Editing Shakespeare: Essays in Honour of Richard Proudfoot*. Edited by Ann Thompson and Gordon McMullan. Arden Shakespeare. London. Thompson. 221–38.

Tonkin, Humphrey. 1972. *Spenser's Courteous Pastoral: Book Six of the Faerie Queene*. Oxford. Clarendon.

Vickers, Brian. 2002. *Shakespeare, Co-Author: A Historical Study of Five Collaborative Plays*. Oxford. Oxford University Press.

Waters, D. Douglas. 1970. *Duessa as Theological Satire*. Columbia. University of Missouri Press.

Watson, Elizabeth See. 2000. "Spenser's Flying Dragon and Pope Gregory XIII." *Spenser Studies*. 14. 293–301.

Wells, Robin Headlam. 1983. *Spenser's Faerie Queene and the Cult of Elizabeth*. London. Croom Helm.

Wells, Stanley, Gary Taylor, John Jowett and William Montgomery. 1987. *William Shakespeare: A Textual Companion*. Oxford. Clarendon Press.

Wells, Stanley, Gary Taylor, John Jowett and William Montgomery. 1989. *William Shakespeare: The Complete Works*. Prepared by William Montgomery and Lou

Burnard. Oxford. Oxford Electronic Publishing, Oxford University Press.

Wells, Stanley. 2002. *Shakespeare: For All Time*. London. Macmillan.

Williams, Gordon. 1994. *A Dictionary of Sexual Language and Imagery in Shakespearean and Stuart Literature*. Vol. 2. 3 vols. London. Athlone.

Wilson Knight, G. 1947. *The Crown of Life: Essays in Interpretation of Shakespeare's Final Plays*. London. Oxford University Press.

Wilson, Richard. 1997. "Shakespeare and the Jesuits: New Connections Supporting the Theory of the Lost Catholic Years in Lancashire." *Times Literary Supplement*. 4942.December. 11–13.

Yates, Frances A. 1947. "Queen Elizabeth As Astraea." *Journal of the Warburg and Courtauld Institutes*. 10. 27–82.

Yates, Julian. 1999. "Parasitic Geographies: Manifesting Catholic Identity in Early Modern England." *Catholicism and Anti-Catholicism in Early Modern English Texts*. Edited by Arthur F. Marotti. Houndmills. Macmillan. 63–84.

Yeats, W. B. 1961. *Essays and Introductions*. London. Macmillan.